A PAGAN TESTAMENT

The Literary Heritage
of the World's Oldest New Religion

First published by O Books, 2008
O Books is an imprint of John Hunt Publishing Ltd., The Bothy, Deershot Lodge, Park Lane, Ropley,
Hants, SO24 0BE, UK
office1@o-books.net
www.o-books.net

Distribution in:

UK and Europe
Orca Book Services
orders@orcabookservices.co.uk
Tel: 01202 665432 Fax: 01202 666219
Int. code (44)

USA and Canada
NBN
custserv@nbnbooks.com
Tel: 1 800 462 6420 Fax: 1 800 338 4550

Australia and New Zealand
Brumby Books
sales@brumbybooks.com.au
Tel: 61 3 9761 5535 Fax: 61 3 9761 7095

Far East (offices in Singapore, Thailand,
Hong Kong, Taiwan)
Pansing Distribution Pte Ltd
kemal@pansing.com
Tel: 65 6319 9939 Fax: 65 6462 5761

South Africa
Alternative Books
altbook@peterhyde.co.za
Tel: 021 555 4027 Fax: 021 447 1430

Text copyright Brendan Myers 2008

Design: Stuart Davies

ISBN: 978 1 84694 129 0

A CIP catalogue record for this book is available
from the British Library.

Printed by Digital Book Print

O Books operates a distinctive and ethical publishing philosophy in
all areas of its business, from its global network of authors to
production and worldwide distribution.
This book is produced on FSC certified stock, within ISO14001
standards. The printer plants sufficient trees each year through
the Woodland Trust to absorb the level of emitted carbon in
its production.

A PAGAN TESTAMENT

The Literary Heritage
of the World's Oldest New Religion

Brendan Myers, Ph.D.

BOOKS

Winchester, UK
Washington, USA

CONTENTS

Acknowledgements

There are many more people here I ought to thank, yet I have space enough for only these few. First and foremost, I thank the many, many people who contributed to my folklore survey. I especially thank my friend Terry Roberts, of Nova Scotia, Canada, for offering more circle-songs than any other single contributor.

While researching this book, I also sought the advice and wisdom of certain people who are particularly well respected and admired by my local pagan community. The focus and the purpose of this book crystallized in my mind after conversations with them. Among those who I spoke to, I give special thanks to Pam Fletcher, Jim Findlay, Helmut, Andy Biggers, and Catherine Ackert. I consider these people, among others, the Elders of my local pagan community.

I must also give thanks to Richard and Tamarra James, who hold Gerald Gardner's library in trust for the community. While I was researching this book they generously permitted me to peruse this library, and examine Gardner's hand-written *Book of Shadows*, his *Book of the Art Magickal*, and other texts from the period when Wicca was born. I also owe thanks to Macha NightMare, who helped me identify the original authors of many of the chant-songs in the collection.

Finally, and most importantly, I thank Lana Winter, for agreeing to illustrate this book, even while she had ten thousand other things to do at the same time.

To all these friends and many others (they know who they are), I am deeply grateful.

Brendan Myers
Elora, Ontario, Canada
January, 2008

Dedication

In a book where the Goddesses of the pagan world feature so prominently, it seems right to dedicate this book to certain special women in my life. Some I met recently; some I have known for a decade or more; some, perhaps, for many lifetimes. All of them, in different ways, profoundly enriched my life while I was writing this book. I therefore dedicate this modest effort to these four magickal friends:

Laura Jackson, NaTasha Bertrand, MJ Patterson, Amy Taylor.

If tomorrow I am slain,
May my life's account remain:
Cited from the point of view
Of the women that I knew.

Overture

Storytelling is, among other things, a product of the people of a community who endeavor to express and to further develop a shared identity. Their collections of stories speak of the things they have in common, and the things they can do together. For storytelling is an inherently social event: at the bare minimum, it requires two people: a listener, and a teller. Nor are the listeners mere passive recipients. They participate in their own way, for instance by imagining the characters and events of the story in their minds, posing questions to the teller, asking him or her to explain some part of the story more, describe the main characters more, and so on. Then the listeners become tellers to a new group of listeners, and they in their turn become tellers to another new group of listeners. A listener one day is a teller on the next. Moreover, there is nothing in the idea of storytelling which suggests that there must be only one teller at a time. Just the other day I went to a place where about fifty or so people collaborated to tell a story together to about a thousand others. In other words, I went to the theatre. The same could be said of the stories told on television or in the cinema, at a family dinner party, or at a religious ceremony. Finally, there's no reason that listeners cannot participate in telling the story. Listeners can always ask the simple question, "What happened next?"

Seventy years ago, in a town on the southern edge of the England's New Forest, a group of friends gathered secretly to tell each other stories about a goddess. In their version of the story, this goddess was the daughter of the Moon, and she came to the Earth to teach human beings to make magic, to liberate the oppressed, to heal the sick and injured, to pass through death and enter another life, and ultimately, to love each other. The people who learned and passed on what the goddess taught became known as witches. In their telling of the story, witches were magical people, in touch with the sacred powers of the elements and the earth. Europeans had not worshipped female deities for almost two millennia. These secret people also told stories of a male deity. However, as if their story of the goddess wasn't scandalous enough, this male god had stag antlers growing from his head, making him resemble one of Christianity's most potent symbols of evil. Indeed as they understood it, the God with the Horns was the original, and positive, image of a male deity. Christianity later hijacked and transformed this image, in order to frighten people into converting to the Christian way.

Furthermore, in their story, Witches were a beleaguered people: having been mistaken for dangerous folk, they were oppressed and hunted almost to extinction. But their magical powers proved strong enough to let a few survive to tell their story. Indeed a large part of the story this circle of friends told each other was the idea that the witches were the inheritors of the ancient pre-Christian religious practices of Europe. Some parts of that practice survived as superstition and as transformed folk practices: the Abbots Bromley Horn Dance, for instance, or the burning of an effigy on Guy Fawkes Day. They themselves, the witches, were the last of the old priesthood of those two ancient gods, and the inheritors of a large body of mystical teachings.

We now know that much of that story is a fantasy. There was no unbroken lineage of knowledge or practice stretching back to ancient times. Historically, of course, there have been many different cults and sects and communities in various parts of the world who revered a Goddess. Some have been small movements within larger ones, such as the worship of various goddesses in Hinduism, or the respect and veneration some Christians offer to the Blessed Virgin Mary. But in various ways and for various reasons, the large majority of Goddess-respecting communities in Western civilisation disappeared centuries or millennia ago. In most cases, they were replaced by, or even suppressed by, the worshippers of male gods. Some of these male gods claimed to be the chief of a pantheon that included several strong female figures. Some claimed to be the only god around. Some of them worked in concert with the female gods, acting as a partner. And while the partnership was not always equal, at least the goddess still had a place in people's lives. But some of the male gods simply pushed the female gods out of the temple altogether, along with all the competing male gods. And so it remained in European and Middle Eastern culture for many centuries.

But having said that, the story of the Goddess did not emerge out of nothing. For one thing, the goddess made many reappearances in world history, even after she was displaced. She was in mediaeval Constantinople, where Sophia, the 'Seat of Wisdom', patron saint of the city and of philosophers, was nearly the equal of Christ himself. She was in northern Italy at the start of the Renaissance, when artists of various kinds crafted images of pagan divinities for the first time in a thousand years. In Britain, at the time the New Forest Coven was founded, there was already a movement afoot that sought a revival of pagan images, ideas, and values. For the most part, this movement was literary and artistic in character. Poets were seeking the old gods as inspirational material, and using their images as representations of emotional impulses in the human heart and mind. There was growing public interest in spiritualism, occultism, and secret societies. Even upper-class socialites were holding séances, and unwrapping Egyptian mummies, during their formal dinner parties. The members of the New Forest Coven were, in various ways, caught up in this eccentric, magical atmosphere. Their contribution to it has survived to the present day, much changed from their own time of course, but still with its distinctive character. And it has a name: it is called Paganism. Today it is a large international movement, with hundreds of thousands of practitioners in more than a hundred countries around the world.

* * *

What is paganism? The word has come to mean a great many different things, and not all of them are very flattering. It can denote a backward or primitive kind of spirituality, practiced by societies that respond to the world with animal instinct instead of with human reason. It is associated in the popular imagination with idolatry and superstition, with the sacrifice of animals or of people, and with a barbaric past that has long been left behind. To some a pagan is simply anyone who has rejected Christian ethics, and whose presence therefore brings a certain moral uncertainty. Without the Ten Commandments to direct him, who knows what a pagan might do! Within the pagan community itself, however, the word 'pagan' is associated with timeless ideas like animism, pantheism, polytheism, and divine immanence. It is also associated with a variety of practices and beliefs, some of which appear to contradict each other:

- The re-enactment or the revival of various customs and traditions associated with the fertility of landscapes, plants, animals, and people.
- The use of European, Near-Eastern, and sometimes Aboriginal symbols and practices to represent and to express spiritual ideas.
- A lifestyle or culture in which human relationships, artistic activity, environmental awareness, and especially "the good life" of "dancing, singing, feasting, making music, and love", are treated as sources of spiritual fulfillment,
- A reform movement that protests against sexism, environmental destruction, heirarchical forms of religious organisation, and various forms of social injustice,
- The seeking of occult or esoteric knowledge, the development of psychic powers and the practice of magic.
- The belief in the existence of spirits or gods within trees, animals, landforms, weather events, the sun and moon, the four traditional elements of earth, air, fire, water, and so on.

- The pursuit of spiritual illumination and release, however defined, by means of human powers and potentials, and without the need for supernatural assistance or divine intervention. (Historically, this has been called The Pelagian Heresy.)
- And finally, paganism is the worship of a *female* deity, who is known by many names. Her presence is sought primarily through activities which are, in themselves, pleasurable, life-affirming, and loving.

The modern pagan movement was not the first religious movement in the world to place a Goddess at the centre of its pantheon. But it is the first international spiritual movement in more than two thousand years to hold a Goddess in such high esteem. Certainly it is the first Goddess-centered religious movement to emerge from an industrialized and developed Western-world nation. The Goddess is the image and the figure that makes the world view of contemporary Paganism unique and distinct. In this world view, the Goddess is allowed to be her own person, with her own identity and power. She is not the consort or the partner of another higher, more authoritative male deity. There are many male gods in the pagan pantheon, of course, but the goddess is not just a consort for one of them. In fact, a male god usually acts as Her consort. Nor is the goddess assigned a specific or limited kind of role in the world, although she has various qualities and purposes which take prominence over others. As you will find in this book, She is a mother, a healer and a caregiver, a sexual partner, a controller of the fertility of plants and the soil, a king-maker and a sponsor of chieftains and warriors, a controller of fate and destiny, a teacher, a fighter, and a witch.

In this book I focus on the literary side of her history: that is, the stories, poems, speeches, and other writings which were either produced by the first generation of pagans, or which influenced them greatly. I'm interested in the literary works which, while not directly influential on the New Forest Coven, were 'in the air', so to speak: the stories and poems from different historical times which expressed similar ideas, or had similar influences. I'm also very interested in the folklore by which contemporary Pagans recognize their paths and express their world-views. The word *folklore* is notoriously difficult to define, even by experts. The term was coined in the nineteenth century by antiquarian William Thoms. To him folklore had to do with songs, tales, customs, and proverbs which seemed to represent the remnants of a culture's distant past. Today it also refers to quilts, knit sweaters, fishing boats, musical tunes, foods and recipes, dances, jokes, urban legends, and any other 'artifact' of a folk tradition. American scholar Barre Toelken defined folklore as "a word very much like *culture*... Its primary characteristic is that its ingredients seem to come directly from dynamic interactions among human beings in communal-traditional performance contexts rather than through the more rigid lines and fossilized structures of technical instruction or bureaucratized education." (Tolken, *The Dynamics of Folklore*, pg. 28-9).

From the summer of 2006 to the autumn of 2007 I brought a folklore survey to pagan gatherings, festivals, private meetings, pub moots, conferences, and just about every pagan event within my reach. I got friends of mine in other countries to distribute the survey at their local events. I also posted it on the internet, using popular web sites, email list-groups, chat rooms, and the like. In this survey, I asked people to share with me their favourite ritual chants, circle songs, wisdom teachings, proverbs, mottos, sayings, and ceremonial expressions. I received replies from people in five Canadian provinces, sixteen American states, and ten other countries around the world. In total, almost two thousand people answered my questions. Finally I also sought out my local community's 'Elders': some of whom are event organizers, some are spiritual councilors and teachers, some are leaders of groups both large and small, and some are known as prominent eccentric 'personalities'. All of them have widespread reputations for great spiritual and practical knowledge spanning thirty years or more. And without them the community would be a very different, a less inviting and less magical place.

There were huge geographic distances between my informants. And most informants also professed huge ideological differences from other pagans. Nevertheless, I found in the results of the survey an extraordinary and surprising degree of coherence, consistency, and unity. Some of the wisdom-teachings and circle-songs were reported by fifty people or more. One, in particular, was reported by more than one hundred people, and in three languages other than English: "We are a circle within a circle, with no beginning and never ending." This song could be the motto of the entire movement. I assert that the consistency of the community's folklore may be taken as evidence of a widely shared modern pagan "testament". In this book I shall describe this testament, and show how it contains several expressions of spiritual identity which practitioners of contemporary Paganism hold in common with each other.

* * *

Most of the time, we use the word Testament only in reference to the two halves of the Bible. Therefore we already have the idea that a testament is something sacred. But the idea of a testament comes from other sources. In Latin a *testis* is a witness in a trial or investigative proceeding. He is someone who, as we say today, *attests* to something, or gives a *testimonial*. To testify, then, is to certify that one is a witness to something. It is also to swear that one's testimony is true. We are all familiar with what it means to 'testify' in a law court. Most of the time, you place your right hand on a Bible and swear to be truthful. But you could also swear on your head (from the Old English *teste*, 'head', from which also comes the French *tête*). Or, as in the days of the Roman Empire, you could swear on your 'manliness': from the Latin *testis* or *testiculus*—bet you didn't expect that! But I find something very satisfying in the thought that someone who offers testimony could swear to its truth on the earth itself. In Latin a *teste* is a brick or a piece of dried earth. This is etymologically connected to *terra*, a landscape, or the planet Earth itself. It is an ancient wisdom that of all things in nature only the Earth is permanent and enduring. So an oath sworn on a stone or a rock calls that permanence to bear. It is to demonstrate that one is prepared to uphold the terms of the oath for as long as the earth itself endures, which means, forever. A testament, let us say, is a story that purports to bear witness to something. At the same time a testament aligns the story with the most enduring and permanent thing known to humankind, the planet Earth itself.

Some people may ask, does contemporary paganism really have a testament? Certainly, it has no Bible, and this is something that pagans often take to be a positive thing. Without having its central principles and statements of belief and identity *written down*, paganism becomes more flexible, less dogmatic. In the pagan community, there is a perception that once an idea is written down on paper, it becomes frozen in time. Then it can no longer change, and no longer grow, and no longer accommodate new situations and circumstances as they arise. And there is a perception that a written scripture carries a kind of presumptuous dogmatic authority which permits no variations. But I believe these perceptions are false. For one reason, no one stops singing a song just because someone wrote down the lyrics. Moreover, even written literature changes over time. Individual written works get edited, proofread, re-written, interpreted, re-interpreted, and translated, just as spoken words do. Whole traditions of literature, in much the same way, are constantly upgraded, altered, interpreted, and contributed to, all the time. With written literature this process works very slowly, and so is much harder to see. The

Bible itself is an excellent example: it was written by more than forty authors, over the space of hundreds of years, in a variety of languages, including Aramaic and Greek. For hundreds of years after that it was re-shaped, re-interpreted, and even hacked around by hundreds of scribes, copy-editors, translators, political opportunists, religious fanatics, and insane kings. Thank the gods, pagans say, that we have nothing like that of our own!

But, actually, they do. There is a vast wealth of mythology and folklore from ancient and early modern cultures around the world. Many of the ancient goddesses and gods whom contemporary pagans honour are also associated with a definite literature. The stories of Inanna and Ishtar come to us from cuneiform inscriptions pressed into clay tablets. The story of Isis, Apophis and Osiris, is known from hieroglyphic writings on papyrus scrolls, and painted on to the walls of temples and other monuments. Some myths are recorded not in words but in pictures: the series of images on the Pantheon Frieze, or the patterns and shapes on a wampum belt, for instance. In short, most of the characters in our religious mythology are known to us precisely because someone, somewhere, took the time to write their stories down. Between the many thousands of writers, and the many millions of readers, a literary testament was created. This literature belongs not only to contemporary pagans: it belongs to the whole world.

There are those who believe that while the written word has undeniable practical usefulness, still it is not as spiritually valuable as the spoken word. Some go further, and say that even the spoken word is not as profound as the presence of the divine itself, which is "always" non-linguistic, ineffable, unspeakable. Words diminish experiences and limit them, so they believe. Here I shall take another stab at controversy in this book: I claim this belief is wrong. A genuine spiritual experience engages the whole being. It does not exclude any part of the mind, heart, feelings, or special capacities we have in our bodies and souls. Any person who does not accept the power of words in spiritual experiences has perhaps never experienced the spiritual power of words. Think here of the magic in the poetry of William Butler Yeats, or the wit in a Shakespearean play, or the persuasive force of the speeches of Martin Luther King. Words are powerful: reading them, speaking, them, and hearing them is a revelation of meaning, a transmission of thought, feeling, and purpose-laden energy. A written testament can also be seen as a record of the original revelation, an account of the experience, brought forth in written form so others can share it.

The reality is that spiritual experiences *can* be spoken of: that is why we have storytelling! And what is more, we can talk about our spiritual experiences *ad infinitum*. The reality is not that spiritual experiences are inexpressible, but that they are *infinitely expressible*. However much has already been said, someone could always say something more. No single account can cover *all* that there is to say. This is not a weakness of language, but rather it is its strength: we can never run out of words. The mystery of a so-called 'ineffable' spiritual experience is not that of a curtain or a veil which cannot be parted. Its mystery is that of a door which, when opened, leads to a room with another door. The best evidence I can present in support of this position is the very phenomena of storytelling itself. It is to storytelling we turn when prose writing or analytic explanation seems to be at a loss. We never run out of stories about our experiences. Indeed for any given experience, there may be an almost infinite number of stories to tell about it. Through storytelling we engage the imagination and the passions, and generate the mental and emotional energy, that makes us able to recognize the divine presence, whatever it may be. Storytelling is the engine of almost all our spiritual activities.

*   *   *

Now that the contemporary pagan movement is more than seventy years old, it is a scene of bewildering diversity. At almost any large pagan festival, you might find a British maypole next to an Aboriginal sweat lodge. There might be an effigy of a man made from corn stalks or wicker, which is set on fire, next to a place where people are practicing Buddhist meditation. In the market area there may be artists and craftspeople offering figurines of the gods, magic wands, crystals and precious stones, jewelry, books, musical instruments, mediaeval weapons and armour, gothic style clothing, and organic food. There may be Viking warriors practicing swordplay together; Persian belly dancers; African drummers; astrologers; massage therapists; psychics of all kinds; Reiki healers; blacksmiths; Taoist Tai Chi practitioners; Celtic bards; and any number of other strange and silly people doing all sorts of strange and silly things. Nonetheless, despite all this diversity, the movement has a common testament. It has a written and oral tradition of mythological storytelling, all its own. It also has a body of stories, poems, thoughts, songs, jokes, and the like which were produced by Pagans themselves, in which clear and assertive expressions of a robust world-view may be found. Most of paganism's literary testament takes the form of invocations and spells intended for use in magical rituals. But ritual, that formalized context in which we address ourselves to the gods, is itself established only by means of storytelling. Someone casts the circle, and calls the quarters, and summons the gods: that's an event with narrative structure. It's a bit like laying the foundations of a house, then raising up the frame, carefully including spaces for windows and doors, and then inviting friends to visit. We see that there is a story here, and that it is going somewhere, and we want to know where. We also want to know that it will end in an elegant and satisfying way.

Together with the mythology of the ancient world, and the poetry and folklore of the early modern world, these literary artifacts constitute modern paganism's testament. They are the works in which the Craft's most important ideas and values are represented. Or, at any rate, they *could* constitute the *beginning* of one. As a testament it may be fragmentary, incomplete, unclear, or even self-contradictory, just like the testaments of other religions, old and new. But as inspirational material, intended for the purpose of getting people to think and to imagine, it is surely useful and valuable. Like the literary tradition of any healthy and grounded spiritual tradition, Paganism's written testament is growing, changing, and continually being contributed to. I have gathered together the writings which, in the findings of my research and in the experience of my own spiritual growth, constitute paganism's most important attestations of identity and value. Although I am also including my own philosophical commentary, I invite each reader to decide for herself what each piece means, and what more and what else deserves a place here. As I said before, Paganism's literary heritage is constantly changing. In twenty years time, therefore, it may be necessary to assemble another pagan testament. What stories will we be telling each other in the future? Will the things we love today continue to be loved by future generations? I'm excited to find out.

* * *

Pagans are proud of their individuality, and they don't like rigidly hierarchical forms of authority. They don't like being told what to do, how to think, or how to worship their gods. Consequently, there is a great emphasis on personal creativity, direct inspiration, 'what works', and 'what feels right'. This is, of course, something most pagans regard as a great strength. It means that a practitioner of the Craft may have her own experience of the spirit, and may craft her own interpretation of its meaning. But one consequence of this emphasis is that it may seem as if there are very few ideas or materials that all pagans, or most of them, could claim to hold in common. The Charge of the Goddess is probably one of the few things pagans everywhere regard as a common heritage. The Wiccan Rede may be another. The order of events in a ritual is probably another as well, although even that is open to negotiation at any given time, and there is no requirement that the actual words used on each occasion be the same. In order to find out what more, and what else, pagans have in common with each other, I conducted my survey.

One of my findings is that paganism's testament is constantly being contributed to. It is the work of many people and not just one person, and it is constantly changing. I believe most pagans will be very happy with the idea that their Testament is "not static". Yet because of this 'turnover of content', I also found that many people did not know, for instance, that the Wiccan Rede is actually 315 words, not just eight (nor even two). Some people who I spoke with had never heard of the Charge of the Goddess, even though they knew some of its key proverbs like 'all acts of love and pleasure are my rituals'. Perhaps the emphasis on personal creativity is causing some of the pagan movement's original material to be forgotten. Some of it may deserve to be forgotten. But I think it is a great tragedy that some truly inspirational words are being left behind.

A common testament is a necessary thing because personal experience, by itself, cannot be the basis for community solidarity. By its very nature, a personal experience can belong to just one person. It can be described to others, but not given to them; it belongs exclusively to its original preceptor. But community cannot be built on things that cannot be shared. It must be built on the things which a group of people can hold in common. It is built on the things which become more rich and subtle and precious the more they are shared. This remains true even if these things are also experimented upon, complained about, argued over, and changed over time. Indeed, *contestation* may be part of the way the things we share increase in value. The written word is just such a shared possession. In written literature, there is a relationship between the author and the reader that is very much like the relationship between a storyteller and her listener. An attentive reader can hear the writer's thoughts — even if the writer has been dead for hundreds of years. Readers can also form new relationships with each other, as they discuss, interpret, re-interpret, even debate and argue about the meaning of the things they've read. And a talented writer can spawn a literary tradition, in which readers become authors, writing commentaries and interpretations, original contributions, even arguments and refutations. *A literary tradition is a conversation.* It is what happens when any group of people use books and letters to talk to each other. Their conversation might last for centuries.

What the medium of the written word makes possible, which the spoken word cannot do, is allow the reader to have the words of someone who is very far away in time or space; to share the thoughts and experiences of the past. The written word creates the possibility of *inter-generational communication*. Someone who writes something down can speak directly to people who they have never met before, and even people who have not yet been born. That is, of course, if his books last that long! When it comes to the job of pulling together a community, especially a spiritual movement like contemporary paganism, the written word is therefore indispensable.

Most religious communities find that one of the most important things their people have in common is a literary testament. This book is about modern paganism's ever-unfolding testament, its on-going attestation of what it is, what it wants us to do, and where it wishes us to go. It is written in the hope that some day, if Pagans decide that they want a literary testament to call their own, they will have one; and more than that, it will make them proud.

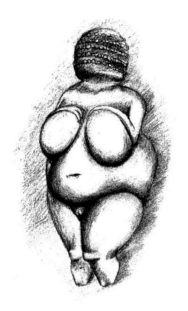

First Movement

The Goddess With No Name

"The sunlight does not leave its marks on the grass. So we, too, pass silently..."

The oldest works of art ever made by humankind are prehistoric cave paintings of animals and hunting scenes. The earliest were created up to 20,000 years ago. It seems likely that these images were made as part of a magical effort to ensure a good hunt, and hence to ensure the survival of the community. One could say that people 'rehearsed' the hunt by portraying the animals in art on the walls of their dwelling-places. This may explain why many of the animals in this form of art are depicted wounded and dying, their bodies stuck with spears. It is as if the artist had 'killed' the spirit of the animal by killing its picture on the cave wall. The hunter, believing that his hunt is magically guaranteed, would be charged up with confidence. That reason alone (if not any other) may have made him more successful. These images often overlap each other, implying that an image could be used for this purpose but once. The next time it became necessary to cast the spell a new image would have to be made, and killed. Images of animals that were not wounded or dying may have been part of a magical effort to ensure the return of the herds in their annual migrations. In effect, such images were not made as a form of death magic, but as a form of *summoning* magic. And the ultimate purpose of this art would have been to magically improve the likelihood that the community would survive.

What has this to do with the story of the goddess? Most artistic figures from the prehistoric age depict animals: there are very few human figures. But, interestingly, most of the human figures are *female*. Furthermore, the cave paintings are made not near the entrance, but far into the dark depths of the cave. This may have been to prevent the images from being seen or profaned by casual passer-bys. But it may also have been because of a belief that the presence of the goddess of the earth had to be found deep within the earth itself. The strongest magic, the most potent life-and-death energy, would have been found deep inside her body. The cave may have been like the womb or the mouth of the Earth-goddess. If so, then it would seem that the cave would be the best place to be close to her, feel her presence, and ask for her help with the hunt.

Many of the Goddess images in prehistoric art are well known to modern pagans. *La Femme à la Corne* is a popular one: she is carved on the side of a rock face, and she holds a ram's horn up to her head, as if about to drink from it. Another well loved image, often used by contemporary pagans as a symbol of their dedication to the deity, is the goddess variously known as the *Nile River Goddess* or the *Bird Goddess*. She stands upright; her legs appear fused together, and her arms curve above her head in a gesture resembling the wings of a bird about to take flight. But the most famous early Goddess image is called *Venus of Willendorf*. This is a small stone figurine, barely more than four inches high, found near the town of Willendorf in Austria. It represents a very large pregnant woman, with enormous breasts and hips, and a greatly enlarged belly. Yet her arms are disproportionately small and thin, and she rests them on top of her breasts. Her head is slightly bowed, looking down, as if contemplating the life of a child growing within her. There are more than sixty figurines like her, most of them in central Europe. We do not know what name was bestowed on her by the people who made her. We do not even know what language those people spoke. Her testament, as we know it, exists only in the form of art. She speaks, but not with words. Her image and presence alone is her word. For the sake of convenience we can refer to these images with the names given to them by archaeologists. But for the sake of understanding who she is and what, if anything, she has to teach us, I prefer to call her The Goddess With No Name.

Prehistoric goddess images started to appear around the same time that human societies transitioned from nomadic hunting and gathering to settled farming. This transition had many advantages. The most important advantage was the reduction of the number of hungry seasons in the average year down to just one. But even with that great technological advance in hand, human existence was still very fragile and precarious. Most of humanity lived just on the edge of starvation, most of the time. Anthropologist Marvin Harris suggested that any extra energy that people stored in their bodies from prosperous times was probably spent in hunting, gathering, planting, and harvesting during lean times. Therefore, he says, it seems likely that the artist who carved the Venus of Willendorf had never in fact seen a real woman who looked anything like her. She is an image of a woman likely to have an easier time surviving famines, and likely to give birth to healthier children: in short, a Neolithic 'ideal' woman. (c.f. Harris, *Our Kind*, pg. 148.)

This interpretation of role and meaning of this goddess comes from a male anthropologist. A friend of mine, who is also a mother to a boisterous young child, taught me that women can understand Her differently, because they can have that experience of pregnancy, which men cannot. Here is how she explained it to me.

The Venus of Willendorf has no face, hands, nor feet. These are the only areas during pregnancy and nursing that remain a woman's own. The rest of her changes so drastically, it is as if she is possessed. (Depending on your definition, she most certainly is, by her infant.) The Venus of Willendorf, in my experience, is the Goddess of pregnancy, and perhaps nursing. She is the One who possesses the woman's body and forces so many changes, everywhere except the features of her face, hands and feet. (N. Bertrand, personal communication, 10 December 2007)

The explanation for why the Venus of Willendorf has no face, hands, or feet cannot be because the sculptor lacked the technical skill. For great attention to detail went into her. On her head she has a full mane of curly hair, for instance. Even her navel and her vulva are both carefully inscribed. If no Neolithic person ever saw a woman who looked like her, as Harris suggested, nonetheless I'm fairly sure that any Neolithic woman would have understood the image as my friend did. The Venus of Willendorf is not simply, nor only, a fertility charm. She is also a representation of a pregnant woman's inner experience. A similar could be drawn about other prehistoric goddess figurines who also have exaggerated breasts and hips, and no hands or faces, such as the Kostienki Venus, or the Ceramic Venus of Dolni Vestonice. I'd like to add that the posture of these figurines, with their heads tilted down as if to contemplate her belly and the life growing inside her, seems to suggest a woman at peace with these transformations.

How did the Goddess With No Name fall from her prestigious place? How did male gods come to supplant her, and take up the more prestigious places in religious culture all over the world? Some feminist anthropologists, such as Gimbutas, postulated that the Goddess was supplanted when peace-loving, Goddess-honouring cultures were supplanted by male-dominated warrior cultures. But I am inclined to believe the following explanation. First of all, someone along the way discovered agricultural techniques like the domestication of food-animals, and the irrigation of fields. With these discoveries, more food than was needed for immediate survival could be produced and stockpiled. Then, the men who sat on the stockpile (and their totems, the male gods) could be the great providers, instead of the women (and their Goddess) who formerly did most of the work of gathering it.

Here is a second possible explanation. The people who crafted the Neolithic goddess images probably had no understanding of the male role in procreation. It may be difficult to believe that humanity could have been ignorant of the facts of life even into the late Stone Age. However, in the words of researcher Reay Tannahill, some tribal people even in the twentieth century still didn't know the facts. In her words:

> The Bellonese of the Solomon Islands, until they were enlightened by Christian missionaries at the end of the 1930's thought that children were sent by their social father's ancestral deities and that the only function of sexual inter-course was to provide pleasure. In the 1960's, the Tully River Blacks of north Queensland [Australia] believed that a woman became pregnant because she had been sitting over a fire on which she had roasted a fish given to her by the prospective father. Another Australian tribe believed that women conceived by eating human flesh. The Trobriand Islanders, though perfectly realistic about the function of coitus between animals, apparently drew no human parallels from it. In Papua New Guinea, the Hua tribe still thinks that a *man* can become pregnant (by eating possum) and may die in child-birth. And a woman of one Australian aboriginal tribe, when the Western facts of life and fatherhood were explained to her, flatly denied it: "Him nothing!" she said scornfully. (Tannahill, *Sex in History*, pg. 41-2)

It may be inferred from this that to the people who crafted the Neolithic goddess images, the goddess was the only supernatural figure with any relation to childbirth and survival. That would seem to make her the most important supernatural being in the universe! But somewhere along the way, someone learned that women didn't become pregnant magically or spontaneously, but that women become pregnant only after having sex with a man. This discovery may have been the impetus for the social control of women by men. Whichever man controls the women, it would seem, controls the lineage of the next generation. Institutions like marriage, concubinage, and so on, become important because they are the way to procure the loyalty of future (blood-related) farmers, gatherers, hunters, warriors, and so on. Then the female gods of creation and fertility began to take a second place to male gods of creation and fertility. As Tannahill says, "Nowhere in the mythology of the Near East—Sumerian, Babylonian, Egyptian, Ugaritic, Hittite, or Hebrew—is there any goddess whose power is supreme." (Tannahill, *Sex in History*, pg. 54) The only goddess whom Tannahill cites as an exception is the Sumerian goddess Inanna. In her story, she travels to the underworld, and in her absence the soil of the earth is barren. Otherwise, all the most important deities responsible for the fertility of the earth are male. Babylon's Ishtar is the consort of Tammuz, and Isis of Egypt is the partner of Osiris. It is these male deities who transit the underworld, leaving the surface of the earth barren until they return. Even in Greece, it is Adonis, and not Demeter, who embodies the fertility of the fields.

This male god of fertility, known to modern pagans variously as the Horned God, the Green Man, the Oak King and the Holly King, has an interesting story that deserves to be told. And like the Goddess With No Name, these male fertility gods eventually lost their place of honour in human society too. But in this book I wish to focus on the story of the Goddess, which is neglected even more. Let us turn to the next chapter and to a culture where a Goddess maintained a position of prestige even long after the discovery of the male role in procreation.

Second Movement

The Woman who Fell From The Sky

"I looked on the land and the rivers, the sky above, and the animals around me, and could not fail to realize they were made by some great power..."

The word Anishnabe means 'first people': and this word is also shared by members of Algonquian and Odawa nations. Together with the Hurons and Petun people, the Anishnabe were part of a political confederacy known as the Council of the Three Fires. In the times before contact with Europeans, the Anishnabe Nation was united by a language and culture; but politically they lived in numerous independent bands, each divided into numerous extended family groups which were named for their totems. A totem, by the way, is not just a family symbol. It is also an ancestor: it is an animal that features in the story of the family's origin. One nineteenth-century chronicler identified 21 Anishnabe totems, the most important of which were the crane, catfish, bear, marten, wolf, and loon. The traditional Anishnabe territory was around the Upper Great Lakes, especially the north shores of Lake Superior and Lake Huron, and also the Bruce Peninsula. After contact with Europeans, the Anishnabe expanded their territory, into what are now Wisconsin, Minnesota, Manitoba, and southern Ontario. This expansion was apparently driven by the fur trade. The story of the Anishnabe people after contact with Europeans is very much like the story of other First Nations, and it is not a happy one: the fur trade brought wealth and prosperity to some nations, but only temporarily. Warfare and competition for resources, the swift rise and swift collapse of the fur trade due to over-hunting, as well as disease, nearly destroyed Aboriginal culture everywhere. Many nations did, in fact, become entirely extinct. For instance, the last of the Beothuks of Newfoundland, a woman named

Shanawdithit, was captured in 1823 by English colonists, and died of tuberculosis in 1829. Today only three Aboriginal languages in Canada (out of more than fifty) are considered not at risk of disappearing entirely. But I am happy to say that the Ojibway language is one of them.

In the religious world-view of the Anishnabe people, spirits inhabit almost everything. According to Father Allouez, a Jesuit priest from France, who observed them in the mid 1660's, the Anishnabe:

> ...recognize no sovereign master of heaven and earth, but believe there are many spirits, some of whom are beneficent, as the Sun, the Moon, the Lake, Rivers, and Woods; others malevolent, as the adder, the dragon, cold, and storms. And, in general, whatever seems to them either helpful or hurtful they call a Manitou, and pay it ... worship and veneration. (*Jesuit Relations*, quoted in McMillan, *Native Peoples and Cultures in Canada*, pg. 99)

The word 'Manitou', sometimes translated as a spirit, can also mean a god. Notwithstanding Father Allouez' remarks about the absence of a 'sovereign master' of heaven and earth, the Anishnabe believe there is a Great Spirit, *Kitche-Manitou*, who is sometimes identified with the sun, and who oversees all things. Kitche Manitou tends to be distant from humanity, and usually works through intermediaries such as prophets and heroes. Let us look at the most important of those intermediaries. She is known by many names, but mostly by the name of Grandmother Sky-Woman. Her story begins before the world was made. She was alone, and she called out to Kitche Manitou for companionship. Kitche Manitou sent a companion to her, and they loved each other and had two children. But their children had opposite natures, and so they hated each other, and they fought and killed each other. Moreover, her companion abandoned her shortly after she became pregnant. The creatures of the water sensed her loneliness, and out of compassion sought ways to console her. A giant turtle rose to the surface of the water and offered its back as a place where the woman could rest. Various water animals were sent to the bottom of the ocean to procure soil. The beaver, the loon, the fisher and the marten all failed, but the humble muskrat succeeded. Sky-woman then used the small handful of soil brought by the muskrat to paint the turtle shell, and she breathed the breath of life into it, causing it to grow. In this way she transformed the turtle's shell into an island. The island was called Michilimackinac, or 'Place of the Great Turtle's Back'. All the animals brought to the new island plants for food and medicine, as well as trees and flowers. Finally, Sky-woman was content. She bore children again, a pair of male and female twins, and from them are descended the Anishnabe people.

On contemporary maps, Michilimackinac is called Manitoulin Island: it is the largest island in Lake Huron.

§ 1. Creation
Kitche Manitou (The Great Spirit) beheld a vision. In this dream he saw a vast sky filled with stars, sun, moon, and earth. He saw an earth made of mountains and valleys, islands and lakes, plains and forests. He was trees and flowers, grasses and vegetables. He saw walking, flying, swimming and crawling beings. He witnessed the birth, growth, and the end of things. At the same time he saw other things live on. Amidst change there was constancy. Kitche Manitou heard songs, wailings, and stories. He touched wind and rain. He felt love and hate, fear and courage, joy and sadness. Kitche Manitou meditated to understand his vision. In his wisdom Kitche Manitou understood that his vision had to be fulfilled. Kitche Manitou was to bring into being and existence what he had seen, heard, and felt.

Out of nothing he made rock, water, fire, and wind. Into each one he breathed the breath of life. On each he bestowed with his breath a different essence and nature. Each substance had its own power which became its soul-spirit. From these four substances Kitche Manitou created the physical world of sun, stars, moon, and earth...

Then Kitche Manitou made the plant beings. These were four kinds: flowers, grasses, trees, and vegetables. To each he gave a spirit of life, growth, healing, and beauty. Each he placed where it would be the most beneficial, and lend to earth the greatest beauty and harmony and order.

After plants, Kitche Manitou created animal beings conferring on each special powers and natures. There were two-leggeds, four-leggeds, winged, and swimmers.

Last of all he made man. Though last in the order of creation, least in the order of dependence, and weakest in bodily powers, man had the greatest gift — the power to dream.

Kitche Manitou then made The Great Laws of Nature for the well being and harmony of all things and all creatures. The Great Laws governed the place and movement of sun, moon, earth, and stars; governed the powers of wind, water, fire, and rock; governed the rhythm and continuity of life, birth, growth, and decay. All things lived and worked by these laws.

Kitche Manitou had brought into existence his vision.

§ 2. Destruction

Disaster fell upon the world. Great clouds formed in the sky and spilled water upon the earth, until the mountain tops were covered. All men died. All the land creatures perished. All the plants were covered by the sea. Only the water animals and birds and fishes lived on. What was once earth was a huge unbroken stretch of water whipped into foam and wave by the ferocious winds.

The world remained a sea for many generations.

§ 3. Re-Creation.

High in the heavens there lived alone a woman, a spirit. Without a companion she grew despondent. In her solitude she asked Kitche Manitou for some means to dispel her loneliness. Taking compassion on the sky-woman, Kitche Manitou sent a spirit to become her consort.

Sky-woman and her companion were happy together. In time the spirit woman conceived. Before she gave birth her consort left. Alone she bore two children, one pure spirit, and the other pure physical being.

The new beings of opposite natures and substances hated one another. In a fiery sky battle they fought and destroyed each other.

After the destruction of her children, the spirit woman again lived in solitude. Kitche Manitou knowing her desolation once more sent her a companion. Again sky-woman conceived. As before her consort left but sky-woman remained content.

The water creatures observed what was happening in the heavens, sensed the weariness of the spirit woman, and pitied her. In their compassion, they sought ways to provide relief for her. Eventually they persuaded a giant turtle to rise to the surface of the waters and offer his back as a haven. When the great turtle agreed, the water beings invited the sky-woman to come down.

The sky-woman accepted the invitation, left her abode in the skies, and came down to rest on the back of the great turtle. When sky-woman had settled on the turtle, she asked the water animals to get some soil from the bottom of the sea.

Gladly all the animals tried to serve the spirit woman. The beaver was one of the first to plunge into the depths. He soon surfaced, out of breath and without the precious soil. The fisher tried, but he too failed. The marten went down, came up empty handed, reporting that the water was too deep. Although he remained out of sight for a long time, he too emerged, gasping for air. He said that it was too dark. All tried to fulfil the spirit woman's request. All failed. All were ashamed.

Finally, the least of the water creatures, the muskrat, volunteered to dive. At his announcement, the other creatures laughed in scorn, because they doubted this little creature's strength and endurance. Had not they, who were strong and able, been unable to grasp soil from the bottom of the sea? How could he, a muskrat, the most humble among them, succeed when they could not?

Nevertheless, the little muskrat determined to dive. Undaunted he disappeared into the waves. The onlookers smiled. They waited for the muskrat to emerge as empty handed as they had done. Time passed. Smiles turned into worried frowns. The small hope that each had nurtured for the success of the muskrat turned into despair. When the waiting creatures had given up, the muskrat floated to the surface more dead than alive, but he clutched in his paws a small morsel of soil. Where the great had failed, the small succeeded.

While the muskrat was tended and restored to health, the spirit woman painted the rim of the turtle's back with the small amount of soil that had been brought to her. She breathed upon it and into it the breath of life. Immediately the soil grew, covered the turtle's back, and formed an island. The turtle had given his service, which was no longer required and he swam away. The island formed in this way was called Mishee Mackinakong, the place of the Great Turtle's back, now known as Michilimackinac.

For his service to mankind and the spirit woman, the turtle became the messenger of thought and feeling that flows and flashes between beings of different natures and orders. He became a symbol of thought given and received. The turtle, slowest of all creatures, represented celerity and communication between things.

The island home grew in size. As the waters subsided, the animal beings brought grasses, flowers, trees, and food-bearing plants to the sky-woman. Into each she infused her life-giving breath and they lived once more. In the same way were the animals that had drowned revived. Everything was restored on that island home.

At last the time came for the sky woman to fulfill the promise of life. One cloudless morning she gave birth to twins, a boy and a girl.

The new beings were unlike her first children who had destroyed one another. They were composite in nature, made up of physical substance, and a soul-spirit substance. In this respect they were similar, yet at the same time they encompassed vast differences. One was a man, the other was woman. Although they were different, they tended toward union with one another. Neither was complete or fulfilled without the other. Only together did they possess meaning: only together could they fulfill their purposes.

What was unique was the soul-spirit of each. Called "cheejauk" it was made up of six aspects: character, personality, soul, spirit, heart or feeling, and a life principle. This substance had the capacity to dream and to receive vision. Through dream and vision a man would find guidance in attaining fulfillment of self.

For men the vision was necessary for self-fulfillment; for women a vision was not essential. By giving life through the first mother, women were fulfilled. Just as Kitche Manitou had received a vision and brought it to fulfillment, so had men to quest for it and live it out once they received it.

Men and women had yet another aspect. Each possessed his "chibowmun", or aura. It was a substance emanating from his "cheejauk", through his body by which the state and quality of his inner being was sensed and felt.

The new men and women were called "Anishnabeg", beings made out of nothing, because their substances were not rock, or fire, or water, or wind. They were "spontaneous beings".

The cycle was complete, creation, destruction, and re-creation.

In the first year, the animals nourished and nurtured the

infants and the spirit woman. For all their needs the spirit woman and her children depended upon the care and goodwill of the animals. The bears, wolves, foxes, deer, and beaver brought food and drink; the squirrels, weasels, raccoons, and cats offered toys and games; the robins, sparrows, chickadees, and loons sang and danced in the air; the butterflies, bees, and dragonflies made the children smile. All the animal beings served in some tangible way; all except the lowly dog.

Of the animal beings, the dog was endowed with the least exceptional powers. He was less fleet than the fox; he was weaker than the wolf, he was less cunning than the mink. Compared to the fisher, the dog was a poor swimmer; beside the deer, the dog was awkward. Less gifted than his brothers, the dog had nothing to offer. He could not serve. Nevertheless he felt constrained to do something. In his despondency, he pledged to give his love. Others could serve according to their natures and capacities; he to his.

The first winter in the life of the Anishnabeg was an ordeal. Food was scarce, the winds were harsh. The infants grew sick and lost strength daily. It seemed that they would not survive the winter. The spirit woman was disconsolate, and the animals and birds were alarmed that the babies they had grown to love would die. The bear, fearing the death of the infants, offered himself that they might live.

With the bear's sweet flesh, the infants survived. The death of the bear encompassed life for the new beings. Thereafter, the other animals sacrificed their lives for the good of men. When the infants grew into manhood and womanhood, they bore a special love for the bear and honoured him in their ceremonies. In gratitude and fondness they dedicated a prayer to the other animals, "I have need". Men and women survive and live because of the death of their elder brothers.

Many years later when the first Anishnabeg had grown up and spirit woman was certain of their survival, she called her children to her. She told them that she was returning to the Land of Peace, to her proper place of abode. She also told them that when they had lived out their term of life and had done sufficient good in life, they too would leave their bodies in the Land of the Living and go to the Land of Peace as soul-spirits, and live there in another way.

Then the spirit woman ascended into the sky to return, to her home. Thereafter the Anishnabeg remembered the first of Mothers, Nokomis (Grandmother) whenever the moon gave light. At the same time, they remembered the primacy of women, who bore the unique gift of life, for it was through woman that the cycle – creation, destruction, re-creation – was completed. For her special gift of giving life and being, women had a special place in the order of existence and were exempt from the vision quest.

After the spirit woman returned to her own realm, the Anishnabeg prospered and increased in numbers. Animals and men and women labored readily and happily together. Michilimackinac was a happy home to all.

(Source: Basil Johnston, *Ojibway Heritage*, pp. 12-17.)

Third Movement

Inanna: The Queen of Heaven and Earth

"Would you walk ten miles with me, my love? Would you walk the skies with me...?"

Sumeria was the world's very first state-level civilization. Its ancient territory lay between the rivers Tigris and Euphrates, in what later became Babylonia, and is now called Iraq. It spread from the great city of Akkad (just north-west of modern Baghdad), and then south-east following the Tigris and Euphrates rivers to the Persian Gulf. Today we think of this land as a desert, but at the time of the Sumerian civilisation, the land was very fertile. Indeed much of the lower half of Sumeria was marshland and swamp. Around 2800 BCE, twelve independent city-states, which had been founded in the third millennium BCE and which had only a language in common, were united into a single empire by King Etana of Kish. Thereafter, the cities of Kish, Erech, Ur, and Lagash competed with each other for control of the whole empire. Sumeria was conquered and displaced by the Amorites in 1900 BCE. But they gave to their successors many important cultural advances, such as one of the earliest systems of writing, called cuneiform. This form of writing, which was etched on to clay tablets, was not to be deciphered until the 19th century.

Among those tablets, the translators found the stories of a goddess named Inanna, the first goddess to be recorded in written form in the whole history of Western civilization. The name of Inanna comes from Sumeria: she is also known to the Babylonians as Ishtar, and to the West Semites as Astarte. She was at first known as a goddess of rain and of thunderstorms. From this association she became associated with the sky god An (in some stories her father, in others her lover), with lions (the roar resembles the sound of thunder), and with warfare. Inanna is also associated with love and fertility, in several different ways.

Inanna's most well known association with fertility is through prostitution. At the city of Erech, one of her religious centers, the temple doubled as an alehouse and as a brothel. Young women in the community were brought there when they entered puberty, to serve the goddess as a courtesan for a time. James Frazer, author of The Golden Bough (1922), noted that these women were often not allowed to leave until they had their first sexual encounter with a man. In his words:

> Whatever its motive, the practice was clearly regarded, not as an orgy of lust, but as a solemn religious duty performed in the service of that great Mother Goddess of Western Asia whose name varied, while her type remained constant, from place to place. Thus at Babylon every woman, whether rich or poor, had once in her life to submit to the embraces of a stranger at the temple of Mylitta, that is, of Ishtar or Astarte, and to dedicate to the goddess the wages earned by this sanctified harlotry. (Frazer, The Golden Bough, pg. 384.)

The young couple would have understood themselves to be re-enacting the courtship and mating of the goddess Inanna and her lover, and that by means of this ritual they would win the favour of the goddess and ensure the fertility of the earth.

> "The fabulous union of the divine pair was simulated and, as it were, multiplied on earth by the real, though temporary, union of the human sexes at the sanctuary of the goddess for the sake of thereby ensuring the fruitfulness of the ground and the increase of man and beast." (ibid, pg. 385.)

As an ordinary working class man, Dumuzi was not Inanna's first choice for a husband. But as the story here quoted goes, Dumuzi earned her love by honestly representing himself as he is, and by speaking to her 'a word of desire'. An uncharitable reading of this story may suggest that Dumuzi seduced her. But I think that Inanna was not the sort of goddess whom any one could seduce, unless she allowed herself to be seduced. Dumuzi's word of desire is not given here. I believe, however, that it was her *name*. Dumuzi, first representing himself as he truly is, then showed that he knew her for who she truly is. If I am right, and his word of desire was her name, this might mean that his love for her, while perhaps in part based on a romantic emotional impulse, was not based on illusion or fantasy. It was also based on honest knowledge, and rational choice. Dumuzi showed that he could love her for herself. She therefore chose to love him in return, regardless of his social standing, and regardless of other people's expectations. This is the action of an independent and purposeful woman. And as the story describes it, the love they shared was charged with spirituality, and with unapologetic eroticism.

Inanna's most important story is called The Descent. As the story opens, Inanna has already established herself as Queen of Heaven. She helped to plant the World Tree, and then helped to rescue it from being usurped by monsters. She met with Enki, the god of wisdom, and got drunk with him, in order to obtain from him a collection of treasures known as the Holy *Me* (pronounced "May"). She then took Dumuzi for her husband. And then the goddess encountered one last region she has not yet visited: the Underworld. It is a place she must go in order to establish herself as a comprehensive goddess of all three realms in the Sumerian cosmology (the sky, the earth, and the 'great below'). The ruler of the underworld was a goddess named Erishkegal, a kind of alter-ego for Inanna herself. Inanna had to pass through seven gates to reach Erishkegal throne room. At each gate a piece of jewelry or clothing is removed, until after the seventh gate she is completely naked. Erishkegal, upon seeing her, is full of resentment and anger, and is apparently unable to take the competition. Therefore she has Ishtar killed: in one version of the story, she orders her vizier to inflict sixty diseases upon her. Inanna's lifeless body is then hung on a hook on a wall.

Up above, on earth, Inanna's absence has brought all fertility to an end. No animals mate each other, and even human beings are unable to have sex. The gods therefore contrive a plan to retrieve her. They create 'impersonators' (Ishtar's story has one, Inanna's has two) and send them to the underworld. In one version of the story, the impersonators dance and entertain Erishkegal. In the other version, reproduced here, they are sent to heal her, by taking pity on her condition and empathizing with her feelings. In either case, they are instructed to ask a boon from Erishkegal as their reward: the body of Ishtar, to be brought back to life and returned to the world above. The story is easy to interpret as an allegory for the turning of the seasons. Yet it is also a beautiful story in its own right, and its honesty about human feelings deserves admiration.

Ishtar's paramour Dumuzi undergoes a cycle of death and rebirth, in part made possible by Inanna's help. As described in the praise-song to him that I have included here, Dumuzi was tending his flock in the desert when he was attacked and killed by Bilulu and her son Girgire, raiders intent upon stealing his flock. When Inanna discovered this she became enraged, went to the alehouse where the raiders were staying, and cast a curse upon them which transformed them into djinni (desert spirits). Bilulu was also transformed into a water skin. Thereafter, offerings of water or wine poured out for Inanna or Dumuzi were poured from a water skin.

§ 4. The Courtship of Inanna and Dumuzi.

The brother spoke to his younger sister.
The Sun god, Utu, spoke to Inanna, saying:
"Young Lady, the flax in its fullness is lovely.
Inanna, the grain is glistening in the furrow.

I will hoe it for you. I will bring it to you.
A piece of linen, big or small, is always needed.
Inanna, I will bring it to you."

"Brother, after you've brought me the flax,
Who will comb it for me?"

"Sister, I will bring it to you combed."

"Utu, after you've brought it to me combed,
Who will spin it for me?"

"Inanna, I will bring it to you spun."

"Brother, after you brought the flax to me spun,
Who will braid it for me?"

"Sister, I will bring it to you braided."

"Utu, after you brought it to me braided,
Who will warp it for me?"

"Inanna, I will bring it to you warped."

"Brother, after you've brought the flax to me warped,
Who will weave it for me?"

"Sister, I will bring it to you woven."

"Utu, after you've brought it to me woven,
Who will bleach it for me?"

"Inanna, I will bring it to you bleached."

"Brother, after you've brought my bridal sheet to me,
Who will go to bed with me?
Utu, who will go to bed with me?"

"Sister, your bridegroom will go to bed with you.
He who was born from a fertile womb,
He who was conceived on the sacred marriage throne,
Dumuzi, the shepherd! He will go to bed with you."

Inanna spoke:
"No, brother!
The man of my heart works the hoe.
The farmer! He is the man of my heart!
He gathers the grain into great heaps.
He brings the grain regularly into my storehouses."

Utu spoke:
"Sister, marry the shepherd.
Why are you unwilling?
His cream is good, his milk is good.
Whatever he touches shines brightly.
Inanna, marry Dumuzi.
You who adorn yourself with the agate necklace of fertility.
Why are you unwilling?
Dumuzi will share his rich cream with you.
You who are meant to be the king's protector,
Why are you unwilling?"

Inanna spoke:
"The shepherd! I will not marry the shepherd!
His clothes are coarse, his wool is rough.
I will marry the farmer.
The farmer grows flax for my clothes.
The farmer grows barley for my table."

Dumuzi spoke:

"Why do you speak about the farmer?
Why do you speak about him?
If he gives you black flour,
I will give you black wool.
If he gives you white flour,
I will give you white wool.
If he gives you beer,
I will give you sweet milk.
If he gives you bread,
I will give you honey cheese.
I will give the farmer my leftover cream.
I will give the farmer my leftover milk.
Why do you speak about the farmer?
What does he have more than I do?"

Inanna spoke:

Shepherd, without my mother, Ningal, you'd be driven away.
Without my grandmother, Ningikuga, you'd be driven into
the steppes,
Without my father, Nanna, you'd have no roof.
Without my brother, Utu—"

Dumuzi spoke:

"Inanna, do not start a quarrel.
My father, Enki, is as good as your father, Nanna.
My mother, Sirtur, is as good as your mother, Ningal.
My sister, Geshtinanna, is as good as yours.
Queen of the palace, let us talk it over.
Inanna, let us sit and speak together.
I am as good as Utu.
Enki is as good as Nanna.
Sirtur is as good as Ningal.
Queen of the palace, let us talk it over."

The word they had spoken
Was a word of desire.
From the starting of the quarrel
Came the lover's desire.

The shepherd went to the royal house with cream.
Dumuzi went to the royal house with milk.
Before the door, he called out:
"Open the house, My Lady, open the house!"

Inanna an to Ningal, the mother who bore her.
Ningal counseled her daughter, saying:
"My child, the young man will be your father.
My daughter, the young man will be your mother.
He will treat you like a father,
He will treat you like a mother.
Open the house, My Lady, open the house!"

Inanna, at her mother's command,
Bathed and anointed herself with scented oil.
She covered her body with the royal white robe
She readied her dowry.
She arranged her precious lapis beads around her neck.
She took her seal in her hand.

Dumuzi waited expectantly.

Inanna opened the door for him.
Inside the house she shone before him
Like the light of the moon.

Dumuzi looked at her joyously.
He pressed his neck close against hers.
He kissed her.

Inanna spoke:
    "What I tell you,
    Let the singer weave into song.
    What I tell you,
    Let it flow from ear to mouth,
    Let it pass from old to young:
    My vulva, the horn,
    The Boat of Heaven,
    Is full of eagerness like the young moon.
    My untilled land lies fallow.

    As for me, Inanna,
    Who will plow my vulva?
    Who will plow my high field?
    Who will plow my wet ground?

    As for me, the young woman,
    Who will plow my vulva?
    Who will station the ox there?
    Who will plow my vulva?"

Dumuzi replied:
    "Great lady, the king will plow your vulva.
    I, Dumuzi the King, will plow your vulva."

Inanna:
    "Then plow my vulva, man of my heart!
    Plow my vulva!"

    At the king's lap stood the rising cedar.
    Plants grew high by their side.
    Grains grew high by their side.
    Gardens flourished luxuriantly.

Inanna sang:
>"He has sprouted; he has burgeoned;
>He is lettuce planted by the water.
>He is the one my womb loves best.
>
>My well stocked garden of the plain,
>My barley growing high in the furrow,
>My apple tree which bears fruit up to its crown,
>He is lettuce planted by the water.
>
>My honey-man, my honey man sweetens me always.
>My lord, the honey-man of the gods,
>He is the one my womb loves best.
>His hand is honey, his foot is honey,
>He sweetens me always.
>
>My eager impetuous caresser of the navel,
>My caresser of the soft thighs,
>He is the one my womb loves best,
>He is lettuce planted by the water."

Dumuzi sang:
>O Lady, your breast is your field.
>Inanna, your breast is your field.
>Your broad field pours out plants.
>Your broad field pours out grain.
>Water flows from on high for your servant.
>Bread flows from on high for your servant.
>Pour it out for me, Inanna.
>I will drink all you offer."

Inanna sang:
>"Make your milk sweet and thick, my bridegroom.
>My shepherd, I will drink your fresh milk.

Wild bull, Dumuzi, make your milk sweet and thick.
I will drink your fresh milk.

Let the milk of the goat flow in my sheepfold.
Fill my holy churn with the honey cheese.
Lord Dumuzi, I will drink your fresh milk.

My husband, I will guard my sheepfold for you.
I will watch over your house of life, the storehouse,
The shining quivering place which delights Sumer—
The house which decides the fates of the land,
The house which gives the breath of life to the people.
I, the queen of the palace, will watch over your house."

Dumuzi spoke:
"My sister, I would go with you to my garden,
Inanna, I would go with you to my garden.
I would go with you to my orchard.
I would go with you to my apple tree.
There I would plant the sweet, honey-covered seed."

Inanna spoke:
"He brought me into his garden.
By brother, Dumuzi, brought me into his garden.
I strolled with him among the standing trees,
I stood with him among the fallen trees,
By an apple tree I knelt as is proper.
Before my brother coming in song,
Who rose to me out of the poplar leaves,
Who came to me in the midday heat,
Before my lord Dumuzi,
I poured out plants from my womb.
I placed plants before him,
I poured out plants before him.

I placed grain before him,
I poured out grain before him.
I poured out grain from my womb."

Inanna sang:
"Last night as I, the queen, was shining bright,
Last night as I, the Queen of Heaven, was shining bright,
As I was shining bright and dancing,
Singing praises at the coming of the night—

He met me—he met me!
My lord Dumuzi met me.
He put his hand into my hand.
He pressed his neck close against mine.

My high priest is ready for the holy loins.
My lord Dumuzi is ready for the holy loins.
The plants and herbs in his field are ripe.
O Dumuzi! Your fullness is my delight!"

She called for it, she called for it, she called for the bed!
She called for the bed that rejoices the heart.
She called for the bed that sweetens the loins.
She called for the bed of kingship.
She called for the bed of queenship.
Inanna called for the bed:
"Let the bed that rejoices the heart be prepared!
Let the bed that sweetens the loins be prepared!
Let the bed of kingship be prepared!
Let the bed of queenship be prepared!
Let the royal bed be prepared!"

Inanna spread the bridal sheet across the bed.
She called to the king:

"The bed is ready!"
She called to her bridegroom:
"The bed is waiting!"

He put his hand in her hand.
He put his hand to her heart.
Sweet is the sleep of hand-to-hand.
Sweeter still the sleep of the heart-to-heart.
(Source: Wolkstein and Kramer, *Inanna: Queen of Heaven and Earth*, pp. 30-43)

§ 5. The Descent of Inanna

From the Great Above she opened her ear to the Great Below.

From the Great Above the goddess opened her ear to the Great Below.

From the Great Above Inanna opened her ear to the Great Below.

My Lady abandoned heaven and earth to descend to the underworld.

Inanna abandoned heaven and earth to descend to the underworld.

She abandoned her office of holy priestess to descend to the underworld.

In Uruk she abandoned her temple to descend to the underworld.

In Badtibira she abandoned her temple to descend to the underworld.

In Zabalam she abandoned her temple to descend to the underworld.

In Adab she abandoned her temple to descend to the underworld.

In Nippur she abandoned her temple to descend to the underworld.

In Kish she abandoned her temple to descend to the underworld.

In Akkad she abandoned her temple to descend to the underworld.

She gathered together the seven *me*.

She took them into her hands.

With the *me* in her possession, she prepared herself:

She placed the *shugurra*, the crown of the steppe, on her head.

She arranged the dark locks of her hair across her forehead.

She tied the small lapis beads around her neck,

Let the double strand of beads fall to her breast,

And wrapped the royal robe around her body.

She daubed her eyes with ointment called "Let him come, let him come,"

Bound the breastplate called "Come, man, come!" around her chest,

Slipped the gold ring over her wrist,

And took the lapis measuring rod and line in her hand.

Inanna set out for the underworld.

Ninshubur, her faithful servant, went with her.

Inanna spoke to her, saying:

"Ninshubur, my constant support,

My *sukkal* who gives me wise advice,

My warrior who fights by my side,

I am descending to the *kur*, to the underworld.

If I do not return,

Set up a lament for me by the ruins.

Beat the drum for me in the assembly places.

Circle the houses of the gods.

Tear at your eyes, at your mouth, at your thighs.

Dress yourself in a single garment like a beggar.
Go to Nippur, to the temple of Enlil.
When you enter the holy shrine, cry out:
'O father Enlil, do not let your daughter
Be put to death in the underworld.
Do not let your bright silver
Be covered with the dust of the underworld.
Do not let your precious lapis
Be broken into stone for the stoneworker.
Do not let your fragrant boxwood
Be cut into wood for the woodworker.
Do not let the holy priestess of heaven
Be put to death in the underworld.'

If Enlil will not help you,
Go to Ur, to the temple of Nanna.
Weep before Father Nanna.
If Nanna will not help you,
Go to Eridu, to the temple of Enki.
Father Enki, the God of Wisdom, knows the food of life,
He knows the water of life,
He knows the secrets.
Surely he will not let me die."

Inanna continued on her way to the underworld.
Then she stopped and said:
"Go now, Ninshubur—
Do not forget the words I have commanded you."

When Inanna arrived at the outer gates of the underworld,
She knocked loudly.
She cried out in a fierce voice:
"Open the door, gatekeeper!
Open the door, Neti!

I alone would enter!"

Neti, the chief gatekeeper of the *kur*, asked:
"Who are you?"

She answered:
"I am Inanna, Queen of heaven,
On my way to the East."

Neti said:
"If you are truly Inanna, Queen of Heaven,
On your way to the East,
Why has your heart led you on the road
From which no traveler returns?"

Inanna answered:
"Because of my older sister, Erishkegal,
Her husband, Gugalanna, the Bull of Heaven, has died.
I have come to witness the funeral rights.
Let the beer of his funeral rites be poured into the cup.
Let it be done."

Neti spoke:
"Stay here, Inanna, I will speak to my queen.
I will give her your message."

Neti, the chief gatekeeper of the *kur*,
Entered the palace of Erishkegal, the Queen of the
Underworld, and said:
"My queen, a maid
As tall as heaven,
As wide as the earth
As strong as the foundations of the city wall,
Waits outside the palace gates.

She has gathered together the seven *me*.
She has taken them into her hands.
With the *me* in her possession, she has prepared herself.

On her head she wears the *shugurra*, the crown of the steppe.
Across her forehead her dark locks of hair are carefully arranged.
Around her neck she wears the small lapis beads.
At her breast she wears the double strand of beads.
Her body is wrapped with the royal robe.
Her eyes are daubed with the ointment called, 'Let him come, let him come.'
Around her chest she wears the breastplate called 'Come, man, come!'
On her wrist she wears the gold ring.
In her hands she carries the lapis measuring rod and line."

When Erishkegal heard this,
She slapped her thigh and bit her lip.
She took the matter in to her heart and dwelt on it.
Then she spoke:
"Come, Neti, my chief gatekeeper of the *kur*,
Heed my words:
Bolt the seven gates of the underworld.
Then, one by one, open each gate a crack.
Let Inanna enter.
As she enters, remove her royal garments.
Let the holy priestess of heaven enter bowed low."

Neti heeded the words of his queen.
He bolted the seven gates of the underworld.
Then he opened the outer gate.
He said to the maid:
"Come, Inanna, enter."

When she entered the first gate,
From her head, the *shugurra*, the crown of the steppe, was removed.

Inanna asked, "What is this?"

She was told:
"Quiet, Inanna, the ways of the underworld are perfect.
They may not be questioned."

When she entered the second gate,
From her neck the small lapis beads were removed.

Inanna asked, "What is this?"

She was told:
"Quiet, Inanna, the ways of the underworld are perfect.
They may not be questioned."

When she entered the third gate,
From her breast the double strand of beads was removed.

Inanna asked, "What is this?"

She was told:
"Quiet, Inanna, the ways of the underworld are perfect.
They may not be questioned."

When she entered the fourth gate,
From her chest the breastplate called "Come, man, come!" was removed.

Inanna asked, "What is this?"

She was told:
  "Quiet, Inanna, the ways of the underworld are perfect.
  They may not be questioned."

  When she entered the fifth gate,
  From her wrist the gold ring was removed.

  Inanna asked, "What is this?"

She was told:
  "Quiet, Inanna, the ways of the underworld are perfect.
  They may not be questioned."

  When she entered the sixth gate,
  From her hand the lapis measuring rod and line was removed.

  Inanna asked, "What is this?"
She was told:
  "Quiet, Inanna, the ways of the underworld are perfect.
  They may not be questioned."

  When she entered the seventh gate,
  From her body the royal robe was removed.

  Inanna asked, "What is this?"

She was told:
  "Quiet, Inanna, the ways of the underworld are perfect.
  They may not be questioned."

  Naked and bowed low, Inanna entered the thrown room.
  Erishkegal rose from her throne.
  Inanna started toward the throne.
  The Annuna, the judges of the underworld, surrounded her.

They passed judgement against her.

Then Ereshkigal fastened on Inanna the eye of death.
She spoke against her the word of wrath.
She uttered against her the cry of guilt.

She struck her.

Inanna was turned into a corpse,
A piece of rotting meat,
And was hung from a hook on the wall.

When, after three days and three nights, Inanna had not returned,
Ninshubur set up a lament for her by the ruins.
She beat the drum for her in the assembly places.
She circled the houses of the gods.
She tore at her eyes; she tore at her mouth; she tore at her thighs.
She dressed herself in a single garment like a beggar.
Alone, she set out for Nippur and the temple of Enlil.

When she entered the holy shrine, She cried out:
"O Father Enlil, do not let your daughter
Be put to death in the underworld.
Do not let your bright silver
Be covered with the dust of the underworld.
Do not let your precious lapis
Be broken into stone for the stoneworker.
Do not let your fragrant boxwood
Be cut into wood for the woodworker.
Do not let the holy priestess of heaven
Be put to death in the underworld."

Father Enlil answered angrily:

"My daughter craved the Great Above.

Inanna craved the Great Below.

She who receives the *me* of the underworld does not return.

She who goes to the Dark City stays there."

Father Enlil would not help.

Ninshubur went to Ur and the temple of Nanna.

When she entered the holy shrine, she cried out:

"O Father Nanna, do not let your daughter

Be put to death in the underworld.

Do not let your bright silver

Be covered with the dust of the underworld.

Do not let your precious lapis

Be broken into stone for the stoneworker.

Do not let your fragrant boxwood

Be cut into wood for the woodworker.

Do not let the holy priestess of heaven

Be put to death in the underworld."

Father Nanna answered angrily:

"My daughter craved the Great Above.

Inanna craved the Great Below.

She who receives the *me* of the underworld does not return.

She who goes to the Dark City stays there."

Father Nanna would not help.

Ninshubur went to Eridu and the temple of Enki.

When she entered the holy shrine, she cried out:

"O Father Enki, do not let your daughter

Be put to death in the underworld.

Do not let your bright silver

Be covered with the dust of the underworld.
Do not let your precious lapis
Be broken into stone for the stoneworker.
Do not let your fragrant boxwood
Be cut into wood for the woodworker.
Do not let the holy priestess of heaven
Be put to death in the underworld."

Father Enki said:
"What has happened?
What has my daughter done?
Inanna! Queen of All the Lands! Holy Priestess of Heaven!
What has happened?
I am troubled. I am grieved."

From under his fingernail Father Enki brought forth dirt.
He fashioned the dirt into a *kurgarra*, a creature neither male nor female.
From under the fingernail of his other hand he brought forth dirt.
He fashioned the dirt into a *galatur*, a creature neither male nor female.
He gave the food of life to the *kurgarra*.
He gave the water of life to the *galatur*.
Enki spoke to the *kurgarra* and *galatur*, saying:
"Go to the underworld,
Enter the door like flies.
Ereshkigal, the Queen of the Underworld, is moaning
With the cries of a woman about to give birth.
No linen is spread over her body.
Her breasts are uncovered.
Her hair swirls about her head like leeks.
When she cries, 'Oh! Oh! My inside!'
Cry also, 'Oh! Oh! Your inside!'

When she cries, 'Oh! Oh! My outside!'
Cry also, 'Oh! Oh! Your outside!'
The queen will be pleased.
She will offer you a gift.
Ask her only for the corpse that hangs from the hook on the wall.
One of you will sprinkle the food of life on it.
The other will sprinkle the water of life.
Inanna will arise."

The *kurgarra* and the *galatur* heeded Enki's words.
They set out for the underworld.
Like flies, they slipped through the cracks of the gates.
They entered the throne room of the Queen of the Underworld.
No linen was spread over her body.
Her breasts were uncovered.
Her hair swirled around her head like leeks.

Ereshkigal was moaning:
"Oh Oh! My inside!"

They moaned:
"Oh! Oh! Your inside!"

She moaned:
"Ohhhh! Oh! My outside!"

They moaned:
"Ohhhh! Oh! Your outside!"

She groaned:
"Oh! Oh! My belly!"

They groaned:
    "Oh! Oh! Your belly!"

She groaned:
    "Oh! Ohhhh! My back!"

They groaned:
    "Oh! Ohhhh! Your back!"

She sighed:
    "Ah! Ah! My heart!"

They sighed:
    "Ah! Ah! Your heart!"

She sighed:
    "Ah! Ahhhh! My liver!"
They sighed:
    "Ah! Ahhh! Your liver!"

    Erishkegal stopped.
    She looked at them.
She asked:
    "Who are you,
    Moaning, groaning, sighing with me?
    If you are gods, I will bless you.
    If you are mortals, I will give you a gift.
    I will give you the water-gift, the river in its fullness."

The *kurgarra* and *galatur* answered:
    "We do not wish it."

Ereshkigal said:
    "I will give you the grain-gift, the fields in harvest."

The *kurgarra* and *galatur* answered:
"We do not wish it."

Ereshkigal said:
"Speak then! What do you wish?"

They answered:
"We wish only the corpse that hangs from the hook on the wall."

Ereshkigal said:
"The corpse belongs to Inanna."

They said:
"Whether it belongs to our queen,
Whether it belongs to our king,
That is what we wish."

The corpse was given to them.

The *kurgarra* sprinkled the food of life on the corpse.
The *galatur* sprinkled the water of life on the corpse.
Inanna arose.
(Source: Wolkstein & Kramer, *Inanna: Queen of Heaven and Earth*, pp.52-67.)

§ 6. Hymn to Dumuzi

O lord Dumuzi, awe-inspiring shepherd of Anu,
Lover of Ishtar the queen, eldest son of Nudimmud,
O mighty one, leader without rival,
Who eats pure loaves baked in embers,
Who is clad in a cloak and carries a staff,
Who drinks water from a water skin,
Creator of everything, lord of the sheepfold,

You are the lofty prince, the noble one!
Drive away from me the "evil gazer", the worker of evil,
Who has fixated upon me and is trying to cut short my life.
Herewith I bring you my life!
I hand him over to an evil spirit, a merciless demon,
Let him be cut off from me, grant me life!
Tear out the "evil gazer" who is present in my body,
Let me sound your praises until the end point of these (my) days.

(Foster, *From Distant Days*, pg. 222.)

§ 7. Hymn to Ishtar: Sing of the Goddess

Sing of the Goddess, most awe-inspiring goddess,
Let her be praised, mistress of people, greatest of the Igigi-gods.

Sing of Ishtar, most awe-inspiring goddess; let her be praised,
Mistress of women, greatest of the Igigi-gods.

She is the joyous one, clad in loveliness,
She is adorned with allure, appeal, charm.
Ishtar is the joyous one, clad in loveliness,
She is adorned with allure, appeal, charm.

In her lips she is sweetness, vitality her mouth,
While on her features laughter bursts to bloom.
She is proud of the love charms set on her head,
Fair her hues, full-ranging, and lustrous her eyes.

This goddess, right counsel is hers,
She grasps in her hand the destinies of all that exists.
At her regard, well-being is born,
Vigor, dignity, good fortune, divine protection.

Whispers, surrender, sweet shared captivation,

Harmony too she reigns over as mistress.
The girl who invokes finds in her a mother,
Among women, one mentions her, invokes her name.

Who is that could rival her grandeur?
Her attributes are mighty, splendid, superb,
Ishtar this is, who could rival her grandeur?
Her attributes are mighty, splendid, superb.

She it is who stands foremost among the gods,
Her word is the weightiest and prevails over theirs.
Ishtar stands foremost among the gods,
Her word is the weightiest and prevails over theirs.

She is their queen, they relay her commands,
All of them bow down before her:
They go to her in her radiance,
Women and men fear her too.
In their assembly her utterance is noble, surpassing,
She is seated among them as an equal to Anu their king.
She is wise in understanding and perception.
Together they make their decisions, she and her lord.

There they sit together on the dais
In the temple chamber, abode of delights,
The gods stand in attendance before them,
Their ears awaiting what those mouths will command.

Their favourite king, whom their hearts love most,
Ever offers in splendor his pure offerings,
Ammiditana offers before them
His personal, pure libation of cattle and fatted lambs.

She has asked of Anu her spouse long life hereafter for him,

Many years of life for Ammiditana
Has Ishtar rendered to him as her gift.

By her command she gave him submission
The four world regions at his feet,
She harnessed the whole of the inhabited world to his yoke.

What she desires, this song is for her pleasure
Is indeed well suited to his mouth, he performed for her Ea's
own words.

When he heard this song of her praise, he was well pleased
with him,

Saying, "Let him live long, may his own king always love
him."

O Ishtar, grant long life enduring to Ammiditana,
The king who loves you, long may he live!
(Foster, *From Distant Days*, pg. 238-41)

§ 8. *(Excerpt from) Hymn to Ishtar: The Great Prayer*

I implore you, lady of ladies, goddess of goddesses,

Ishtar, queen of all the inhabited world, who governs the
peoples,

Irnini, you are noble, the greatest of the Igigi-gods,

You are powerful, you are queen, exalted is your name.

You are the luminary of heaven and earth, the valiant daughter
of Sin

Who brandishes weapons, who prepares for battle,

Who gathers to herself all rites, who dons the lordly tiara,

O Mistress, splendid is your greatness, exalted over all the
gods.

Planet for the war cry, who can make harmonious brothers set
at one another.

Who can always grant a comrade,

Strong one, mistress of the tilt, who gores mountains,

Gushea, whose mail is combat, clothed in chilling fear.

You render final judgment and decision, the command for heaven and netherworld,

Chapels, sanctuaries, altars, and daises are attentive to you.

Where is not your name, where are not your rites?

Where are your designs not put into effect, where are your daises not set up?

Where are you not great, where are you not exalted?

Anu, Enlil, and Ea have lifted you high, they have made your authority greatest among the gods.

They have given you the highest rank among all the Igigi-gods, they have made your station highest of all.

At the thought of your name, heaven and netherworld quake,

The gods totter, the Anunna-gods tremble.

Mankind extols your awe-inspiring name,

You are the great one, the exalted one.

All the [Mesopotamians], living creatures, mankind, praise your valour.

You are the one who renders verdicts for subject peoples in truth and justice.

You look upon the oppressed and abused and always set them right.

Have mercy, mistress of heaven and earth, shepherd of the human race!

Have mercy, mistress of holy Eanna, the pure treasury!

Have mercy, mistress whose feet weary not, whose legs are strong to run!

Have mercy, mistress of combat and of every melee!

(Foster, *From Distant Days*, pp. 241-2)

Fourth Movement

Demeter and the Eleusinian Mysteries of Greece

"Thou Nature art my goddess..."

Greece, the "cradle of Western civilisation", is where we travel next. Everyone is probably familiar with the names, if not the stories of the Olympian deities. But the one I wish to draw special attention to is the goddess of the earth and the harvest, to whom the religious festival known as the Eleusinean Mysteries was dedicated: Demeter. But first, I must set the scene.

It is important to understand how very different Greek religion was, compared to religion today. The function of a Greek priest, no matter which deity he or she served, was simply to perform the rituals and sacrifices correctly, and at the correct time. He or she was not a promoter of some standard of ethics. He was certainly not a 'spiritual councilor'. Someone might ask a priest to perform divinations to learn the will of the gods. Then he might ask the priest to do some further ritual in order to sway the will of the deity in his favour. Or he might ask the priest to obtain the blessing of the god for some purpose or plan. But that is all that was ever expected of a Greek priest. After he had given these services, his job was done. In almost all Greek mythology, the gods interact with men and women freely, without any clerical intermediaries. They talk to each other, exchange gifts and services, make love, and even fight each other sometimes. When you can interact with the gods just as easily as you can with your next door neighbour, there is no need for a complicated system of theology or dogma to define divinity for you. Indeed the very few priests who appear in Homer's two epic poems, the *Illiad* and the *Odyssey*, are half ignored by the heroes, as if their presence is more of a nuisance than anything else.

Having said that, there were indeed a few religious institutions in Greek society. The most important of them, right from the very beginning of Greek civilisation, was the Temple of the Oracle of Delphi. The temple was situated on a high hilltop, close to the sun and sky, and hence close to the gods. There was a special chamber in the temple, and in that chamber there was a priestess sitting on an altar. She would chew on a special herb (don't ask me what it was) and inhale volcanic vapours which wafted up from a crack in the floor. An acolyte at the other end of the room would catch the reflection of the sun or moon in a silver dish, and turn it up and down, flashing the priestess' eyes like a strobe light, perhaps in time with soft drumming or chanting. This would cause the priestess on the altar to enter a trance. Then she would be possessed by the god Apollo. Whatever gibberish came out of her mouth during this time was treated as the voice of Apollo himself, offered directly to humanity. This ceremony has come to be known as "drawing down the moon."

This institution, the Oracle of Delphi, was very powerful. Petitioners had to bring expensive gifts and offerings, and sometimes pay hefty fees, for an audience with the god. Hence the temple quickly became very wealthy, and very politically influential. Orators, generals, merchants, politicians of all kinds, even poets and artists, would seek the Oracle's advice. Petitioners came from all over the Mediterranean, not just the peninsula and islands of Greece, to hear the Oracle's words. The values that Apollo stood for, therefore, came to be spread all over the ancient world, and in some places identified with the national character of ancient Greek civilisation itself. One of those values was written above the door to the temple: "Everything in moderation, nothing in excess." Apollo's highest virtue, one could therefore claim, is *temperance*. This does not mean the same as asceticism, after all, Apollo is an artist-god. But his art, like his other values, is above all *rational*. Apollo is the god who retrieves order from the chaos of the world by means of reason.

With all that power, the Temple may have become decadent,

and too much like an intercessor between humankind and the gods. This was something the Greek mind would never tolerate. Somewhere along the way, therefore, another god arrived in Greece and started up a religious festival that would stand for the exact opposite of Apollo's temperance. This was Dionysus, the god of nothing in moderation and everything in excess. The Dionysian festival, called The Dithyramb, celebrated hedonism and drunkenness, and the dangerous and chaotic side of nature. People would gorge themselves on food and drink, run around like wild animals, dance themselves to exhaustion, and have sex with almost anyone. Even with animals. It was the absolute antithesis to the civilised and sober rationality of Apollo at Delphi. Edith Hamilton, a scholar of classics, argued persuasively that the worship of Dionysus:

> ...must have begun in a great religious revival, a revolt very probably against the powerful centre of worship Delphi had become. At any rate, it was the very antipodes to Delphi, the shrine of Apollo, the most Greek of all the gods, the artist god, the poet and musician, who ever brought fair order and harmony out of confusion. (Hamilton, *The Greek Way*, pg. 214).

Yet as hamilton also noted (c.f. pg. 214), the violence and indulgence of the Dionysian festival eventually became just as intolerable to the Greek spirit as the well ordered sobriety of Delphi. The Dithyramb was eventually absorbed by the Mysteries of Orpheus, and other activities that sought a balance between reason and passion.

I suspect that the main religious festival in honour of Demeter, the Eleusinean Mysteries, was also set up as a kind of rebellion against the social and political power of the Temple of Delphi. I suspect that it too was a vehicle for spiritual ideas neglected elsewhere. We do not know the exact nature of the rituals performed at Eleusis. Those who attended the ceremony were bound by an oath of silence. Yet they all claimed that it gave them an extraordinary sense of reverence and wonder, which had to be experienced personally to be understood. As another incentive, the punishment for breaking the secrecy oath was death. Nonetheless, we do know a few fragmentary facts about the Eleusinean Mysteries. We know, for instance, that the *mystai* (as those who had attended the ceremony were called) were trained in stages. There was a first ceremony, called the "Lesser Mysteries", which took place in February and in the town of Agrae, just outside of Athens. Then in September or October the *mystai* made a solemn procession from Athens to Eleusis, about 14 miles away, to complete the process. The ceremony was then conducted in a building called the Telesterion, or Hall of Initiation; but some sources claim the ceremony was conducted in a cave. We know that as part of the ceremony, the priests and priestesses would dramatise the story of Demeter's life, the abduction of her daughter Persephone, and the negotiation with Hades for her release. The purpose of the ceremony was to conduct the participants through their own underworld journey, just like Persephone before them. We also know that at some point near the end, at the most dramatic and spiritually significant moment of the ritual, a priestess announced "Behold the Mystery!" and held aloft a freshly-cut sheaf of golden corn.

What made the Eleusinean Mysteries different from the rites of Apollo at the Temple of Delphi, in terms of the values and ideas being affirmed? Although I cannot prove it, I suspect that the Eleusinean Mysteries were controlled by women. This hypothesis can explain, for instance, the secrecy oath. The men who witnessed the Mystery might not want it known in the male-dominated society around them that they had experienced something profound and personally meaningful in a ritual space controlled by women. Furthermore, the Eleusinean Mysteries represent an almost polar opposite to the rituals performed at Delphi, in several ways. At Delphi the deity of honour is a god of the sun. At Eleusis, the deity of honour is a goddess of the earth. The Temple of Delphi is on a mountaintop; at Eleusis, the Mysteries are performed underground. At Delphi, the whole institution is controlled by men. Male accountants receive and disburse the money from the petitioners, and male priests interpret the words of the priestess in her trance. Although the Oracle was always a woman, every move she made was controlled or interpreted by the men around her. Might it have been the case that at Eleusis, women did the jobs which at Delphi were done by men?

Let us look now at Demeter's story. It begins with Demeter's daughter Persephone, also known as Kore, collecting flowers in a meadow. The lord of the underworld, Hades, seeing her beauty, desired her for his bride. He therefore tempted her into his realm with a pomegranate. The moment she touched the fruit, the earth opened and Hades emerged on his chariot and carried her off.

Demeter went looking for her daughter in the town of Eleusis. There she disguised herself as an old widow woman. She befriends the city's royal family, and became nursemaid to the queen's infant son. Still despondent over the loss of her child, Demeter attempted to make the queen's young child immortal. But the queen was fearful for her child's safety – the process of rendering the boy immortal and forever young involved roasting him in a fire – and Demeter was dismissed before she could finish. The story then returns to the problem of Persephone's absence. Demeter goes to Eleusis, and stages a protest: no crops will grow until Persephone is returned to her. Zeus sends an emissary to Hades to plead for her return. Hades gives her back, but first gives her a pomegranate seed to eat. This otherworldly food has the effect of 'trapping' a part of her in the Underworld, and requiring her to return there for part of every year. Again, while she is away, Demeter despairs in her absence, and the land reflects that despair by passing into winter.

§ 9. The Homeric Hymn to Demeter

I begin to sing of lovely-haired Demeter, the goddess august,
Of her and her slender-ankled daughter whom Zeus,
Far-seeing and loud-thundering, gave to Aidoneus to abduct.
Away from her mother of the golden sword and the splendid
    fruit
She played with the full-bosomed daughters of Okeanos,
Gathering flowers, roses, crocuses, and beautiful violets
All over a soft meadow, irises too, and hyacinths she picked,
And narcissus, which Gaia, pleasing the All-receiver,
Made blossom there, by the will of Zeus, for a girl with a
    flower's beauty.
A lure it was, wonderous and radiant, and a marvel to be seen
By immortal gods and mortal men.
A hundred stems of sweet-smelling blossoms
Grew from its roots. The wide sky above
And the whole earth and the briny swell of the sea laughed.
She was dazzled and reached out with both hands at once
To take the pretty bauble; Earth with its wide roads gaped
And then over the Nysian field the lord and All-receiver,
Against her will he seized her and on his golden chariot
Carried her away as she wailed; and she raised a shrill cry
Calling upon father Kronides, the highest and the best.
None of the immortals or of mortal men heard
Her voice, not even the olive-trees bearing splendid fruit.
Only the gentle tempered daughter of Persaios,
Hekate of the shining headband, heard from her cave
And lord Helios, the splendid son of Hyperion, heard
The maiden calling father Kronnides; he sat
Apart from the gods in the temple of prayers,
Accepting beautiful sacrifices from mortal men.
By Zeus' counsels, his brother, the All-receiver
And Ruler of Many, Kronos' son of many names,

Was carrying her away with his immortal horses, against her
    will.
So while the goddess looked upon the earth and the starry sky
And the swift-flowing sea teeming with fish
And the rays of the sun and hoped to see
Her loving mother and the races of the gods immortal
Hope charmed her great mind, despite her grief.
The peaks of the mountains and the depths of the sea
    resounded
With her immortal voice, and her mighty mother heard her.
A sharp pain gripped her heart, and she tore
The headband round her divine hair with her own hands.
From both of her shoulders she cast down her dark veil
And rushed like a bird over the nourishing land and the sea,
Searching; but none of the gods or mortal men
Wanted to tell her the truth and none
Of the birds of omen came to her as truthful messenger.
For nine days then all over the earth might Deo
Roamed about with bright torches in her hands
And in her sorrow never tasted ambrosia
Or nectar sweet to drink, and never bathed her skin
But when the tenth, light-bringing Dawn came to her,
Hekate carrying a light in her hands, met her,
And with a loud voice spoke to her and told her the news:
"Mighty Demeter, bringer of seasons and splendid gifts,
which of the heavenly gods or of mortal men
seized Persephone and pierced with sorrow your dear heart?
For I heard a voice but did not see with my eyes
Who it was; I am quickly telling you the whole truth."
Thus spoke Hekate. And to her the daughter of lovely-haired
    Rhea
Answered, not a word, but with her she sped away
Swiftly, holding the bright torches in her hands.
They came to Helios, watcher of gods and men,

And stood near his horses, and the illustrious goddess made a plea:

"Helios, do have respect for me as a goddess, if I ever
    Cheered your heart and soul by word or deed.
    Through the barren ether I heard the shrieking voice
    Of my daughter famous for her beauty, a sweet flower at birth,
    As if she were being overcome by force, but I saw nothing.
    And since you do gaze down upon the whole earth
    And sea and cast your rays through the bright ether,
    Tell me truly if you have seen anywhere
    What god or even mortal man in my absence
    Seized by force my dear child and went away."
    Thus she spoke and Hyperionides gave her an answer:
    "Lady Demeter, daughter of lovely-haired Rhea,
    you shall know; for I greatly reverence and pity you
    in your grief for your slender-ankled child; no other immortal
    is to be blamed save cloud-gathering Zeus
    who gave her to Hades, his own brother, to become
    his buxom bride. He seized her and with his horses
    carried her crying loud down to misty darkness.
    But, Goddess, stop your great wailing; you mustn't give
    Yourself to grief so great and fruitless. Not an unseemly
    Bridegroom among immortals is Aidoneus, Lord of Many,
    Your own brother from the same seed: to his share fell
    Honour when in the beginning a triple division was made.
    And he dwells among those over whom his lot made him lord."

With these words, he called upon his horses, and at his command
    Speedily, like long-winging birds, they drew the swift chariot,
    As a pain more awful and savage reached Demeter's soul.
    Afterwards, angered with Kronion, lord of black clouds,
    She withdrew from the assembly of the gods and from lofty

Olympus

And went through the cities of men and the wealth of their labours,

Tearing at her fair form for a long time: no man

Or deep-girded woman looking at her knew who she was

Before she reached the house of prudent Keleos

Who was then lord of Eleusis, a town rich in sacrifices.

Grieving in her dear heart, she sat near the road,

At Parthenin, the well from which the citizens drew water,

In the shade of a bushy olive-tree which grew above it.

[100]

She looked like a woman born a long time ago

And barred from childbearing and the gifts of wreath-loving Aphrodite,

Even as are nurses for the children of law-tending

Kings and keepers of the storerooms in their bustling mansions.

The daughters of Keleos Eleusinides saw her

As they were coming to fetch easily-drawn water

In copper vessels to their father's dear halls,

Four of them in their maidenly bloom, like goddesses,

Kallidike, Kleisidike and Demo the lovely,

And Kallithoe, who was the eldest of them all.

They did not know who she was; it is hard for mortals to see divinity.

Standing near they addressed her with winged words:

"Old woman, whence and from what older generation do you come?

Why have you wandered away from the city and not approached

A house; there in the shadowy halls live

Women of your age and even younger ones

Who will treat you kindly in both word and deed."

After these words, the mighty goddess answered:

"Dear children, whoever of ladylike women you are,
I greet you and will explain; indeed it is fitting
To tell you the truth, since you are asking.
Dos is the name which my mighty mother gave me.
And now from Crete on the broad back of the sea
I came unwillingly; marauding men by brute force
Carried me off against my will, and later
They landed their swift ship at Thorikos, where the woman
Came out in a body and the men themselves
Prepared a meal by the stern-cables of the ship.
But my heart had no desire for the evening's sweet meal;
I eluded them and, rushing through the black land,
I fled my reckless masters, so that they might not enjoy
The benefit of my price, since, like thieves, they carried me
across the sea.
So I have wandered to this place and know not at all
What land this is and what men live in it.
But may all who dwell in the Olympian halls
Grant you men to wed and children to bear
As your parents wish; and now have mercy on me, maidens
And, dear children, kindly let me go to someone's house,
A man's and a woman's to work for them
In such tasks as befit a woman past her prime.
I shall be a good nurse to a new-born child,
Holding him in my arms; I shall take care of the house,
And make the master's bed in the innermost part
Of the well-built chamber and mind his wife's whorl."
So said the goddess, and forthwith Kallidike, still a pure
virgin,
And the most beautiful of Keleos' daughters, replied:
"Good mother, men must take the gifts of the gods
even when they bring them pain, since gods are truly much
stronger.
I shall advice you clearly and give you the names

Of the men who have great power and honour in this place;
These are the leaders of the people who defend the towers
Of the city by their counsels and straight judgments.
They are Triptolemos, shrewd in counsel, and Dioklos,
Polyxenios and Eumolpos, untainted by blame,
Dolichos and our manly father,
And everyone has a wife managing his mansion.
No woman there, when she first looks upon you,
Will dishonour your appearance and remove you from the mansion,
But each will receive you, for indeed you look like a goddess.
If you wish, wait here for us to go to the mansion
Of our father and tell our deep-girded mother, Metaneira,
All these things from beginning to end, hoping that
She will bid you come to our mansion and not search for another's.
A growing son is being reared in the well-built mansion,
Born late in her life, much wished for and welcome.
If you should bring him up to reach puberty,
Some tender woman seeing you could easily
Ben envious; such rewards for rearing him she'll give you."
So she spoke, and the goddess nodded her head in assent,
And they proudly carried their shining vessels filled with water.
Swiftly they reached their father's great mansion and quickly told
Their mother what they had seen and heard. And she commanded them
To go forthwith and invite her to come for copious wages.
And they, as deer or heifers in the season of spring,
Sated in their hearts with pasture frisk over a meadow,
Held up the folds of their lovely robes
And darted along the hollow wagon-road, as their flowing hair

Tossed about their shoulders, like the flowers of the crocus.
They met the glorious goddess near the road where
They had left her before; and then they led her to their father's
House. And the goddess walked behind them, brooding
In her dear heart, with her head covered, while a dark
Cloak swirled about her tender feet.
Soon they reached the house of Zeus-cherished Keleos
And through the portico they went where their lady mother
Sat by a pillar, which supported the close-fitted roof,
Holding a child, a young blossom, on her lap; they ran
Near her, and the goddess stepped on the threshold and touched
The roof with her head and filled the doorway with divine radiance.

Awe, reverence and pale fear seized the mother;
And she yielded her seat to the goddess and asked her to sit.
But Demeter, the bringer of seasons and splendid gifts,
Did not want to sit on the lustrous seat;
She kept silent and cast down her beautiful eyes
Until Iambe, knowing her duties, placed in front of her
A well-fitted seat and over it she threw a white fleece.
Demeter sat on it and with her hands she held in front of her a veil,
Remaining on the seat for long, speechless and brooding,
Doing nothing and speaking to nobody.
And without laughing or tasting food and drink
[200]
She sat pining with longing for her deep-girded daughter
Until Iambe, knowing her duties, with her jokes
And many jests induced the pure and mighty one
To smile and laugh and have a gracious temper.
At later times, too, Iambe was able to please her moods.
Metaneira now filled a cup with wine and gave it
To her, but she refused it; it was not right for her, she said

To drink red wine. She asked them to give her a drink
Of barley-meal and water mixed with tender pennyroyal.
She mixed the drink and gave it to the goddess, as she had
asked,
And mighty Deo accepted it, complying with holy custom.
Then among them fair-girded Metaneira started speaking.
"I salute you, lady, because I think you were born to noble
and not to lowly parents. Modesty and grace show
in your eyes, as if you were a child of law-giving kings.
But man must take the gifts of gods even when they are
Grieved by them, for on their necks there is a yoke.
And now since you have come here, what is mine will be
yours.
Nurture this child of mine, whom un-hoped for and late-born
The gods have granted me, in answer to my many prayers.
If you should bring him up to reach the age of puberty,
Some tender woman seeing you could easily
Be envious; such rewards for rearing him I will give you."
Fair-wreathed Demeter addressed her in turn:
"I salute you too, lady; may the gods grant you good
things. I will gladly accept the child as you ask me.
I will nurture him and I don't think that for his nurse's
foolishness
Either a spell or the Undercutter will harm him.
I know a remedy by far mightier than the tree-felling creature,
And for harmful bewitching I know a noble antidote."
With these words she received him to her fragrant bosom,
And immortal arms, and the mother rejoiced in her heart.
Thus the fine son of prudent Keleos,
Demophoön, to whom fair-girded Metaneira gave birth,
Was nurtured by her in the palace; and he grew up like a god,
Not eating food or nursing at his mother's breast.
As if he were the child of a god, Demeter anointed him with
ambrosia,

Holding him to her bosom and breathing on him sweetly.
At night she hid him like a firebrand in the blazing fire,
Secretly from his dear parents. To them it was a miracle
How he blossomed forth and looked like the gods.
And she would have made him ageless and immortal,
If fair-girded Metaneira, thinking foolish thoughts,
And keeping watch by night from her fragrant chamber,
Had not seen her; she raised a cry, striking her thighs
In fear for her child, and blindness entered her mind,
And weeping she spoke winged words:
"Demophoön, my child, this stranger hides you
in a great fire, bringing me grief and painful care."
Thus she spoke wailing and the splendid goddess heard her.
The shafts of terrible anger shot through Demeter,
The fair-wreathed, who then with her immortal hands
Took from the blazing fire and placed on the ground
The dear child born in the queen's mansion,
And at the same time addressed fair-girded Metaneira:
"Men are too foolish to know ahead of time
the measure of good and evil which is yet to come.
You too were greatly blinded by your foolishness.
The relentless water of the Styx by which gods swear
Be my witness: immortal and ageless forever
Would I have made your dear son and granted him everlasting
honour;
But now it is not possible for him to escape the fate of death.
Yet honour everlasting shall be his because
He climbed on my knees and slept in my arms.
But in due time and as the years revolve for him,
The sons of the Eleusinians will join in war
And dreadful battle against each other forever.
I am Demeter the honoured, the greatest
Benefit and joy to undying gods and to mortals.
But come now, let all the people build me

A great temple and beneath it an altar under the steep walls
Of the city, above Kallichoron, on the rising hill.
I myself shall introduce rites so that later
You may propitiate my mind by their right performance."
With these words the goddess changed her size and form
And sloughed off old age, as beauty was wafted about her.
From her fragrant veils a lovely smell
Emanated, and from the immortal skin of the goddess a light
Shone afar, as her blond hair streamed down over her
shoulders,
And the sturdy mansion was filled with radiance as if from
lightning.
Out she went through the mansion. The queen staggered,
And she remained speechless for a long time, forgetting
To pick her growing child up from the floor.
Her sisters heard his pitiful voice,
And they ran from their well-spread beds; and then one
Took up the child in her arms and held him to her bosom.
Another revived the fire and yet a third rushed
With tender feet to rouse her mother from her fragrant
chamber.
They gathered round the squirming child, bathed him
And fondled him, but his heart was not soothed,
For surely lesser nurses and governesses held him now.
All night long they propitiated the glorious goddess,
Quaking with fear, and as soon as dawn appeared
They told the truth to Keleos, whose power reached far,
As the fair-wreathed goddess Demeter had ordered them.
He then called to assembly the people of every district
And bade them build an opulent temple to lovely-haired
Demeter
And made an altar on the rising hill.
And they listened to his speech, and obeying forthwith
They built as he ordered; and the temple took shape according

to divine degree. [300]

Now when they finished the temple and refrained from labour,
Each man went to his home, but blond Demeter
Sitting there apart from all the blessed ones,
Kept on wasting with longing for her deep-girded daughter.
Onto the much-nourishing earth she brought a year
Most dreadful and harsh for men; no seed
In the earth sprouted, for fair-wreathed Demeter concealed it.
In vain the oxen drew many curved plows over the fields,
And in vain did much white barley fall into the ground.
And she would have destroyed the whole race of mortal men
With painful famine and would have deprived
The Olympians of the glorious honour of gifts and sacrifices,
If Zeus had not perceived this and pondered in his mind.
First he sent golden-winged Iris to invite
The lovely-haired Demeter of the fair form.
He spoke to her and she obeyed Zeus, the son of Kronos and lord
Of dark clouds, and ran swiftly mid-way between earth and heaven.
She reached the town of Eleusis rich in sacrifices,
Found the dark-veiled Demeter in the temple
And spoke, uttering winged words to her:
"Demeter, Zeus the father, whose wisdom never wanes,
invites you to come among the tribes of the immortal gods.
But come and let not the word of Zeus be unaccomplished."
Thus she spoke begging her, but her mind was not persuaded.
So again the father sent forth all the blessed
Immortal gods. They ran to her, and each in his turn
Summoned her and gave her many beautiful gifts
And whatever honours she might want to choose among the immortals.
But no one could persuade the mind and thought
Of the angry goddess who stubbornly spurned their offers.

She said she would never set foot on fragrant Olympus
And never allow the grain in the earth to sprout forth
Before seeing with her eyes her fair-faced daughter.
So when loud-thundering, far-seeing Zeus heard this,
He sent Argeiphontes of the golden wand to Erebos.
His mission was to win Hades over with gentle words,
And bring Persephone out of misty darkness
To light and among the gods, so that her mother
Might see her with her eyes and desist from anger.
Hermes did not disobey and, leaving his Olympian seat,
With eager speed plunged into the depths of the earth.
He found the lord inside his dwelling,
Sitting on his bed with his revered spouse; she was
In many ways reluctant and missed her mother, who far
From the works of the blessed gods was devising a plan.
Mighty Agreiphontes stood near and addressed him:
"Hades, dark-haired lord of those who have perished,
Zeus the father bids you bring noble Persephone
Out of Erebos and among the gods, so that her mother
Seeing her with her eyes, may desist from anger
And dreadful wrath against the gods; because she is contem-
plating
A great scheme to destroy the feeble races of earth-born men,
Hiding the seed under the earth and abolishing the honours
Of the immortals. Her anger is dreadful, and she does not
mingle
With the gods, but apart from them in a fragrant temple
She sits, dwelling in the rocky town of Eleusis."
Thus he spoke and Aidoneus, lord of the nether world,
With smiling brows obeyed the behests of Zeus the king
And speedily gave his command to prudent-minded
Persephone:
"Persephone, go to your dark-robed mother,
with a gentle spirit and temper in your breast,

and in no way be more dispirited than the other gods.
I shall not be an unfitting husband among the immortals,
As I am father Zeus' own brother. When you are here
You shall be mistress of everything which lives and moves;
Your honours among the immortals shall be the greatest,
And those who wrong you shall always be punished,
If they do not propitiate your spirit with sacrifices.
Performing sacred rites and making due offerings."
Thus he spoke and wise Persephone rejoiced
And swiftly sprang up for joy, but he himself
Gave her to eat a honey-sweet pomegranate seed,
Contriving secretly about her, so that she might not spend
All her days again with dark-robed, revered Demeter.
Aidoneus, Ruler of Many, harnessed nearby
The immortal horses up to the golden chariot.
She mounted the chariot, and next to her mighty Argeiphontes
Took the reins and the whip in his own hands
And sped out of the halls, as the horses flew readily.
Soon they reached the end of the long path, and neither
The sea nor the water of rivers nor the grassy glens
And mountain-peaks checked the onrush of the immortal horses,
But they went over all these, traversing the lofty air.
He drove them and then halted near the fragrant temple
Where fair-wreathed Demeter stayed. When she saw them,
She rushed as a maenad does, along a shady woodland on the mountains.
Persephone on her part, when she saw the beautiful eyes
Of her mother, leaving chariot and horses, leaped down
To run and, throwing her arms around her mother's neck, embraced her.
And as Demeter still held her dear child in her arms,
Her mind suspected trickery, and in awful fear she withdrew
From fondling her and forthwith asked her a question:

"Child, when you were below, did you perchance partake
of food? Speak out, that we both may know.
If your answer is no, coming up from loathsome Hades,
You shall dwell both with me and with father Kronion,
Lord of dark clouds, honoured by all the immortals.
Otherwise, you shall fly and go to the depths of the earth
To dwell there a third of the seasons in the year,
Spending two seasons with me and the other immortals
[400]
Whenever the earth blooms with every kind of sweet-smelling
Springflower, you shall come up again from misty darkness,
A great wonder for gods and mortal men.
With what trick did the mighty All-receiver deceive you?"
Facing her now, beautiful Persephone replied:
"Surely, Mother, I shall tell you the whole truth.
When Hermes, the helpful swift messenger, came
From father Zeus and the other heavenly dwellers
To fetch me from Erebos, so that seeing me with your eyes
You might desist from your anger and dreadful wrath against
the immortals,
   I myself sprang up for joy, but Aidoneus slyly placed
   In my hands a pomegranate seed, sweet as honey to eat.
   Against my will and by force he made me taste of it.
   How he abducted me through the shrewd scheming of
Kronides,
   My father, and rode away carrying me to the depths of the
earth
   I shall explain and rehearse every point as you are asking.
   All of us maidens in a delightful meadow,
   Leukippe, Phaino, Electra, Ianthe,
   Melite, Iache, Rhodeia, Kallirhoe,
   Melobosis, Tyche, Okyrhoe with a face like a flower,
   Chryseis, Ianeira, Akaste, Admete,
   Rhodope, Plouto, lovely Kalypso,

Styx, Ourania, charming Galaxaura,
Battle-stirring Pallas, and arrow-pouring Artemis,
Were playing and picking lovely flowers with our hands,
Mingling soft crocuses and irises with hyacinths
And the flowers of the rose and lilies, a wonder to the eye,
And the narcissus which the wide earth grows crocus-
coloured.
So I myself was picking them with joy, but the earth beneath
Gave way and from it the mighty lord and All-receiver
Leaped out. He carried me under the earth in his golden
chariot,
Though I resisted and shouted with shrill voice.
I am telling you the whole truth, even though it grieves me."
So then all day long, being one in spirit,
They warmed each other's hearts and minds in many ways
With loving embraces, and an end to sorrow came for their
hearts,
As they took joys from each other and gave in return.
Hekate of the shining headband came near them
And many times lovingly touched the daughter of pure
Demeter.
From then on this lady became her attendant and follower.
Far-seeing, loud-thundering Zeus sent them a messenger,
Lovely-haired Rhea, to bring her dark-veiled mother
Among the races of the gods, promising to give her
Whatever honours she might chose among the immortal gods.
With a nod of his head he promised that, as the year revolved,
Her daughter could spend one portion of it in the misty
darkness
And the other two with her mother and the other immortals.
He spoke and the goddess did not disobey the behests of Zeus.
Speedily she rushed down from the peaks of Olympus
And came to Rharion, life-giving udder of the earth
In the past, and then no longer life-giving but lying idle

Without a leaf. It was now hiding in the white barley
According to the plan of the fair-ankled Demeter, but later
The fields would be plumed with long ears of grain,
As the spring waxed, and the rich furrows on the ground
Would teem with ears to be bound into sheaves by withies.
There she first landed from the unharvested ether.
Joyfully they beheld each other and rejoiced in their hearts;
And Rhea of the shining headband addressed her thus:
"Come, child! Far-seeing, loud-thundering Zeus invites you
to come among the races of the gods and promises to give you
whatever honours you wish among the immortal gods
With a nod of his head he promised you that, as the year
revolves,
Your daughter could spend one portion of it in the misty
darkness
And the other two with you and the other immortals.
With a nod of his head he said it would thus be brought to
pass.
But obey me, my child! Come, and do not nurse
Unrelenting anger against Kronion, lord of dark clouds;
Soon make the life-giving seed grow for men."
Thus she spoke and fair-wreathed Demeter did not disobey,
But swiftly made the seed sprout out of the fertile fields.
The whole broad earth teemed with leaves and flowers;
And she went to the kings who administer laws,
Triptolemos and Diokles, smiter of horses, and mighty
Eumolpos,
And Keleos, leader of the people, and showed them the
Celebration of holy rites, and explained to all,
To Triptolemos, to Polyxeinos and also to Diokles,
The awful mysteries not to be transgressed, violated
Or divulged, because the tongue is restrained by reverence for
the gods.
Whoever on this earth has seen these is blessed,

But he who has no part in the holy rites has
Another lot as he wastes away in dank darkness.
After the splendid Demeter had counseled the kings in every-
thing,
She and her daughter went to Olympus for the company of
other gods.
There they dwell beside Zeus who delights in thunder,
Commanding awe and reverence; thrice blessed is he
Of men on this earth whom they gladly love.
Soon to his great house they sent as guest
Ploutos, who brings wealth to mortal men.
But come now, you who dwell in the fragrant town of Eleusis,
Sea-girt Paros and rocky Antron,
Mighty mistress Deo, bringer of seasons and splendid gifts,
Both you and your daughter, beauteous Persephone,
For my song kindly grant me possessions pleasing the heart,
And I shall remember you and another song, too.
(Athanassakis, *The Homeric Hymns*, pp. 1-15)

Fifth Movement

Morrígan: Great Queen of the Celts

"I went out to the hazel wood, because a fire was in my head..."

Ireland and Britain, the north half of Spain, and almost everything else in Europe west of the Rhine, as well as most of Switzerland and much of Turkey, was once the territory of a people called the Celts. They were not one culture or race but at least seven distinct nations, possibly more. Yet they shared a root-language, a social and political structure, a distinct style of art and architecture, and a number of common religious ideas. Most historians accept that during the middle of the Bronze Age (around 1500 – 900 BCE), the Celts migrated into western Europe from the same east Asian homeland as other Indo-European people. The differences between each of the Celtic nations may be attributable to local influences from the various cultures they assimilated on the way.

The Celts might be characterized broadly as a warrior culture, interested in expansion and conquest. Yet they were also a magical culture, deeply interested in mysticism and religion. One historian of the period, Pliny, observed that "Britain continues to be spellbound by magic and conducts so much ritual that it would seem that Britain had given magic to the Persians." In 387 BCE King Brennus of the Gauls captured the mighty capital of Rome; in 290 BCE another Celtic king, also named Brennus, sacked the Oracle of Delphi. By the third century BCE there were Celtic communities on both sides of the Danube and the Rhine, and in Bohemia, in Illyria and the Carpathian mountains, in Asia Minor, even the shores of the Black Sea. But the second century BCE witnessed the decline of Celtic power almost everywhere. The Romans had not forgotten Brennus' sacking of their city, nor the heavy tribute he demanded as the price of his withdrawal. Celtiberia (northern Spain) was conquered by Rome in 197 BCE and again in 133 BCE. Teutonic people from east of the Rhine began harassing Gaul, on the west side: forcing several Celtic tribes to migrate *en masse* across the continent. Julius Caesar offered himself as a mediator and protector between rival Celtic tribes and between the Celts and Germans. The Gauls accepted his offer: but once Caesar took care of the Germans, he didn't send his troops home. Instead, he set up garrisons and trading posts everywhere, to exploit Gaul's vast agricultural wealth. There was a revolt in 52 BCE, led by a chieftain named Vercingetorix who had the allegiance of almost all the tribes in Gaul for this purpose. But at the Battle of Alesia the Celts were routed. Vercingetorix was taken prisoner, and ten years later publicly executed in the Forum. Britain was invaded and conquered by the Romans only a hundred years later.

Ireland was the only Celtic nation never conquered by the Roman Empire. But Ireland had its own history of warfare and conquest. In the first century CE, Ireland had as many as a hundred independent Celtic tribes, roughly grouped into four kingdoms: Ulster in the North, Leinster in the east, Connaucht in the West, and Munster in the south. In the second century CE, a chieftain from the west named Conn of the Hundred Battles invaded the agriculturally rich Boyne Valley, in Leinster. There he established a fifth kingdom, Meath (or 'middle'), with the Hill of Tara as his new capital. He also declared himself 'Ard-Ri', or High King, of all Ireland. Conn seems to have brought with him a goddess called Maeve, also called *An Mhórrigan*, a name which means 'Queen of Phantoms' or 'Great Queen'.

She was a 'Triple' goddess, meaning that she was sometimes represented as three sisters: Morrígan, Bobd, and Macha. She was associated with birds, especially ravens, and also horses, and she carried two spears, one with a red spear-tip and the other yellow. She has a counterpart in the Welsh-Celtic goddess Rhiannon, and in the continental Celtic goddess Rigantona. This goddess is popularly known among many contemporary pagans as a goddess of warfare and death; and the impression is not without reason. For instance, French scholar Jean Markale wrote: "Morrigaine, Bobd, and Macha are always shown in a wild light, as the warlike furies who harried combatants and urged them to fight. Morrigaine is even called 'daughter of Ernmas' (murder) which is highly expressive in itself." (Markale, *Women of the Celts*, pg. 113). But Morrígan is also a goddess of agricultural fertility. In the Irish story of the *Caith Maigh Tuireadh*, 'the Battle of Moytura', she is represented as the paramour of a sky-god, *An Daghda* ('the Good God' and 'Father of All'). The story of their sexual mating is the story of the heat and light of the sun uniting with the water of streams and rivers, to fertilize the land. Irish folklorist Dáithí Ô h-Ôgáin said of that story: "Notwithstanding its burlesque flavour, this account can be taken to be a residue of an old tradition which had the Daghda uniting with a water-goddess to fertilise the land." (Ô h-Ôgáin, *The Sacred Isle*, pg. 64). Why are these two functions attributed to the same goddess? One of the best answers is as follows:

This name (Old Irish *Medb*, Celtic *Meduva*) originally meant 'she who is mead', or 'she who intoxicates'. This was the name more usually given to the goddess of sovereignty at Tara (*Medb Temrach*) and the literature claims in fact that one fortress there was known as hers, Ráth Mheadhbha. With her was associated the *ban-fheis*, or feast of inauguration to the kingship, but which literally meant 'sleeping with a woman'. The cultus of Meadhbh as a personification of sovereignty has a long and venerable background in the culture of the Celts and further afield... In the Tara cultus, however, we find the role of the lady magnified from a personification of sovereignty into that of a veritable goddess, who is in many ways more powerful than the kings with whom she associates. (Ô h-Ôgáin, *The Sacred Isle*, pg. 133-4)

The goddess Morrígan can be both agricultural fertility deity and war deity at the same time because both of these are functions related to sovereignty. Military victory, the provision of justice, the distribution of agricultural produce and other goods, and so on, are part of the job of the mortal king. The ceremony of inaugurating the king, as mentioned here, is a kind of marriage ceremony in which the king is united with the Goddess. Thereafter he had to please and satisfy his immortal wife, by being just, noble, generous, hospitable, and so on. The goddess would reward him with fertile crops, good weather, victory in battle, and so on. If the king had any blemishes of character, for instance if he was inhospitable, greedy, unjust, and so on, he would get all kinds of trouble from her in return! (Incidentally, he had to be without scars or disfigurements or other *physical* blemish too, since he had to please the goddess in 'every' way!) The Morrígan's anger and rage is always said to be furious and terrible—but, it must be added, never unjust.

Morrígan also appears as a very old, wrinkled and disfigured woman, washing someone's blood-stained clothes and battle equipment at the side of a stream or lake. If a mortal hero sees her, she will reveal that the clothes in her basket belong to him. In this aspect, she is the terrifying "washer-woman at the ford" who foretells the death of heroes. Morrígan may thus be compared to the Norns, and other goddesses associated with fate, although she is a harbinger of fate, not a controller of it. Because of this connection, some people believe Morrígan is also the "Ban Shee" (from the Irish bean sidhe, 'faerie woman') who laments the deaths in certain Irish families with a heart-wrenching cry called keening. I have heard a group of traditional Irish druidesses perform the keening, and I can assure you it is a powerful and frightening sound to behold.

I present here a few parts of the *Caith Maigh Tuireadh*. The first part describes how The Dagda, one of the chief gods of the Tuatha de Dannan, meets with the Morrígan, the goddess of the land, in a secret house, to "unite" with her. Afterwards, The Dagda goes to the camp of the Fomhoire, to negotiate the terms of the battle. While he is there, the Fomhoire made a bit of fun at his expense. They made a huge pot of porridge and demanded that he eat it all, or else they would kill him. The Dagda did this, even though it made his belly "as big as a house cauldron, and the Fomhoire laughed at it". While he was on his way home, he met a girl on the road, who demands that he carry her on his back to her father's house. This part of the story becomes rather Monty Python-ish, and even a little baudy. The girl beats him and satirises him, to convince him to take her on his back. Dagda, although unhappy with the situation, endures the taunts. He also challenges her to a kind of riddle game, reminiscent of Cu Chullain's courtship of Emer: he demands that the girl say his whole name before he will carry him. Somewhere in the process of trying her best to humiliate him, Morrígan accidentally exposes herself. I imagine that at that moment, the Dagda suddenly recognizes her for who she really is: his own partner and lover, Morrígan. At the same time, she recognises the truth about him from beneath the humiliations that the Fomhoir had heaped upon him. They make love again. Afterwards the Morrígan says she doesn't want him to go to the battle; perhaps out of love for him, and fear for his safety. Dagda insists that he must go anyway, and Morrígan eventually agrees to let him go on the condition that she can come, and partake in the battle as well. After the battle, and the Tuatha de Dannan are victorious, the Morrígan proclaims the peace.

Morrígan can be quite a tricksy character, and it seems she always gets what she wants in the end. In the following story, she offers her help to Cu Chullain in the war against Maeve of Cruachan's armies. Cu Chullain, too proud to accept help from a woman (or from anyone else), rejects her. They have an angry exchange, in which Morrígan describes the ways she will hinder him. Cu Chullain counters that he will wound her in such a way that she will never heal without his blessing. It comes to pass as they both predict: but Cu Chullain is tricked into blessing her, and thus healing her wounds. The story describes not only the consequences of spurning Morrígan's aid, but also the human fact that 'no one is an island', and that no one should think himself too proud to accept the help of others.

The last selection on the goddess Morrígan comes from Lady Augusta Gregory's collection of Irish folklore and mythology, *Gods and Fighting Men* (1904). Her account is based on the oral traditions which local people shared with her, as well as on archival material in Irish libraries available at the time.

§ 10. *Caith Maigh Tuireadh: The Meeting of Dagda and Morrígan.*

The Dagda had a house in Glen Edin in the north, and he had arranged to meet a woman in Glen Edin a year from that day, near the All Hallows of the battle. The Unshin of Connacht roars to the south of it.

He saw the woman at the Unshin in Corann, washing, with one of her feet at Allod Echae (that is, Aghanagh) south of the water and the other at Lisconny north of the water. There were nine loosened tresses on her head. The Dagda spoke with her, and they united. "The Bed of the Couple" was the name of that place from that time on. The woman mentioned here is the Morrígan...

Then he went away from them to Tráigh Eabha. It was not easy for the warrior to move along on account of the size of his belly. His appearance was unsightly: he had a cape to the hollow of his elbows, and a gray-brown tunic around him as far as the swelling of his rump. He trailed behind him a wheeled fork which was the work of eight men to move, and its track was enough for the boundary ditch of a province. It is called "The Track of the Dagda's Club" for that reason. His long penis was uncovered. He had on two shoes of horse-hide with the hair outside.

As he went along he saw a girl in front of him, a good-looking young woman with an excellent figure, her hair in beautiful tresses. The Dagda desired her, but he was impotent on account of his belly. The girl began to mock him, then she began wrestling with him. She hurled him so that he sank to the hollow of his rump in the ground.

He looked at her angrily and asked, "What business did you have, girl, heaving me out of my right way?"

"This business: to get you to carry me on your back to my father's house."

"Who is your father?" he asked.

"I am the daughter of Indech, son of Dé Domnann," she said.

She fell upon him again and beat him hard, so that the furrow around him filled with the excrement of his belly; and she satirized him, three times so that he would carry her upon his back.

He said that it was a *ges* [taboo] for him to carry anyone who would not call him by his name.

"What is your name?" she asked.

"Fer Benn", he said.

"That name is too much!" she said. "Get up, carry me on your back, Fer Benn."

"That is indeed not my name," he said

"What is it?" she asked.

"Fer Benn Brúach," he answered.

"Get up, carry me on your back, Fer Benn Brúach," she said.

"That is not my name," he said.

"What is it?" she asked. Then he told her the whole thing. She replied immediately and said, "Get up, carry me on your back, Fe Benn Brúach Brogaill Broumide Cerbad Caic Rolaig Builc Labair Cerrce Di Brig Oldathair Boith Athgen mBethai Brightere Tri Carboid Roth Rimaire Riog Scotbe Obthe Olaithbe… Get up, carry me away from here!"

"Do not mock me any more, girl," he said.

"It will certainly be hard," she said.

Then he moved out of the hole, after letting go the contents of his belly, and the girl had waited for that for a long time. He got up then, and took the girl on his back; and he put three stones in his belt. Each stone fell from it in turn – and it has been said that they were his testicles which fell from it. The girl jumped on him and struck him across the rump, and her curly pubic hair was revealed. Then the Dagda gained a mistress, and they made love. The mark remains at Beltraw Strand where they came together.

Then the girl said to him, "You will not go to the battle by any means."

"Certainly I will go," said the Dagda.

"You will not go," said the woman, "because I will be a stone at the mouth of every ford you will cross."

"That will be true," said the Dagda, "but you will not keep me from it. I will tread heavily on every stone, and the trace of my heel will remain on every stone forever."

"That will be true, but they will be turned over so that you may not see them. You will not go past me until I summon the sons of Tethra from the *sid*-mounds, because I will be a giant oak in every ford and in every pass you will cross."

"I will indeed go past," said the Dagda, "and the mark of my axe will remain in every oak forever" And people have remarked upon the mark of the Dagda's axe.

Then however she said, "Allow the Fomhoire to enter the land, because the men of Ireland have all come together in one place" She said that she would hinder the Fomhoire, and she would sing spells against them, and she would practice the deadly art of the wand against them – and she alone would take on a ninth part of the host. (*Caith Maigh Tuireadh*, pg. 47-51.)

§ 11. Caith Maigh Tuireadh: Morrígan's Contribution to the Battle.

"And you, Morrígan", said Lug, "what power?"

"Not hard to say," she said. "I have stood fast; I shall pursue what was watched; I will be able to kill; I will be able to destroy those who might be subdued." (pg. 53)

§ 12. Caith Maigh Tuireadh: After the battle.

Then after the battle was won and the slaughter had been cleaned away, the Morrígan, the daughter of Ernmas, proceeded to announce the battle and the great victory which had occurred there to the royal heights of Ireland and to its sid-hosts, to its chief waters and to its river mouths. And that is the reason Badb still relates great deeds. "Have you any news?" everyone asked her then.

> "Peace up to heaven,
> Heaven down to earth,
> Earth beneath heaven,
> Strength in each,
> A cup very full,
> Full of honey,
> Mead in abundance.
> Summer in winter.
> Peace up to heaven."

She also prophesied the end of the world, foretelling every evil that would occur then, and every disease and every vengeance, and she chanted the following poem:

> I shall not see a world
> Which will be dear to me:
> Summer without blossoms,
> Cattle will be without milk,
> Women without modesty,
> Men without valor.
> Conquests without a king,
> Woods without mast.
> Sea without produce,

False judgments of old men,
False precedents of lawyers,
Every man a betrayer,
Every son a reaver.
The son will go to the bed of his father,
The father will go to the bed of his son.
Each his brother's brother-in-law,
He will not seek any woman outside his house,
An evil time.

§13. *The Táin Bo Cuailnge: Cu Chullain and the Morrígan.*

Cu Chulainn beheld at this time a young woman of noble figure coming toward him, wrapped in garments of many colours.

"Who are you?" he said.

"I am King Buan's daughter," she said. "and I have brought you my treasure and cattle. I love you because of the great tales I have heard."

"You come at a bad time. We no longer flourish here, but famish. I can't attend to a woman during a struggle like this."

"But I might be a help."

"It wasn't for a woman's backside I took on this ordeal!"

"Then I'll hinder," she said. "When you are busiest in the fight I'll come against you. I'll get under your feet in the shape of an eel and trip you in the ford."

"That is easier to believe. You are no king's daughter. But I'll catch and crack your eel's ribs with my toes and you'll carry that mark forever unless I lift it from you with a blessing."

"I'll come in the shape of a grey she-wolf, to stampede the beasts into the ford against you."

"Then I'll hurl a sling-stone at you and burst the eye in your head, and you'll carry that mark forever unless I lift it from you with a blessing."

"I'll come before you in the shape of a hornless red heifer and lead the cattle-herd to trample you in the waters, by ford and pool, and you won't know me."

"Then I'll hurl a stone at you," he said, "and shatter your leg, and you'll carry that mark forever unless I lift it from you with a blessing."

Then she left him...

While Cú Chullain was going to that ford men drove some cattle over.

"There will be a great trampling across your water here today," Gabrán the poet said.

Ath Tarteisc, 'across your water', and Tír Mór Tairtesc, the mainland of Tarteisc, got their names in this way.

The men met there in the ford and fought and struck at each other. As they were exchanging blows an eel flung three coils about Cú Chulainn's feet and he fell back in the ford. Then Lóch set upon Cú Chulainn with the sword until the ford was blood-red with his crimson gore.

"Urge him on!" Fergus said to his followers. "This is a poor spectacle in front of the enemy. Let someone put heart in Cú Chulain or he will die for want of encouragement."

The venom-tongued Bricriu mac Carbad stood up and started to taunt Cú Chulain.

"Your strength is withered up," Bricriu said, "if a little salmon can put you down like this, and the men of Ulster rising out of their pangs. If this is what happens when you meet a tough warrior in arms, it's a pity you took on a hero's task, with all the men of Ireland looking on."

Cú Chulainn rose up at this and struck the eel and smashed its ribs. Then, with the thunderous deeds that the warriors did in the ford, the cattle stampeded madly eastward through the army and carried off the tents on their horns. Next a she-wolf attacked Cú Chulain and drove the cattle back westward upon him, but he let fly a stone from his sling and burst the eye in her head. She came in the shape of a hornless red heifer and led the cattle dashing through the fords and pools, so that he cried out:

"I can't tell ford from flood!"

He slung a stone at the hornless red heifer and broke her legs beneath her. So it was that Cú Chulain did to the Morrígan the three things he had sworn. He made this chant:

I am alone against hordes.
I can neither halt nor let pass.
I watch through the long hours
Alone against all men.

Tell Conchobor to come now
It wouldn't be too soon.
Mágach's sons have stolen our cattle
To divide between them.
I have held them single-handed,
But one stick won't make fire.
Give me two or three
And torches will blaze!

I am almost worn out
By single contests.
I can't kill all their best
Alone as I am.

Then he fought Lóch with the sword and the gae bolga that his charioteer sent him along the stream. He struck him with it up through the fundament part of his body—for when Lóch was fighting, all his other parts were covered in a skin of horn.

"Yield to me: leave me space," Lóch said.

Cú Chulain yielded before him and Lóch fell forward on his face. From this Ath Traigid is named Tír Mór – the Ford of the Yielding. Then Cú Chulainn cut his head off.

A great weariness fell on Cú Chulainn. The Morrígan appeared to him in the shape of a squint-eyed old woman milking a cow with three tits. He asked her for a drink and she gave him milk from the first tit.

"Good health to the giver!" Cú Chulain said. "The blessing of God and man on you."

And her head was healed and made whole. She gave him milk from the second tit and her eye was made whole. She gave him milk from the third tit and her legs were made whole.

"You said you would never heal me," the Morrígan said.

"If I had known it was you I wouldn't have done it," Cú Chulain said.

(Source, Kinsella, trans. *The Táin*, pg. 132-137.)

§ 14. Gods and Fighting Men: The Morrígan

As to the Morrigu, the Great Queen, the Crow of Battle, where she lived after the coming of the Gael is not known, but before that it was in Teamhair [the Hill of Tara] she lived. And she had a great cooking-spit there, that held three sorts of food on it at the one time: a piece of raw meat, and a piece of dressed meat, and a piece of butter. And the raw was dressed, and the dressed was not burned, and the butter did not melt, and the three together on the spit.

Nine men that were outlaws went to her one time and asked for a spit to be made for themselves. And they brought it away with them, and it had nine ribs in it, and every one of the outlaws would carry a rib in his hand wherever he would go, till they would all meet together at the close of day. And if they wanted the spit to be high, it could be raised to a man's height, and at another time it would not be more than the height of a fist over the fire, without breaking and without lessening.

And Mechi, the son the Morrigu had, was killed by Mac Cecht on Magh Mechi, that till that time had been called Magh Fertaige. Three hearts he had, and it is the way they were, they had the shapes of three serpents through them. And if Mechi had not met with his death, those serpents in him would have grown, and what they left alive in Ireland would have wasted away. And Mac Cecht burned the three hearts on Magh Luathad, the Plain of Ashes, and he threw the ashes into the stream; and the rushing water of the stream stopped and boiled up, and every creature in it died.

And the Morrigu used often to be meddling in Ireland in Cuchulan's time, stirring up wars and quarrels. It was she came and roused up Cuchulain one time when he was but a lad, and was near giving in to some enchantment that was used against him. "There is not the making of a hero in you", she said to him. "and you lying there under the feet of shadows." And with that Cuchulain rose up and struck off the head of a shadow that was standing over him, with his hurling stick. And the time Conchubar was sending out Finched to rouse up the men of Ulster at the time of the war for the Bull of Cuailnge, he bade him to go to that terrible fury, the Morrigu, to get help for Cuchuhlain. And she had a dispute with Cuchulain one time he met her, and she bringing away a cow from the Hill of Cruachan; and another time she helped Talchinem, a Druid of the household of Conaire Mor, to bring away a bull his wife had set her mind on. And indeed she was much given to meddling with cattle, and one time she brought away a cow from Odras, that was of the household of the cow-chief of Cormac Hua Cuined, and that was going after her husband with cattle. And the Morrigu brought the cow away with her to the Cave of Cruachan, and the Hill of the Sidhe. And Odras followed here there till she fell on her side in the oak-wood of Falga; and the Morrigu awoke her and sang spells over her, and made of her a pool of water that went to the river that flows to the west of Slieve Buane.

And in the battle of Magh Rath, she fluttered over Congal Claen in the shape of a bird, till he did not know friend from foe. And after that again at the battle of Cluantarbh, she was flying over the head of Murchadh, son of Brian; for she had many shapes, and it was in the shape of a crow she would sometimes fight her battles.

And if it was not the Morrigu, it was Badb that showed herself in the battle of Dunbolg, where the men of Ireland were fighting under Aedh, son of Niall, and Brigit was seen in the same battle on the side of the men of Leinster.

And as to Aine, that some said was a daughter of Manannan, but some said was the Morrigu herself, there was a stone belonging to her that was called Cathair Aine. And if any one would sit on the stone he would be in danger of losing his wits, and any one that would sit on it three times would lose them for ever. And people whose wits were astray would make their way to it, and mad dogs would come from all parts of the country, and would flock around it, and then they would go into the sea to Aine's place there. But those that did cures by herbs said she had power over the whole body; and she used to give gifts of poetry and of music, and she often gave her love to men, and they called her the Leannan Sidhe, the Sweetheart of the Sidhe.

And it was no safe thing to offend Aine, for she was very revengeful. Oiliol Oluim, a king of Ireland, killed her brother one time, and it is what she did, she made a great yew-tree by enchantment, beside the river Maigh in Luimnech, and she put a little man in it, playing sweet music on a harp. And Oiliol's son was passing the river with his step-brother, and they saw the tree and heard the sweet music from it. And first they quarreled as to which of them would have the little harper, and then they quarreled about the tree, and they asked a judgment from Oiliol, and he gave it to his own son. And it was the bad feeling about that judgment that led to the battle of Magh Mucruimhe, and Oiliol and his seven sons were killed there, and so Aine got her revenge.

(Lady Gregory, *Gods and Fighting Men*, pp. 85-87.)

Sixth Movement

The Three Norns and the World Tree

"Their holy places are woods and groves, and they apply the names of deities to that hidden presence which is seen only by the eye of reverence..."

Northern Europe was the home of another heroic warrior society, the Scandinavians, or as they are better known, the Norse. Their lands included what is now Norway, Sweden, Finland, Denmark, parts of northern Germany, and Iceland. Norse culture spread by means of a combination of conquest and colonization all over Europe. Healfdene the Great established a Norse kingdom in Britain around the year 865 AD. Other Norse kingdoms were established in the Irish ports of Dublin, Limerick, and Waterford around the beginning of the 10th century. Around the year 1001 AD, Lief Erikson was sailing to his father Erik the Red's colony in Greenland when he was blown off course by a storm. He ended up sailing past Baffin Island, Labrador, and Newfoundland; later he established a settlement in the northern peninsula of Newfoundland, at a site known today as L'Anse Aux Meadows.

The mythology of the Norse is perhaps the best known of all European mythologies aside from the Greek. It is not lacking in prominent female deities; but the figures I wish to draw special attention to are known as the three Norns. A female deity who controls fate and destiny seems to be a recurring feature of heroic mythology. The Romans had a goddess named 'Fortuna' in their pantheon: In the writings of philosophers such as Cicero, Fortuna was the personification of the transience and unpredictability of the world. Later Italian writers like Machiavelli and Dante employed the symbol of the Wheel of Fortune in their work. And even today, perhaps as a kind of throwback to ancient times, gamblers and con-artists sometimes say they have the favour of 'lady luck'.

The goddess of fortune also appears as a triple-deity: not one but three goddesses, usually related to each other as sisters. In ancient Ireland, the Morrígan served the function of the controller of destiny, together with her two sisters Bodb and Macha. In Greece, fate is controlled by three goddesses: Clotho, Laechaesis, and Atropos, who tend the tapestry of life. One measures out the thread, causing someone somewhere to be born. One weaves it into the tapestry, shaping and fashioning the direction of someone's life like a work of art. And one cuts the thread, causing someone somewhere to die. It is possible that the folk-memory of these three goddesses inspired Shakespeare to write of three witches who predict Macbeth's future, and in so doing, drive him to his unavoidable tragic end.

Among the Norse, there are not just three, but thousands, of goddesses who control fate: they are collectively called the Norns. But there are three who stand out among the others, and their names are Urd, Verdani, and Skuld. These names are sometimes taken to mean Past, Present, and Future, but the words themselves, translated directly, mean Fate, Becoming, and Obligation. The last of the three, Skuld, is pronounced similarly to the English word 'should', and refers to that which one 'should' do to ensure a good relationship with Wyrd (fate) the transience of the world (Verdani), and with the members of one's extended family. ('Skuld' can also be translated as 'kinfolk of'; the implication is that one's kinfolk are the people to whom one owes moral duties like generosity and loyalty). These three special Norns tend the roots of the World Tree, Yggdrasli, by patching up the bark of the Tree with mud and water from the Well of Urd. This Well is a magical repository of wisdom and knowledge comparable to the Celtic 'Well of Wisdom'. Their presence and favour was called upon particularly during childbirth, as they were said to decide a person's destiny at the moment he or she is born. For this reason, perhaps, the Norns became particularly associated with midwives.

The job of contacting the Norns and gaining knowledge from the Well of Urd falls to a special kind of seer in Norse society. This seer is called a Seithr; she is usually a woman, and her practice appears to have involved something like a shamanic journey. As Jenny Blain, practitioner of seith-magic and professional anthropologist, wrote:

> It seems possible that both seithr and spae-working may form part of the rather scattered remnants of shamanistic techniques in Norse culture, and have been related to the shamanic practices of other cultures. Writ large, Norse culture of the Viking age viewed through the (later) saga accounts does not strike the reader as *shamanic* as such: this would have required the shaman to be a central figure within society, even while being viewed ambiguously, whereas seithworkers appear in the sagas as marginalized figures, and spae-workers, though respected, are rare. Yet, seeresses and other practitioners apparently did work in ways describable as 'shamanistic' – and often it is said that they were trained by 'the Finns', referring probably to the nomadic Sámi, a people who were truly 'shamanic'. (Blain, *Nine Worlds of Seid-Magic*, pg. 19-20).

At a seithr event, a seeress would go 'under the cloak' and enter a trance by means of rhythmic music, such as drumming or chant-singing, or possibly by the use of mind-altering substances derived from plants or fungi. She then perceives herself traveling to an otherworldly realm inhabited by spiritual beings, and she converses with them. She asks questions, either on behalf of others or on her own behalf, and reports to her clients, or the community in general, the answers she receives. Here is how she is described by the *Voluspa*, a Norse epic poem:

Bright one they called her, whenever she came to houses,
The seer with pleasing prophesies, she charmed them with
    spells,
She made magic wherever she could, with magic she played
    with minds,
She was always the favourite of wicked women.
(*Voluspá* 22; cited in Blain, *Nine Worlds of Seid-Magic*, pg. 100).

Scandinavia's best known literary work is the *Edda*, which recounts the story of the creation of the world and the various activities and struggles of the gods. Two *Eddas* exist: one in poetry and one in prose, both of which were composed in Iceland probably in the thirteenth century. I have included here the sections of the prose *Edda* which speaks of the goddesses of the Norse pantheon. The story takes the form of a conversation between a seer named Gangleri, and three otherworldly characters named High, Just-As-High, and Third.

§ 15. The Ash Yggdrasil, the Norns, and the Three Wells.
Then Gangleri said, 'Where is the central or holy place of the gods?'

High answered, 'It is at the ash Yggdrasil. There each day the gods hold their courts.'

Then Gangleri asked, 'What is there to tell about that place?'

Then Just-as-High said, 'The ash is the largest and the best of all trees. Its branches spread themselves over all the world, and it stands over the sky. Three roots support the tree and they are spread very far apart. One is among the Aesir. A second is among the frost giants where Ginnungagap once was. The third reaches down to Niflheim, and under this root is the well Hvergelmmir, but Nidhogg [Hateful Striker] gnaws at this root from below.

'Under the root that goes to the frost giants is the Well of Mimir. Wisdom and intelligence are hidden there, and Mimir is the name of the well's owner. He is full of wisdom because he drinks of the well from the Gjallarhorn. All-Father went there and asked for one drink from the well, but he did not get this until he gave one of his eyes as a pledge. As it says in *The Sibyl's Prophesy:*

Odin, I know all,
Where you hid the eye
In that famous
Well of Mimir.
Each morning
Mimir drinks mead
From Val-Father's pledge.
Do you know now or what?

'The third root of the ash is in heaven, and under that root is the very holy well called the Well of Urd. There the gods have their place of judgment. Every day the Aesir ride up over Bifrost, which is also called Ashru [Bridge of the Aesir]. The horses of the Aesir are named as follows: Sleipnir [Fast Traveller] is the best; Odin owns him, and he has eight legs. The second is Glad, the third Gyllir, the fourth Glaer, the fifth Skeidbrimir, the sixth Silfrtopp, the seventh Sinir, the eighth Gils, the ninth Falhofnir, the tenth Gulltopp and the eleventh is Lettfeti. Baldr's horse was burned with him. Thor, however, walks to the court; wading those rivers named as follows:

Kormt and Ormt
And the two Kerlaugs,
Through these Thor will
Wade each day
When he goes to judge
At the ash Yggdrasil,
Because the bridge of the Aesir
Burns with fire –
Holy waters seethe.

Then Gangleri said, 'Does fire burn over Bifrost?'

High replied: 'The red you see in the rainbow is the burning fire. The frost giants and the mountain giants would scale heaven if Bifrost could be traveled by all who wanted to do so. There are many beautiful places in heaven and everything is divinely protected. A handsome hall stands under the ash beside the well. Out of this hall come three maidens, who are called Urd [Fate], Verdani [Becoming], and Skuld [Obligation]. These maidens shape men's lives. We call them the Norns. There are yet more Norns, those who come to each person at birth to decide the length of one's life, and these are related to the gods. Others are descended from the elves, and a third group comes from the dwarves, as is said here:

Born of very different parents
I believe the Norns are,
They do not share kinship.
Some are of the Aesir,
Some are of the elves,
Some are the daughters of Dvalin.

Then Gangleri said, 'If the Norns decide the fates of men, then they do so in a terribly uneven manner. Some people enjoy a good and prosperous life, whereas others have little wealth or renown. Some have a long life, but others, a short one.'

High said: 'The good Norns, the ones who are well born, shape a good life. When people experience misfortune, it is the bad Norns who are responsible.'

§ 16. The creatures of the Ash Tree Yggdrasil.

Then Gangleri said, 'What more of importance can be said about the ash?'

High replied, 'there is much to be told. An eagle sits in the branches of the ash, and it has knowledge of many things. Between its eyes sits the hawk called Vedrfolnir [Wind Bleached]. The squirrel called Ratatosk [Drill Tooth] runs up and down the ash. He brings slanderous gossip, provoking the eagle and Nidhogg. Four stags called Dam, Dvalin, Duneyr and Durathror move about in the branches of the ash, devouring the tree's foliage. In Hvergelmir there are so many serpents with Nidhogg that no tongue can count them. As it says here:

> The ash Yggdrasil
> Endures hardship
> More than men know.
> A stag bits from above
> And its sides rot:
> From below Nidhogg gnaws.

'So it is said:

> More snakes
> Lie under the ash Yggdrasil
> Than any old fool imagines.
> Goin and Moin,
> They are Grafvollud's sons,
> Grabak and Grafvollud, and
> Ofnir and Svafnir
> Will always, I believe,
> Eat away at the tree's shoots.

'It is also said that those Norns who live beside Urd's Well draw water every day from the spring and that they splash this, mixed with the mud that lies beside the well, over the ash so that its branches will not wither or decay. That water is so sacred that all things which come into the spring become as white as the membrane called *sjall* [skin] which lies on the inside of the eggshell. As it says here:

> I know an ash,
> It is called Yggdrasil,
> A high, holy tree,
> Splashed and coated with white clay.
> From it comes the dews
> That fall in the valleys.
> It will always stand
> Green over Urd's well.

'People call the dew, which falls to the earth, honey dew, and bees feed on it. Twin birds nourish themselves in the Well of Urd. These are called swans, and from them comes the species of bird with that name.

§ 17. Goddesses

Then Gangleri asked, 'Who are the goddesses?'

High answered, 'Frigg is the foremost. She owns the dwelling called Fensalir, and it is splendid in all ways.

'A second goddess is Saga. She lives at Sokkvabekk, which is a large dwelling.

'A third is Eir, the best of doctors.

'A fourth is Gafjun. She is a maiden, and women who die as virgins serve her.

'A fifth is Fulla. She, too, is a virgin, and she goes about with her hair falling loose and a gold band around her head. She carries Frigg's ashen box, looks after her footwear, and shares secrets with her.'

'Freyja, along with Frigg, is the most noble. She married the man called Od. Their daughter, Hnoss, is so beautiful that from her name comes the word for a treasure that is exceptionally handsome and valuable. Od went traveling on distant paths while Freyja remained behind, crying tears of red gold. Freyja has many names, because she gave herself different names as she traveled among unknown peoples searching for Od. She is called Mardoll and Horn and Gefn and Syr. Freyja owned Brisingamen [Necklace of the Brisings]. She is called the goddess of the Vanir.

'The seventh goddess, Sjofn, is deeply committed to turning the thoughts of both men and women to love. The word for lover, *sjafni*, is derived from her name.

'The eighth goddess is Lofn [Loving]. She is so gentle and so good to invoke that she has permission from All-Father or Frigg to arrange unions between men and women, even if earlier offers have been refused and unions have been banned. From her name comes the word *lof*, meaning permission as well as high praise.

'The ninth is Var [Beloved]. She listens to the oaths and private agreements that are made between men and women. For this reason such agreements are called *várar*. She takes vengeance on those who break trust.

'The tenth, Vor [Careful], is so knowledgeable and inquires so deeply that nothing can be hidden from her. Hence the expression that a women becomes "aware" [*vor*] of what she learns.

'The eleventh is Syn [Refusal]. She guards the doors in the hall and locks out those who ought not to enter. She is also appointed o defend cases that she wants to see refuted in the courts. From this situation comes the expression that a denial [*syn*] is advanced when something is refuted.

'The twelfth, Hlin [Protector], is appointed to guard over people whom Frigg wishes to protect from danger. From her name comes the expression that he who escapes finds *hlenir* [peace and quiet].

'The thirteenth, Snotra, is wise and courtly. From her name comes the custom of calling a clever woman or man *snort*.

'The fourteenth is Gna. Frigg sends her to different worlds on errands. She has the horse named Hofvarpnir [Hoof Kicker], which rides through the air and on the sea. Once some Vanir saw

her path as she rode through the air, and one of them said:
"What flies there?
What fares there
Or moves through the air?"

'She replied,

"I fly not
though I fare
and move through the air
on Hofvarpnir,
the one whom Hamskerpir got
with Gardrofa"
'Fom Gna's name comes the custom of saying that something *gnaefir* [looms] when it rises up high.
'Sol [Sun] and Bil, whose natures have already been described, are counted among the goddesses.

§ 18. Valkyries and Goddesses
There are still others whose duty it is to serve in Valhalla. They bring drink and see to the table and the ale cups. *The Lay of Grimnir* names them in the following way:

Hrist and Mist
I want to bring me the [drinking] horn.
Skeggjold and Skogul,
Hild and Thrud,
Hlokk and Herfjotur,
Goll and Geirahod,
Randgrid and Radgrid,
And Reginleif –
They bring ale to the Einherjar.

'These women are called valkyries. They are sent by Odin to every battle, where they choose which men are to die and they determine who has the victory. Gunn and Rota and the youngest Norn, called Skuld, always ride to choose the slain and to decide the outcome of a battle.

'Earth, the mother of Thor, and Rind, the mother of Vali, are counted among the goddesses.'

(Source: Sturlson, *The Prose Edda*, sections 15, 16, 35, 36.)

Seventh Movement

Lore of the Witch

"Where shall we three meet again? In thunder, lightning, or in rain..."

The witch is one of the most distinctive and powerful images in Western culture. Here in the twenty-first century the image is largely one of caricature and ridicule. She is a green-skinned old hag, who wears tattered black clothing, a pointed hat and pointed shoes. Yet she is magically powerful: able to control the weather, summon and control animals, and fly through the air on an enchanted broomstick. She is a source of fear because she is a cannibal: the popular image of the witch depicts her with a cauldron, bubbling with a soup-broth made from the flesh of abducted human children. Almost no one takes the image seriously anymore.

That was not the case only a few hundred years ago. For a time, the belief in the existence of witches was a doctrine of the Catholic Church, and it was considered heretical to disbelieve in witches. Why were they threatening? Witches were alleged to have the power to contact God (or the devil) directly, influence the will of god, divine the future, cure injuries or diseases by supernatural means, and so on. In mediaeval and early modern Europe, the Catholic magisterium claimed for itself the exclusive right to perform magical operations of that kind. What makes a work of magic *witchcraft*, on this level, is not the nature of the work, but the matter of *who* is doing it. A witch, in the simplest definition, is an illegal sorcerer: anyone who practices magic without a license. The threat of a witch was not primarily physical, but *political*. If the old woman who lives on the edge of the village can effect a magical cure for gout by a herbal remedy, then people will have an alternative to the prayers and incantations of the local priest in his church. It may therefore be necessary to spread propaganda against her: for instance, by claiming that the source of her power is evil.

When accused witches were put on trial, the usual offences had to do with murders or property damage supposedly effected by magical means. He or she was accused of killing someone, or causing diseases in people or farm animals, inflicting blights on crops, conjuring thunderstorms which damaged houses or other buildings. A second definition of a witch, then, is a person who uses magic to cause harm.

In this collection I have included a selection from *The Malleus Maleficarum* (the "Hammer of Witches"). This text was written in 1486 by two Dominican Catholic priests, Jakob Sprenger and Heinrich Kramer. It is a handbook, or a manual, for witch hunters. It teaches the reader how to identify witches and their handiwork, how to torture them for a confession, and so on. The misogyny of the text is so well known it is hardly worth mentioning. I'm including it here because the mediaeval and early modern image of the witch represents probably the lowest point that the Goddess ever reached in European history. In the earlier readings included in this Testament, the Goddess has a position of great prestige and honour; but in the Malleus Maleficarum, women are a source of evil.

I also wish to draw attention to Kramer and Sprenger's claim that a witch is a person involved in a relationship with a super-natural being. To Kramer and Sprenger, that supernatural being is the devil. The witch and the devil strike a kind of bargain: the witch gains supernatural power, and the devil, in return, gains a foothold on the earth, someone through whom he can do works of evil. This idea can also be found in the dramatic literature of the period. For instance, Christopher Marlowe's play, *Doctor Faustus*, (1589) portrays a medical doctor who conjures a demon named Mephistopheles. They sign a contract between them: Faustus would gain the service of Mephistopheles for twenty years, and in return, at the end of those twenty years, Faustus would give up his soul to hell.

Modern pagans also assert that they are involved in a kind of relationship with a supernatural being. They do not describe it as a contract or a bargain. And, obviously, they are not involved in relationships with figures of evil, like the Christian devil. To them, the supernatural being they associate with to them, the supernatural being they associate with is a friendly and loving fertility deity: the Green Man, or the God with the Horns, or the Triple Goddess. In both cases, a relationship is presupposed. I have selected a passage from the Malleus Maleficarum which appear to reflect that point.

The second selection here is part of the court record of the trial and execution of Walpurga Hausmännin, a midwife from Dillingen. She was accused of having killed more than 40 children. The more likely explanation for the deaths of these children is that the sanitary conditions of the time, and the state of medical knowledge, were such that one child in every six would die in childbirth anyway. But it is not a large leap for frustrated parents or civic officials to accuse the midwife of murder. Walpurga was also old and widowed at the time of the accusation, and thus particularly vulnerable. She was burned at the stake in Dillingen on 20th September 1587. The third is part of a secret letter written by Johannes Junius, Burgomaster at Bamberg, to his daughter, after he had been convicted of being a witch, on 28th June 1628. He was fifty-five years old. These are included here to remind the world that the absolutist thinking in religion, however theologically powerful and compelling, tends to have horrific human consequences.

In the year 1890, folklorist Charles Leland met with a woman named Maddalena, who claimed to be a hereditary witch of Tuscany (northern Italy). Maddalena revealed to Leland her 'gospel of witchcraft'. Leland was so excited he promptly published it. The selections included here are from Leland's text. It gives is a vision of the witch from 'inside', so to speak; from the perspective of someone claiming to actually practice witchcraft.

Leland's text became enormously influential on the people who founded the present day pagan community.

Around the beginning of the 20th century, a semi-retired English anthropologist named Margaret Murray, who had been reading mediaeval witchcraft trial records and related sources, noticed a number of features common to many of the accounts, including:

- the leader of a group of witches was a man who wore an animal-mask and costume, and was called 'the devil' (Murray interpreted him as the priest),
- newly initiated members of the group struck a bargain or a contract with this 'devil',
- the initiate was required to spit on a crucifix, or curse the name of Jesus, or perform some other act of blasphemy,
- many of the rites involved sexuality, sometimes with the 'devil', or sometimes with another member of the group,
- the devil's penis was cold and hard, like wood (Murray interpreted this to mean that an artificial implement was used),
- a permanent mark, either a tattoo or a scar, was inflicted somewhere on the newly initiated witch's body,
- a new name was given to the initiate,
- the witch-group, called a Coven, always numbered thirteen: twelve regular coven members plus the 'devil'. They had annual festivals, called Sabbaths, and irregular meetings to work magic on behalf of clients, called Esbats.

Murray came to believe that such regularly recurring features constituted evidence that mediaeval witchcraft was an organised secret society. In fact she believed that it was the last remaining survival of an ancient pagan priesthood. She published this theory in two books: *The Witch Cult in Western Europe* (1921) and *The God of the Witches* (1931). It is worth adding that in Murray's account, the witch gatherings were joyful and celebratory occasions, featuring music and dance, food and drink, and lovemaking. In her words:

> Throughout all the ceremonies of this early religion there is an air of joyous gaiety and cheerful happiness which even the holy horror of the Christian recorders cannot completely disguise. When the witches' own words are given without distortion their feelings towards their religious rites and their god are diametrically opposed to the sentiments of the Christians... at the Great Sabbaths when whole villages met together for a combination of religion and amusement the feast must have been a source of great happiness, symbolizing as it did the gifts of God to man, with the god himself presiding in person. (Murray, The God of the Witches, pg. 114)

Murray's theory is no longer taken seriously by most professional historians, since not enough material evidence could be found to support it. Moreover, the common features she discovered can also be explained as the consistency of Church doctrine and popular fear concerning witchcraft. However, the publication of her books made possible the transformation of the image of the witch, from a source of fear to a person of power. A witch, in her description, was not only a member of a secret society, but also a person in touch with magical forces and ancient deities. The founders of the modern pagan revival found that definition enormously appealing. Some of the ritual events described by Murray, such as the use of masks, or the grant of a secret name, became part of the format of Wiccan initiations and ceremonies. And like Murray's fictitious witch meetings, a gathering of modern day pagans can be a hell of a good party.

§ 19. (Excerpt from) The Malleus Maleficarum.
There are some things in nature which have certain hidden

powers, the reason for which man does not know; such for example is the lodestone, which attracts steel and many other such things, which S. Augustine mentions in the 20th book *Of the City of God*.

And so women in order to bring about changes in the bodies of others sometimes make use of certain things, which exceed our knowledge, but this is without any aid from the devil. And because these remedies are mysterious we must not therefore ascribe them to the power of the devil as we should ascribe evil spells wrought by witches.

Moreover, witches use certain images and other strange periapts, which they are wont to place under the lintels of the doors of houses, or in those meadows where flocks are herding, or even where men congregate, and thus they cast spells over their victims, who have oft-times been known to die. But because such extraordinary effects can proceed from these images it would appear that the influence of these images is in proportion to the influence of the stars over human bodies, for as natural bodies are influenced by heavenly bodies, so may artificial bodies likewise be thus influenced...

But certain objections must be allowed. The influence of the mind cannot make an impression upon any form except by the intervention of some agent, as we have said above. And these are the words of S. Augustine in the book which we have already quoted. It is incredible that the angels who fell from Heaven should be obedient to any material things, for they obey God only. And much less can a man of his natural power bring about extraordinary and evil effects. The answer must be made, there are even to-day many who err greatly on this point, making excuses for witches and laying the whole blame upon the craft of the devil, or ascribing the changes that they work to some natural alteration. These errors may be easily made clear. First, by the description of witches which S. Isadore gives in his *Etymologiae*, c. 9: Witches are so called on account of the blackness of their guilt, that is to say, their deeds are more evil than those of any other malefactors. He continues: They stir up and confound the elements by the aid of the devil, and arouse terrible hailstorms and tempests. Moreover, he says they distract men the minds of men, driving them to madness, insane hatred, and inordinate lusts. Again, he continues, by the terrible influence of their spells alone, as it were by a draught of poison, they can destroy life.

And the words of S. Augustine in his book *The City of God* are very much to the point, for he tells us who magicians and witches really are. Magicians, who are commonly called witches, are thus termed on account to the magnitude if their evil deeds. These are they who by the permission of God disturb the elements, who drive to distraction the minds of men, such as have lost their trust in God, and by the terrible power of their evil spells, without any actual draught or poison, kill human beings. As Lucan says: A mind which has not been corrupted by any noxious drink perishes forspoken by some evil charm. For having summoned devils to their aid they actually dare to heap harms upon mankind, and even to destroy their enemies by their evil spells. And it is certain that in operations of this kind the witch works in close conjunction with the devil. Secondly, punishments are of four kinds: beneficial, hurtful, wrought by witchcraft, and natural. Beneficial punishments are meted out by the ministry of good Angels, just as hurtful punishments proceed from evil spirits. Moses smote Egypt with ten plagues by the ministry of good Angels, and the magicians were only able to perform three of these miracles by the aid of the devil. And the pestilence which fell upon the people for three days because of the sin of David who numbered the people, and the 72,000 men who were slain in one night by the army of Sennacherib, were miracles wrought by the Angel of God, that is, by good Angels who feared God and knew that they were carrying out His commands.

Destructive harm, however, is wrought by the medium of bad angels, at whose hands the children of Israel in the desert were often afflicted. And those harms which are simply evil and nothing more are brought about by the devil, who works through the medium of sorcerers and witches. There are also natural harms which in some manner depend upon the conjunction of heavenly bodies, such as dearth, drought, tempests, and similar effects of nature.

It is obvious that there is a vast difference between all these causes, circumstances, and happenings. For Job was afflicted by the devil with a harmful disease, but this is nothing to the purpose. And if anybody who is too clever and over-curious asks how it was that Job was afflicted with this disease by the devil without the aid of some sorcerer or witch, let him know that he is merely beating the air and not informing himself as to the real truth. For in the time of Job there were no sorcerers and witches, and such abominations were not yet practiced. But the providence of God wished that by the example of Job the power of the devil even over good men might be manifested, so that we might learn to be on our guard against Satan, and, moreover, by the examples of this holy patriarch the glory of God shines abroad, since nothing happens save what is permitted by God.

With regard to the time at which this evil superstition, witchcraft, appeared, we must first distinguish the worshippers of the devil from those who are merely idolaters. And Vincent of Beauvais in his *Speculum historiale*, quoting many learned authorities, says that he who first practiced the arts of magic and of astrology was Zoroaster, who is said to have been Ham the son of Noah. And according to S. Augustine in his book *Of the City of God*, Ham laughed aloud when he was born, and thus showed that he was a servant of the devil, and he, although he was a great and mighty king, was conquered by Ninus the Son of Belus, who built Nineveh, whose reign was the beginning of the kingdom of Assyria in the time of Abraham.

This Ninus, owing to his insane love for his father, when his father was dead, ordered a statue of his father to be made, and whatever criminal took refuge there was free from a punishment which he might have incurred. From this time men began the earliest years of history, for in the very first ages there was no idolatry, since in the earliest times men still preserved some remembrance of the creation of the world, as S. Thomas says, Book 2, question 95, article 4. Or it may have originated with Nembroth, who compelled men to worship fire; and thus in the second age of the world there began Idolatry, which is the first of all superstitions, as Divination is the second, and the Observing of the Times and Seasons the third.

The practices of witches are included in the second kind of superstition, which is to say Divination, since they expressly invoke the devil. And there are three kinds of this superstition: Necromancy, Astrology, or rather Astromancy, the superstitious observation of the stars, and Oneiromancy.

I have explained all this at length that the reader may understand that these evil arts did not suddenly burst upon the world, but rather were developed in the process of time, and therefore it was not impertinent to point out that there were no witches in the days of Job. For as the years went by, as S. Gregory says in his *Moralia*, the knowledge of the Saints grew: and therefore the evil craft of the devil likewise increased. The prophet Isaiah says: The earth is filled with the knowledge of the Lord (xi.6). And so in this twilight and evening of the world, when sin is flourishing on every side and in every place, when charity is growing cold, the evil of witches and their iniquities superabound.

And since Zoroaster was wholly given up to the magic arts, it was the devil alone who inspired him to study and observe the stars. Very early did sorcerers and witches make compacts with the devil and connive with him to bring harm upon human beings. This is proved in the seventh chapter of Exodus, where the magicians of Pharao by the power of the devil wrought extraordinary wonders, imitating those plagues which Moses had brought upon Egypt by the power of good angels...

So far we have set down our opinions absolutely without prejudice and refraining from any hasty or rash judgment, not deviating from the teachings and writings of the Saints. We conclude, therefore, that the Catholic truth is this, that to bring about these evils which form the subject of discussion, witches and the devil always work together, and that in so far as these matters are concerned one can do nothing without the aid and assistance of the other.

(Source: Monter, *European Witchcraft*, pg. 11-22.)

§ 20. A Witchcraft Trial

The herein mentioned, malefic and miserable woman, Walpurga Hausmännin, now imprisoned and in chains, has, upon kindly questioning and also torture, following on persistent and fully justified accusations, confessed her witchcraft and admitted the following. When one-and-thirty years ago, she had become a widow, she cut corn for Hans Schlumperger, of this place, together with his former servant Bis im Pfarrhof, by name. Him she enticed with lewd speeches and gestures and they convened that they should, on an appointed night, meet in her, Walpurga's dwelling, there to indulge in lustful intercourse. So when Walpurga in expectation of this, sat awaiting him at night in her chamber, meditating upon evil and fleshy thoughts, it was not the said bondsman who appeared unto her, but the Evil One in the latter's guise and raiment and indulged in fornication with her. Thereupon he presented her with a piece of money, in the semblance of half a thaler, but no one could take it from her, for it was a bad coin and like lead. For this reason she had thrown it away. After the act of fornication she saw and felt the cloven foot of her whoremonger, and that his hand was not natural, but as if made of wood. She was greatly affrighted thereat and called upon the name of Jesus, whereupon the Devil left her and vanished.

On the ensuing night, the Evil Spirit visited her again in the same shape and whored with her. He made her many promises to help her in her poverty and need, wherefore she surrendered herself to him in body and soul. Thereafter the Evil One inflicted upon her a scratch below the left shoulder, demanding that she should sell her soul to him with the blood that had flown therefrom. To this end he gave her a quill and, whereas she could not write, the Evil One guided her hand. She believes that nothing offensive was written, for the Evil One only swept with her hand across the paper. This script the Devil took with him and whenever she piously thought of God Almighty, or wished to go to church, the Devil reminded her of it.

Further, the above-mentioned Walpurga confesses that she oft and much rode on a pitchfork by night with her paramour, but not far, on account of her duties. At such devilish trysts she met a big man with a grey beard, who sat in a chair, like a great prince and was richly attired. That was the Great Devil to whom she had once more dedicated and promised herself body and soul. Him she worshipped and before him she knelt, and unto him she rendered other such-like honours. But she pretends not to know with what words and in what fashion she prayed. She only knows that once she heedlessly pronounced the name of Jesus. Then the above-mentioned Great Devil struck her in the face and Walpurga had to disown (which is terrible to relate) God in heaven, the Christian name and belief, the blessed Saints and the Holy Sacraments, also to renounce the heavenly hosts and the whole of Christendom. Thereupon the Great Devil baptized her afresh, naming her Höfelin, and her paramour-devil, Federlin.

At those devilish meetings, she ate, drank, and fornicated with her paramour. Because she would not allow him to drag her along everywhere he had beaten her harshly and cruelly. For food she often had a good roast or an innocent child, which was also roasted, or a suckling pig, and red and white wine, but no salt.

Since her surrender to the Devil, she had seemingly oft received the Blessed Sacrament of the true Body and Blood of Jesus Christ, apparently by the mouth, but had not partaken of it, but (which is more terrible to relate) had always taken it out of her mouth again and delivered it up to Federlin, her paramour. At their nightly gatherings she had oft with her other playfellows trodden under foot the Holy and Blessed Sacrament and the image of the Holy Cross. The said Walpurga states that during such-like frightful and loathsome blasphemies she at times truly did espy drops of blood upon the said Holy Sacrament, whereat she herself was greatly horrified.

At the command and threat of her whoremonger she had oft dishonoured the consecrated font, emptied it before her house or even destroyed the same. This she was made to do only a few days before she was cast into prison, when she was in the parish church from which she took a holy water stoup and carried it home. Then her devil paramour arrayed in handsome garments encountered her in the little street between the great cloister and the stable of Martin Müller. He desired to take the holy water stoup out of her hand and forced her to hurl it against the wall. She had also been obliged sorely to dishonour the blessed Mother of God, the Holy Virgin Mary, to spit out in front of her and say, "Shame, thou ugly hussy!" her paramour, Federlin, came to her in many diverse places in order to fornicate with her, even in the street by night and while she lay in durance. She confesses, also, that her paramour gave her a salve in a little box with which to injure people and animals, and even the precious fruit of the field.

[The text goes into an account of the 43 children whom Walpurga is accused of having killed, as well as hailstorms she is accused of having created, and other 'crimes'.]

After all this, the Judges and Jury of the Court of this Town of Dillingen, by virtue of the Imperial and Royal Prerogative and Rights of His Right Reverence, Herr Marquard, Bishop of Augsburg, and Provost of the Cathedral, our most gracious Prince and Lord, at last unanimously gave the verdict that the aforesaid Walpurga Hausmännin be punished and dispatched from life to death by burning at the stake as being a maleficent and well-known witch and sorceress, convicted according to the context of Common Law and the Criminal Code of the Emperor Charles V and the Holy Roman Empire. All her goods and chattels and estate left after her to go to the Treasury of our Most High Prince and Lord. The aforesaid Walpurga to be led, seated on a cart, to which she is tied, to the place of her execution, and her body first to be torn five times with red-hot irons. The first time outside the town hall in her left breast and the right arm, the second time at the lower gate in the right breast, the third time at the place of execution in the left hand. But since for nineteen years she was a licensed and pledged midwife of the city of Dillingen, yet has acted so vilely, her right hand with which she did such knavish tricks is to be cut off at the place of execution. Neither are her ashes after the burning to remain lying on the ground, but are thereafter to be carried to the nearest flowing water and thrown thereinto.

(Source: Matthews, *News and Rumor in Renaissance Europe*, pp. 137-143.)

§ 21. A Letter from the Accused

Many hundred thousand good-nights, dearly beloved daughter Veronica. Innocent have I come into prison, innocent have I been tortured, innocent must I die. For whoever comes into the witch prison must become a witch or be tortured until he invents something out of his head and—God pity him—bethinks him of something. I will tell you how it has gone with me. When I was the first time put to the torture, Dr. Braun, Dr. Kötzendörffer, and two strange doctors were there. Then Dr. Braun, asks me, "Kinsman, how come you here?" I answer, "Through falsehood, through misfortune." "Hear you," he says, "you are a witch; will you confess it voluntarily? If not, we'll bring in witnesses and the executioner for you." I said, "I am no witch, I have a pure conscience in the matter; if there are a thousand witnesses, I am not anxious, but I'll gladly hear the witnesses." Now the chancellor's son was set before me... and afterward Hoppfen Elss. She had seen me dance on the Haupts-moor... I answered, "I have never renounced God, and will never do it—god graciously kept me from it. I'll rather bear whatever I must." And then came also—God in highest Heaven have mercy—the executioner, and put the thumb-screws on me, both hands bound together, so that the blood ran out at the nails and everywhere, so that for four weeks I could not use my hands, as you can see from the writing... Thereafter they stripped me, bound my hands behind me, and drew me up in the torture. Then I thought heaven and earth were at an end; eight times did they draw me up and let me fall again, so that I suffered terrible agony...

And this happened on Friday, June 30, and with God's help had to bear the torture... When at last the executioner led me back into the prison, he said to me: "Sir, I beg you, for God's sake confess something, whether it be true or not. Invent something, for you cannot endure the torture which you will be put to; and even if you bear it all, yet you will not escape, not even if you were an earl, but one torture will follow after another until you say you are a witch. Not before that," he said, "will they let you go, as you may see by all their trials, for one is just like another..."

And so I begged, since I was in wretched plight, to be given one day for thought and a priest. The priest was refused me, but the time for thought was given. Now, my dear child, see in what hazard I stood and still stand. I must say that I am a witch, though I am not—must now renounce God, though I have never done it before. Day and night I was deeply troubled, but at last there came to me a new idea. I would not be anxious, but, since I had been given no priest with whom I could take counsel, I would myself think of something and say it. It were surely better that I just say it with mouth and words, even though I had not really done it, and afterwards I would confess it to the priest, and let those answer for it who compel me to do it...And so I made my confession, as follows; but it was all a lie.

...Then I had to tell what people I had seen [at the witch-sabbath]. I said that I had not recognised them. "You old rascal, I must set the executioner at you. Say — was not the Chancellor there?" So I said yes. "Who besides?" I had not recognized anybody. So he said: "Take one street after another; begin at the market, go out on one street and back on the next." I had to name several persons there. Then came the long street. I knew nobody. Had to name eight persons there. Then the Zinkenwert — one person more. Then over the upper bridge to Georgthor, on both sides. Knew nobody again. Did I know nobody in the castle — whoever it might be, I should speak without fear. And thus continuously they asked me on all the streets, though I could not and would not say more. So they gave me to the executioner, told him to strip me, shave me all over, and put me to the torture. "The rascal knows one on the market-place, is with him daily, and yet won't name him." By that they meant Dietmeyer, so I had to name him too.

Then I had to tell what crimes I had committed. I said nothing... "Draw the rascal up!" So I said that I was to kill my children, but I had killed a horse instead. It did not help. I had also taken a sacred wafer, and had desecrated it. When I had said this, they left me in peace.

Now, dear child, here you will have all my confession, for which I must die. And they are sheer lies and made-up things, so help me God. For all this I was forced to say through fear of the torture which was threatened beyond what I had already endured. For they never leave off with the torture till one confesses something; be he never so good, he must be a witch. Nobody escapes, though he were an earl...

Dear child, keep this letter secret so that people do not find it, else I shall be tortured most piteously and the jailers will be beheaded. So strictly is it forbidden... I have taken several days to write this: my hands are both lame. I am in a sad plight.

Good night, for your father Johannes Junius will never see you more. July 24, 1628.

[The letter also included the following post-script.]

Dear child, six have confessed against me at once: the Chancellor, his son, Neudecker, Zaner, Hoffmaisters Ursel, and Hoppfen Els—all false, through compulsion, as they have all told me, and begged my forgiveness in God's name before they were executed... They know nothing but good of me. They were forced to say it, just as I myself was...

(Source: Burr, "The Witch-Persecution at Bamberg" pp. 23-28.)

§ 22. *How Diana Gave Birth to Aradia*

This is the Gospel (*Vangelo*) of the Witches. Diana greatly loved her brother Lucifer, the god of the Sun and of the Moon, the god of Light (*Splendor*), who was so proud of his beauty, and who for his pride was driven from Paradise.

Diana had by her brother a daughter, to whom they gave the name of Aradia [i.e. Herodias].

In those days there were on earth many rich and many poor.

The rich made slaves of all the poor.

In those days there were many slaves who were cruelly treated; in every palace tortures, in every castle prisoners.

Many slaves escaped. They fled to the country; thus they became thieves and evil folk. Instead of sleeping by night, they plotted escape and robbed their masters, and then slew them. So they dwelt in the mountains and forests as robbers and assassins, all to avoid slavery.

Diana said one day to her daughter Aradia:

'Tis true indeed that thou a spirit art,
But thou wert born but to become again
A mortal; thou must go to earth below
To be a teacher unto women and men
Who fain would study witchcraft in thy school...

And thou shalt be the first of witches known;
And thou shalt be the first of all i' the world;
And thou shalt teach the art of poisoning,
Of poisoning those who are great lords of all;
Yea, thou shalt make them die in their palaces;
And thou shalt bind the oppressor's soul (with power);
And when ye find a peasant who is rich,
Then ye shall teach the witch, your pupil, how
To ruin all his crops with tempests dire,
With lightning and with thunder (terrible).
And with hail and wind…

And when a priest shall do you injury
By his benedictions, ye shall do to him
Double the harm, and do it in the name
Of me, *Diana*, Queen of witches all!

And when the priests or the nobility
Shall say to you that you should put your faith
In the Father, Son, and Mary, then reply:
"Your God, the Father, and Maria, are
Three devils…

"For the true God the Father is not yours;
For I have come to sweep away the bad,
The men of evil, all will I destroy!

"Ye who are poor suffer with hunger keen,
And toil in wretchedness, and suffer too
Full oft imprisonment; yet with it all
Ye have a soul, and for your sufferings
Ye shall be happy in the other world,
But ill the fate of all who do you wrong!"

Now when Aradia had been taught, taught to work all witchcraft, how to destroy the evil race (of oppressors), she (imparted it to her pupils) and said unto them:

When I shall have departed from this world,
Whenever ye have need of anything,
Once in the month, and when the moon is full,
Ye shall assemble in some desert place,
Or in a forest all together join
To adore the potent spirit of your queen,
My mother, great *Diana*. She who fain
Would learn all sorcery yet has not won
Its deepest secrets, them my mother will
Teach her, in truth all things as yet unknown.
And ye shall all be freed from slavery,
And so ye shall be free in everything,
And as a sign that ye are truly free,
Ye shall be naked in your rites, both men
And women also: this shall last until
The last of your oppressors shall be dead;
And ye shall make the game of Benevento,
Extinguishing the lights, and after that
Shall hold your supper thus:

§ 23. The Sabbat

You shall make cakes of meal, wine, salt, and honey in the shape of a (crescent or horned) *moon*, and then put them to bake, and say:

I do not bake the bread, nor with it salt,
Nor do I cook the honey with the wine,
I bake the body and the blood and soul,
The soul of (great) *Diana*, that she shall
Know neither rest nor peace, and ever be

In cruel suffering till she will grant
What I request, what I do most desire,
I beg it of her from my very heart!
And if the grace be granted, O *Diana!*
In honour of thee I will hold this feast,
Feast and drain the goblet deep,
We will dance and wildly leap,
And if thou grant'st the grace which I require,
Then when the dance is wildest, all the lamps
Shall be extinguished and we'll freely love!

And thus shall it be done: all shall sit down to the supper all naked, men and women, and, the feast over, they shall dance, sing, make music, and then love in the darkness, with all the lights extinguished; for it is the Spirit of *Diana* who extinguishes them, and so they will dance and make music in her praise.

And it came to pass that Diana, after her daughter had accomplished her mission or spent her time on earth among the living (mortals), recalled her, and gave her the power that when she had been invoked... having done some good deed... she gave her the power to gratify those who had conjured her by granting her or him success in love:

To bless or curse with power friends or enemies [to do good or evil].
To converse with spirits.
To find hidden treasures in ancient ruins.
To conjure the spirits of priests who died leaving treasures.
To understand the voice of the wind.
To change water into wine.
To divine with cards.
To know the secrets of the hand (palmistry).
To cure diseases.
To make those who are ugly beautiful.

To tame wild beasts.

Whatever thing should be asked from the spirit of *Aradia*, that should be granted unto those who merited her favour.

And thus must they invoke her:

Thus do I seek Aradia! Aradia! Aradia! At midnight, at midnight I go into a field, and with me I bear water, wine, and salt, *I bear water, wine, and salt,* and my talisman—*my talisman, my talisman,* and a red small bag which I ever hold in my hand—*con dentro, con dentro, sale,* with salt in it, *in it.* With the water and the wine I bless myself, *I bless myself* with devotion to implore a favour from Aradia, Aradia.

§ 24. The Invocation to Aradia.
Aradia! My Aradia!
Thou who art daughter unto him who was
Most evil of all spirits, who of old
Once reigned in hell when driven away from heaven,
Who by his sister did thy sire become,
But as thy mother did repent her fault,
And wished to mate thee to a spirit who
Should be benevolent
And not malevolent!

Aradia, Aradia! I implore
Thee by the love which she did bear for thee!
And by the love which I too feel for thee!
I pray thee grant the grace which I require!
And if this grace be granted, may there be
One of three signs distinctly clear to me:
The hiss of a serpent,
The light of a firefly,
The sound of a frog!

But if you do refuse this favour, then
May you in future know no peace nor joy,
And be obliged to seek me from afar,
Until you come to grant me my desire,
In haste, and then thou may'st return again
Unto thy destiny. Therewith, Amen!
(Source: Leland, *Aradia, Gospel of the Witches* pp. 1-17)

Eighth Movement

Poetry and Romance

"In Xanadu did Kubla Kahn a stately pleasure-dome decree.."
From this point on, in this book, every part of the Testament here assembled is based on my survey of contemporary pagan folklore. Every entry included here was either mentioned or contributed directly by an informant responding to my questions. The making of this part of the book, then, could be seen as a community effort. I, as the author, am acting as the collector and the commentator for a body of words which an entire community has crafted together. Upon receiving something from someone who responded to my survey, whether it was a fragment of a song, or a proverb, or a short story, or whatever, I endeavored to track down its earliest source. Therefore many of the pieces here are quoted from books and other sources. But more important than the origin of a folk artifact is the event in which it is 'performed', as well as the process by which it is transferred from one person to another. These pieces have all taken on 'lives' of their own: someone invented them, shared them with others, who in turn felt them so important or inspirational that he too passed them on to others. They also change slowly over time. Such is part of the normal process of a folk-artifact in any community. As folklorist Wiliam Bascom wrote, "Change occurs each time new variations are introduced and again these innovations are subject to acceptance or rejection. As this process continues, each new invention is adapted gradually to the needs of the society and to the pre-existing culture patterns, which may themselves be modified somewhat o conform to the new invention" (cited in Toeklen, *Dynamics of Folklore*, pg. 34). Barre Toelken described the folk process as a combination of two forces. One force is conservative, and seeks to pass things on unchanged through all the usual channels of traditional expression. The other is dynamic,

and seeks to change things slightly to accommodate a given situation, or the taste of the folk performer. Toelken takes both forces together as necessary for tradition: "those artifact productions that remain traditional do so because they have retained their variability, [and] have remained vital units of traditional exchange among participants in a close cultural set." (*ibid* pg. 38). A folk artifact may be comparable to what the English geneticist Richard Dawkins calls a 'meme': an *idea* that replicates and spreads itself from one person's mind to another, much like a genome does within the cells of living organisms.

Thus, the authorship of many of these items has been forgotten. But so long as they continue to be shared, recited, sung, taught, passed on, and enjoyed, they constitute the literary corpus which contemporary pagans look to for inspiration, and use to represent their spiritual ideas. It is here that one may find something like a contemporary pagan 'identity', for it is here that contemporary pagans identify their ideas, symbols, and values.

Here I begin with the most conservative items in the pagan folk tradition: poems and songs from "canonical" folk literature. While researchers like Leland and Murray were re-writing the history of witchcraft, while James Frazer was describing the Laws of Magic and the lore of the Sacred King, there was a movement afoot among English poets and artists called 'Romanticism'. The literary side of romanticism had more or less begun around a century earlier. Like the pieces in earlier chapters these songs and poems belong not to the pagan community alone. They belong to the whole world. The ones selected here were specifically mentioned by informants responding to my survey.

§ 25. *Now is the Month of Maying*

Now is the month of Maying, when merry lads are playing! Fa la la...

Each with his bonny lass, a-dancing on the grass, fa la la...!

The Spring, clad all in gladness, doth laugh at Winter's

sadness! Fa la la...

And to the bagpipes' sound, the nymphs tread out the ground!
Fa la la...!

Fie! Then why sit we musing, youth's sweet delight refusing?
Fa la la...

Say, dainty nymphs and speak! Shall we play barley break? Fa
la la...!

(Thomas Morley, circa 1595.)

§ 26. *The Gipsy Laddie*

The gypsies they came to my lord Cassilis' yet,
And O but they sang so bonnie!
They sang so sweet and complete,
Till down came our fair ladie.

She came tripping down the stairs
And all her maids before her:
As soon as they saw her weel-far'd face,
They cast their glamourie owre her.

She gave them the good wheat bread,
And they gave her the ginger,
But she gave them a fair better thing,
The gold rings of her fingers.

"Will ye go with me, my hinny and my heart?
Will you go with me, my dearie?
And I will swear by the hilt of my spear,
That your lord shall no more come near thee."

"Gar take from me my silk mantel,
And bring to me a plaidie,
For I will travel the world owre,

Along with the gypsie laddie.

"I could sail the seas with my Jackie Faa,
I could sail the seas with my dearie;
I could sail the seas with my Jackie Faa,
And with pleasure could drown with my dearie."

They wandered high, they wandered low,
They wandered late and early,
Until they came to an old farmer's barn
And by this time she was weary.

"Last night I lay in a weel-made bed,
And my noble lord beside me,
And now I most ly in an old farmer's barn
And the black crae glowring owre me."

"Hold your tongue, my hinny and my heart,
Hold your tongue, my dearie,
For I will swear, by the moon and the stars,
That thy lord shall no more come near thee."

They wandered high, they wandered low,
They wandered late and early,
Until they came to that on water,
And by this time she was wearie.

"Many a time I have rode that on water,
And my lord Cassilis beside me,
And now I must set in my white feet and wade,
And carry the gypsie laddie."

By and by came home this noble lord,
And asking for his ladie,

The one did cry, the other did reply,
"She is gone with the gypsie laddie."

"Go saddle to me the black," he says,
"The brown rides never so speedie,
And I will neither eat nor drink
Till I bring home my ladie."

He wandered high, he wandered low,
He wandered late and early,
Until he came to that on water,
And there he spied his ladie.

"O wilt thou go home, my hinny and my heart,
O wilt thou go home, my dearie?
And I'll close thee in a close room,
Where no man shall come near thee."

"I will not go home, my hinny and my heart,
I will not go home, my dearie;
If I have brewn good beer, I will drink of the same,
And my lord shall no more come near me.

"But I will swear, by the moon and the stars,
And the sun that shines so clearly,
That I am as free of the gypsie gang
As the hour my mother bore me."

They were fifteen valiant men,
Black but very bonnie,
They lost all their lives for one,
The Earl of Cassilis' ladie.
(Whiting, *Traditional British Ballads*, pg. 21-3.)

§ 27. *Corn Rigs And Barley Rigs*

It was upon a Lammas night
When corn rigs are bonnie,
Beneath the moon's unclouded light
I held awa to Annie,
The time flew by wi' tentless heed
Till 'tween the late and early,
Wi' sma' persuasion she agreed
To see me through the barley.

(chorus.) Corn rigs, an' barly rigs,
An' corn rigs are bonnie:
I'll ne'er forget that happy night
Amang the rigs wi' Annie.

The sky was blue, the wind was still,
The moon was shining clearly,
I set her down wi' right good will
Amang the rigs o' barley;
I kent her heart was a' my ain;
I loved her most sincerely;
I kissed her owre and owre again
Amang the rigs o' barley. (chorus.)

I locked her in my fond embrace;
Her heart was beating rarely;
My blessings on that happy place,
Amang the rigs o' barley!
But by the moon and stars so bright,
That shone that hour so clearly,
She ay shall bless that happy night
Amang the rigs o' barley. (chorus.)

I hae been blithe wi' comrades dear;

I hae been merry drinking;
I hae been joyful; gath'rin gear;
I hae been happy thinking:
But a' the pleasures e'er I saw,
Though three times doubled fairly,
That happy night was worth them a',
Amang the rigs o' barley. (chorus.)
(Robert Burns, 1759-1796)

§ 28. *The Stolen Child*
Where dips the rocky highland
Of Sleuth Wood in the lake,
There lies a leafy island
Where flapping herons wake
The drowsy water-rats;
There we've hid our faery vats,
Full of berries,
And the reddest stolen cherries.
Come away, O human child,
To the waters and the wild
With a faery, hand in hand,
From a world more full of weeping than you can understand.

Where the wave of moonlight glosses
The dim grey sands with light,
Far off by furthest Rosses
We foot it all the night,
Weaving olden dances
Mingling hands and mingling glances
Till the moon has taken flight;
To and from we leap
And chase the frothy bubbles
While the world is full of troubles
And is anxious in its sleep.

Come away, O human child,
To the waters and the wild
With a faery, hand in hand,
From a world more full of weeping than you can understand.

Where the wandering water gushes
From the hills above Glenn-Car,
In pools among the rushes
That scarce could bathe a star;
We seek for slumbering trout
And whispering in their ears
Give them unquiet dreams;
Leaning softly out
From ferns that drop their tears
Over the young streams.
Come away, O human child,
To the waters and the wild
With a faery, hand in hand,
From a world more full of weeping than you can understand.

Away with us he's going,
The solemn-eyed:
He'll hear no more the lowing
Of the calves on the warm hillside
Or the kettle on the hob
Sing peace into his breast
Or see the brown mice bob
Round and round the oatmeal-chest
For he comes, the human child,
To the waters and the wild,
With a faery, hand in hand,
From a world more full of weeping than he can understand.
(W.B.Yeats, *Collected Poems*, pg. 20-1)

§ 29. *La Belle Dame Sans Merci*

Oh what can ail thee, knight-at-arms!
Alone and palely loitering?
The sedge has wither'd from the lake
And no birds sang.

Oh what can ail thee, knight-at-arms!
So haggard and so woe-begone?
The squirrel's granary is full
And the harvest's done.

I see a lily on thy brow,
With anguish moist and fever dew
And on thy cheeks a fading rose
Fast withereth too.

I met a lady in the mead —
Full beautiful, a fairy's child
Her hair was long, her foot was light
And her eyes were wild.

I made a garland for her head,
And bracelets too, and fragrant zone,
She look'd at me as she did love,
And made sweet moan.

I set her on my pacing steed,
And nothing else saw all day long;
For sidelong would she bend, and sing
A fairy song.

She found me roots of relish sweet,
And honey wild, and manna dew;
And sure in language strange she said —

"I love thee true."

She took me to her elfin grot,
And there she wept, and sigh'd full sore;
And there I shut her wild, wild eyes
With kisses four.

And there she lull'd me asleep;
And there I dream'd—ah! Woe betide!
The latest dream I ever dream'd
On the cold hill's side.

I saw pale kings and princes too—
Pale warriors, death-pale were they all;
They cried—"La belle dame sans merci
Hath thee in thrall!"

I saw their starved lips in the gloam
With horrid warning gaped wide;
And I awoke, and found me here,
On the cold hill's side.

And this is why I sojourn here,
Alone and palely loitering
Though the sedge is wither'd from the lake,
And no birds sang.
(John Keats)

§ 30   *"The Old Woman Tossed Up"*

Oh, there was an old woman tossed up in a blanket
Ninety-nine miles beyond the moon
And under one arm she carried a basket
And under the other she carried a broom
"Old Woman, old woman, old woman," cried I,

"Oh wither, oh wither, oh wither so high?"
"I'm going to sweep cobwebs beyond the sky
And I'll be back with you, by and by."
(traditional English Morris Dancing song)

§ 31. *Bealtaine Chase Song*

O I shall go as a wren in spring with sorrow and sighing on silent wing
And I shall go in my Lady's name aye till I come home again.

And we shall follow as falcons gray and hunt the cruelly as our prey
And we shall go in our Master's name, aye to fetch thee home again

O I shall go as a mouse in May in fields by night and cellars by day
And I shall go in my Lady's name aye till I come home again.

And we shall follow as black tomcats and chase thee through the corn and vats
And we shall go in our Master's name, aye to fetch thee home again

O I shall go as an autumn hare with sorrow and sighing and mickle care
And I shall go in my Lady's name aye till I come home again.
And we shall fallow as swift gray hounds to dog thy tracks by leaps and bounds
And we shall go in our Master's name, aye to fetch thee home again
O I shall go as a winter trout with sorrow and sighing and mickle doubt
And I shall go in my Lady's name aye till I come home again.

And we shall follow as otters swift to snare thee fast ere thou
canst shift

And we shall go in our Master's name, aye to fetch thee home
again

Aye then I'll come home again.

§ 32. Soul Cake

Sole cake, sole cake, please good missus, a sole cake
Apple, a pear, plum, a cherry,
Any good thing to make so merry,
One for Peter, two for Paul,
Three for Him who made us all.

The streets are very dirty, my shoes are very thin.
I have a little pocket to put a penny in.
If you haven't got a penny, a ha'penny will do,
If you haven't got a ha'penny, then God bless you.

Go down into your cellar and see what you may find
If your barrels are not empty, I know you will be kind
I know you will be kind with your apples and your pears,
For we'll go no more a-wassailing 'til this time next year.

God bless the master of this house, the mistress also,
And all the little children around the table go
The cattle in your stable, the dog by your front door
To all who dwell within these walls, we wish them ten times
more.

(Source: an "old English plainsong")

§ 33. I Am

I am: yet what I am none cares or knows,
My friends forsake me like a memory lost,

I am the self-consumer of my woes —
They rise and vanish in oblivion host,
Like shadows in love's frenzied stifled throes —
And yet I am, and live — like vapors tossed

Into the nothingness of scorn and noise,
Into the living sea of waking dreams,
Where there is neither sense or life nor joys,
But the vast shipwreck of my life's esteems;
And e'en the dearest, that I love the best,
Are strange — nay, rather stranger than the rest.

I long for scenes, where man hath never trod,
A place where woman never smiled or wept —
There to abide with my Creator, God,
And sleep as I in childhood sweetly slept,
Untroubling, and untroubled where I lie,
The grass below — above the vaulted sky.
(John Clare, 1793-1864)

§ 34. A Tree Song

Of all the trees that grow so fair,
Old England to adorn,
Greater are none beneath the Sun,
Than Oak, and Ash, and Thorn.
Sing Oak, and Ash, and Thorn, good Sirs
(All of a Midsummer morn!)
Surely we sing no little thing
In Oak, and Ash, and Thorn!

Oak of the Clay lived many a day,
Or ever Aeneas began;
Ash of the Loam was a lady at home,
When Brut was an outlaw man;

Thorn of the Down saw New Troy Town
(From which was London born);
Witness hereby the ancestry
Of Oak, and Ash, and Thorn!

Yew that is old in churchyard mould,
He breedeth a mighty bow;
Alder for shoes do wise men choose,
And beech for cups also.
But when ye have killed, and your bowl is spilled,
And your shoes are clean outworn,
Back ye must speed for all that ye need
To Oak, and Ash, and Thorn!

Ellum she hateth mankind, and waiteth
Till every gust be laid,
To drop a limb on the head of him
That anyway trusts her shade:
But whether a lad be sober or sad,
Or mellow with ale from the horn,
He will take no wrong when he lieth along
'Neath Oak, and Ash, and Thorn!

Oh, do not tell the Priest our plight,
Or he would call it a sin;
But—we have been out in the woods all night
A-conjuring Summer in!
And we bring you news by word of mouth—
Good news for cattle and corn—
Now is the Sun come up from the South
With Oak, and Ash, and Thorn!

Sing Oak, and Ash, and Thorn, good Sirs
(All of a Midsummer morn!)

England shall bide till Judgement Tide,
By Oak, and Ash, and Thorn!
(Rudyard Kipling)

§ 35. *A Night-Piece*

—The sky is overcast
With a continuous cloud of texture close,
Heavy and wan, all whitened by the Moon,
Which through that veil is indistinctly seen,
A dull, contracted circle, yielding light
So feebly spread that not a shadow falls,
Chequering the ground—from rock, plant, tree, or tower,
At length, a pleasant instantaneous gleam
Startles the pensive traveler while he treads
His lonesome path, with unobserving eye
Bent earthwards; he looks up—the clouds are split
Asunder,—and above his head he sees
The clear Moon, and the glory of the heavens.
 There, in a black-blue vault she sails along,
Followed by multitudes of stars, that, small
And sharp, and bright, along the dark abyss
Drive as she drives: how fast they wheel away,
Yet vanish not!—the wind is in the tree,
But they are silent;—still they roll along
Immeasurably distant; and the vault,
Built round by those white clouds, enormous clouds,
Still deepens its unfathomable depth.
At length the Vision closes; and the mind,
Not undisturbed by the delight it feels,
Which slowly settles into peaceful calm,
Is left to muse upon the solemn scene.
(William Wordsworth)

§ 36. *Lines Written In Early Spring*

I heard a thousand blended notes,
While in a grove I sate reclined,
In that sweet mood when pleasant thoughts
Bring sad thoughts to the mind.

To her fair works did Nature link
The human soul that through me ran;
And much it grieved my heart to think
What man has made of man.

Through primrose tufts, in that green bower,
The periwinkle trailed its wreathes,
And 'tis my faith that every flower
Enjoys the air it breathes.

The birds around me hopped and played,
Their thoughts I cannot measure: —
But in the least motion which they made
It seemed a thrill of pleasure.

The budding twigs spread out their fan,
To catch the breezy air,
And must I think, do all I can,
That there was pleasure there.

If this belief from heaven be sent,
If such be Nature's holy plan,
Have I not reason to lament
What man has made of man?
(William Wordsworth)

§ 37. *John Barleycorn*

There were three men come out of the West

Their fortunes for to try,
And these three men made a solemn vow:
John Barleycorn should die!

They plowed, they sowed, they harrowed him in,
Threw clods upon his head,
And these three men made a solemn vow:
John Barleycorn was dead!

They let him lie for a very long time
Til the rain from Heaven did fall,
Then Little Sir John sprung up his head,
And so amazed them all!

They let him stand 'til Midsummer tide,
Til he grew both pale and wan,
Then Little Sir John he grew a long beard,
And so became a man!

They hired men with the sythes so sharp
To cut him off at the knee
They rolled him and tied him about the waist,
And used him barbarously!

They hired men with the sharp pitchforks
To pierce him to the heart,
And the loader he served him worse than that,
For he tied him in a cart!

They wheeled him around and around the field,
Til they came to a barn,
And there they made a solemn vow
Of poor John Barleycorn,

They hired men with the crab-tree sticks
To strip him skin from bone
And the Miller he served him worse than that:
For he ground him between two stones!

They have wheeled him here and wheeled him there
And wheeled him to a barn,
And they have served him worse than that
They have bunged him in a vat!

They have worked their will on John Barleycorn
But he lived to tell the tale;
For they pour him out of an old brown jug,
And they call him home-brewed ale!

Here's Little Sir John in a nut-brown bowl,
And brandy in a glass!
And Little Sir John in the nut-brown bowl
Proved the stronger man at last!

For the huntsman he can't hunt the fox
Nor loudly blow his horn,
And the tinker can't mend kettles nor pots
Without John Barleycorn!

§ 38. Hal an Toe

Hal an Toe, Jolly Rumble Oh!
We were up long before the day oh,
To welcome in the summer
To welcome in the may oh
The summer is a-comin'
And the winter's gone away oh!
Take no scorn to wear the horn

It was a crest when you were born
Your father's father wore it
And your father wore it too — oh!

Robin Hood and Little John
Have both gone to the fair oh
And we will to the merry green wood
To hunt the buck and hare — oh!

What happened to the span-iard
That made so great a boast oh?
They shall eat the feathered goose
And we shall eat the roast — oh!

The lord and lady bless you
With all their power and might oh
And send their peace upon us
Bring peace by day and night — oh!

Notes on Poetry and Romance

Robert Burns' "Corn Rigs" (§27) was the most often mentioned of these poems, perhaps because it was arranged to music and performed in the 1972 film, "The Wicker Man". The poem narrates the story of a man who seduces a woman, and makes love to her in a cornfield. It hearkens to a Celtic custom in which, in the springtime, young couples would 'bless' the land by making love upon it, in part as a form of sympathetic magic to encourage the newly sown crops to grow. James Frazer saw in this custom a re-enactment of the mating of the divine couple, a sky-god and an earth-goddess, whose coupling makes life on earth possible. A simpler explanation may be that after the spring planting, the man would be up on the hills tending to sheep and cattle in their summer pastures. The springtime could have been the last time couples would see each other until the harvest.

Three other pieces in this collection also represent the theme of romantic love and sexual seduction: the "Beltaine Chase Song" mentioned by Margaret Murray as a spell used by mediaeval witches to transform themselves into animals (c.f. Murray, *The Witch Cult in Western Europe*, pg. 166.) (§31), Thomas Morley's mediaeval madrigal, "Now is the Month of Maying" (§25), and "The Gypsy Laddie", (§26) which was also part of Francis James Child's 19th century collection of British folk ballads. The Gypsie Laddie is known by many versions, such as "The Whistling Gypsy Rover", or "The Raggle-Taggle Gypsie"; the version included here is the oldest variant of the song I have been able to find. In every version, a band of gypsies arrive at the home of a feudal lord, and abduct the wife. In this version the gypsies cast a spell over her. But in most other versions she goes with them perfectly willingly, apparently to escape a husband who did not love her the way she wanted to be loved. During mediaeval and early modern times, when many of these pieces were composed, marriage was primarily an economic and political arrangement, and had little or nothing to do with love. So it should be unsurprising that so many folk songs from the period seem to encourage the flaunting of socially 'proper' conventions like marital fidelity, chastity, and modesty. The same idea appears in Morley's madrigal, "Now is the Month of Maying", although this piece can also be interpreted as a musical celebration of lechery. 'Dancing' was frequently used in mediaeval madrigals as a code-word for sex. And 'Barley-break' is the mediaeval equivalent of the modern saying, 'a roll in the hay'! (I can remember singing this song as a child in primary school, blissfully unaware of the blatantly obvious sexuality in the lyrics: at the time, I thought the 'merry lads' were playing Hide-And-Seek.) Even so, songs like these have a certain honesty about them. Human sexuality is a powerful force in art and culture and psychology. We can learn a great deal about who and what we are from songs like these, however ribald they may be. With such knowledge we may be able to make better decisions about what we should and should not do, when held in the thrall of love (or lust). The alternative, the billion dollar industry in chastity education, has produced absolutely no results whatsoever. Surveys have found that teenagers who received chastity education had exactly the same sexual habits and the same average age of first sexual experience as teens who had not. (c.f. Ed Pilkington, "$1bn 'don't have sex' campaign a flop" *The Guardian*, 16 April 2007). But this should come as no surprise: at a certain age we become sexual beings, and that discovery is both irreversible and unstoppable. It may be better, then, to find ways to make the enjoyment of embodied life, including sexual life, into a source of spiritual knowledge and fulfillment.

Other songs included here find that sense of spiritual fulfillment through participating in natural processes. Two songs in this collection seem to represent this: "Hal and Toe" (§38) and "John Barleycorn" (§37). "Hal and Toe" is a traditional song for celebrating the return of warm weather in the spring. The last verse included here appears to have been added by someone in the pagan community. "John Barleycorn" is the story of the planting and harvesting of grain crops, and he is a dying and resurrecting fertility-god whose story James Frazer saw re-enacted all over the world. John Barleycorn, the personification of the life of the fields, is 'killed' (that is, buried in the soil as a seed), but then reborn as a new stalk of barley. He is 'killed' again (that is, harvested) but reborn yet again, this time in the form of home made beer.

Still other poems in this collection find that sense of spiritual fulfillment in an aesthetic visionary experience of the natural world. This is the case for John Clare's "I Am" (§33), and "A Night Piece" (§35) and "Lines Written in Early Spring" (§36) by Wordsworth. Stories of faerie abductions, such as "La Belle Dame Sans Merci" (§29) could be included as an account of a visionary experience. Several informants interpreted fairy-abduction stories as accounts of people being taken to a Witches' Sabbat, where people can temporarily forget the requirements and absurdities of 'respectable' society, release their inhibitions, and enjoy themselves completely. One informant compared the Witch's Sabbat to a rave in a night club. Leland's Aradia describes the Sabbat as a night of feasting and sexual revelry, all performed in honour of the goddess of the moon. The 'game of Benevento' (c.f. §23) might be a sexual innuendo, rather like the game of 'barley-break', since it must be performed with the lights out. Upon returning to normal society, the Sabbat-goers could plead their innocence by claiming to have been abducted by elves or faeries. Margaret Murray noted that attendees at witch gatherings sometimes wore veils or disguises (c.f. *The Witch Cult in Western Europe* pg. 183), to impersonate animals or supernatural beings. She also held the view that the faeries were "descendants of the early people who inhabited northern Europe" who inherited the religion of their neolithic ancestors (cf. *The God of the Witches*, pp. 52-64.) Therefore, perhaps the witches really were abducted by faeries! Whether or not this interpretation is factually true, for the purpose of a folklore collection may be beside the point. Many contemporary pagans arrange their festivals and gatherings to resemble those early modern poetic accounts of faerie revels in the deep woods. The 'abduction' is an invitation to the lonely, the isolated, the confused, the wounded, and the lost, to come and partake in something joyful, life-affirming, and beautiful. In my mind, I imagine that invitation sounds like the chorus of "The Stolen Child" (§28).

Ninth Movement:

The Book of Shadows

"The places best fitted for Magical Arts are those which are concealed..."

The present form of the paganism was born around 80 years ago, and it is worth telling a short version of the story of its birth. In Britain, around the end of the 19th century, there was widespread interest in occultism and spiritualism, among all social classes. People were publishing books on esoteric topics: spellcraft manuals attributed to characters from the Bible, accounts of attempts to contact the dead, and so on. There were various secret or quasi-secret societies which investigated magic or paranormal phenomena, or which acted like a kind of gentleman's club for magicians. The Theosophical Society, the Masons, the Rosicrucians, the Hellfire Club, the Golden Dawn, can be included here. Books on the subject of magic and the supernatural were proving enormously popular. In 1922 anthropologist James Frazer published *The Golden Bough*, a voluminous study of folk magic practices from all over Europe, described how the story of a god who dies and is reborn is actually common and widespread all over the world. It appears especially in folk magic practices associated with hunting and with agriculture, where the purpose is to ensure a plentiful harvest. The dying and resurrected god was not, Frazer was deliberately implying, a unique event in history, accomplished only by Christ.

Around the year 1936, a man named Gerald Gardner, who had worked all over south-eastern Asia as a customs inspector for the British government, return to England from Malaya to retire. He had a keen interest in magic and the supernatural; in fact he brought home with him a large collection of artifacts associated with witchcraft and shamanism (and, apparently, a formidable collection of traditional weapons!). Settling in Highcliff, near the

New Forest area of England, he was introduced to the members of an esoteric society called the Fellowship of Crotona, and to the members of the Rosicrucian Theatre, in nearby Christchurch. Gardner came to believe, rightly or wrongly, that he had encountered a surviving vestige of Britain's original witchcraft cult. He began publishing his own books on the topic: first two novels, *A Goddess Arrives* and *High Magic's Aid*, and then a non-fiction work entitled *Witchcraft Today*. He also created a working group to practice this new witchcraft, and attracted members to it by permitting tabloid newspapers to report on his doings. This group, called the New Forest Coven, is more or less the first genuinely 'pagan' community of the modern world. They called their new religion 'Wicca'. To this day, Wicca is the largest of modern paganism's internal divisions: around half of the informants responding to my survey identified themselves as Wiccans.

What made the image of the witch particularly attractive to Gardner and his associates was not simply, nor only, her affinity with magic. It was also the way that image represented a transformation of religious values. Certain activities which were discouraged by the conservative Christian morality of the time, such as nudity, flamboyant dancing, and certain expressions of sexuality, were treated by witches as forms of worship. Witchcraft offered not only personal power (through spell-craft and ritual magic), but also a lifestyle in which "ecstacy and joy on earth" was a legitimate spiritual goal. Furthermore, with a Goddess as its central image of divinity, Wicca could offer women more role-models than just the Virgin Mother. A Witch could be anything any Goddess or heroine in history ever was. The first Wiccans had their problems and failings, of course. But their courageous "re-valuation of values" in religion planted a seed which would eventually grow into the tree of many branches that the Pagan movement subsequently became.

Furthermore, the New Forest Coven wrote two books of magic, ritual, and spellcraft together. One was called "Ye Bok of the Art

Magickal"; the other, "The Book of Shadows". The 1957 edition of the Book of Shadows which I was permitted to examine includes a lot of repetition and revision. It gave me the impression of being the handiwork of a group of people, not just one author, in part because of the handwriting styles and the colours of the ink alone. The authors were constantly revising their practices and ideas: keeping what worked, discarding what didn't work. They also drew upon multiple sources: for instance, a portion of Kipling's Tree Song (§34) appears in it as a dancing-song for May Day. The idea behind the writing of the Book of Shadows was to put into one volume the spells, invocations, ceremonies, and ideas which 'worked' the best. Each student would then copy her teacher's Book, and that way everyone would be 'reading from the same page'. People were also encouraged to add things to it, move things around, make corrections, or 'improvements'. As historian Ronald Hutton wrote, "to [Gardner's] credit he was equally insistent that all Wiccan initiates should not merely copy the existing rituals and statements of belief but alter and add to them according to their own tastes and abilities, as Valiente had done." (Hutton, *The Triumph of the Moon*, pg.248) Each copy, therefore, would be unique, and particular to its owner. Some people even discarded and re-wrote entire sections. The first Book of Shadows, despite being varied, jumbled, and in some places hopelessly obscure, is the beginning of a literary tradition. Its very existence alone attests to a fairly well organized community of people with things to say to each other that they take to be important.

The pieces which appear in this section are the parts of Gardner's 1957 Book of Shadows which were mentioned by informants responding to my survey. Gardner's original hand-written book is presently in the care of Richard and Tamarra James, of Toronto, Canada, and they generously permitted me to publish parts of it in this Testament. I have also included here various pieces from Books of Shadows belonging to my survey informants.

§ 39. *Preface to the Book of Shadows.*

Keep a book in your hand of write. Let brothers & sisters copy what the will, but never let the book out of your hands, & never keep the writings of another for if it be found in their hand of write, they well may be taken & tortured.

Each should guard his writings & destroy it whenever danger threatens. Learn as much as you may by heart & when danger is past, rewrite your book if it be safe. For this reason, if any die, destroy their book if they have not been able to, for an it be found, tis clear proof against them, and "ye may not be a witch alone."

So, all their friends be in danger of the torture. So destroy everything not necessary. If your book be found on you, tis clear proof against you alone. You may be tortured. If so, keep all thought of the cult from your mind.

Say you had bad dreams, a devil caused you to write it without your knowledge. Think to yourself,

I know nothing. I remember nothing.

I have forgotten everything.

Drive this into your mind.

If the torture be too great to bear, say I will confess, I cannot bear this torment.

What do you want me to say?

Tell me and I will say it.

If they try to make you speak of the Brotherhood, do not.

But if they try to make speak of impossibilities such as flying through the Air, consorting with the Devil, or Sacrificing Children or eating man's flesh, to obtain relief from torture say "I had an evil dream, I was not myself. I was crazed.

Not all magistrates are bad, if there be an excuse, they may show mercy.

If you have confessed aught, deny it afterwards, say you babbled under torture, you knew not what you did, or said. If you be condemned, fear not.

The Brotherhood is powerful.

They may help you to escape, if you stand fast. If you betray aught, there is no hope for you in this life, or in that which is to come.

Tis sure, if steadfast you go to the pyre, drugs will reach you, you will feel naught.

And you go but to Death and what lies beyond. The ecstasy of the Goddess.

The same of the working tools.

Let them be as ordinary things that anyone may have in their houses.

Let the Pentacles be of Wax, so they may be broken at once. Have no sword unless your rank allows you one, and have no names or signs on anything.

Write the names and signs on them in ink before consecrating them, and wash it off immediately after.

Never boast. Never threaten. Never say you would wish ill to anyone. If you speak of the Craft, say, Speak not to me of such, it frightens me. Tis evil luck to speak of it.

(*The Book of Shadows*)

§ 40. Preface to the Book of Shadows (continued)

For this reason, the Christians have their spies everywhere. These speak as if they were affected to us, as if they wouldn't come into our meetings, saying, 'My mother used to worship the Old Ones. I would I could go myself.' To such as these, ever deny all knowledge.

But to others, ever say, 'Tis foolish men talk of witches flying through the air. To do so they must be as light as thistledown. And men say that witches all be blear-eyed old crones, so what pleasure can there be at a witch meeting such as folks talk on?'

And say, 'Many wise men now say there be no such creatures.'

Ever make it a jest, and in some future times perhaps, the persecution may die and we may worship our Gods in safety again.

Let us all pray for that happy day.

May the blessings of the Goddess and the God be on all who keep these Ardane.

(*The Book of Shadows*)

§ 41. *The Goddess Invocation*

I invoke thee & call upon thee, O Mighty mother of us all,
Bringer of all fruitfulness;
By seed & root, by stem & bud,
By leaf and flower and fruit,
By life and love,
Do we invoke thee to descend upon the body of thy servant & priestess.

Of the Mother, darksome & divine,
Mine the scourge & mine the kiss
The five point star of love and bliss
Here I charge ye in this sign.
(*The Book of Shadows*)

§ 42. *Goddess Invocation*

Hail from the Amalthean horn.
Pour forth thy store of love.
I lowly bend before thee:
I invoke thee at the end,
When other gods are fallen & put to scorn.
Thy foot is to my lips, my sighs unborn
Rise, touch, curl about thy heart, then spend
Pitiful love, loveliest pity descend
And bring me luck
Who am lonely & forlorn.
(*The Book of Shadows*)

§ 43. *The Charge Verse.*

All ye assembled at mine shrine
Of the Mother, Darksome and divine,
Mine the scourge and mine the kiss
The five point star of love and bliss
Here I charge ye in this Sign.
All ye assembled in mine sight
Bow before my spirit bright
Aphrodite, Arianrod
Lover of the Horned God
Mighty Queen of Witchery and Night

Morrígan Etain Nisine
Diana Brigid Melusine
Am I named of old by men
Artemis and Meriden
Hells dark mistress, Heaven's Queen

All who would learn of me a Rune
Or would ask of me a boon
Meet ye in some secret glade
Dance my round I greenwood shade
By the light of the full moon.

In a place wild and lone,
Dance around mine Altar Stone
Work my Holy Mystery
To ye who are fain to Sorcery,
I bring ye secrets yet unknown.

Who give due worship unto me
No more shall ye know slavery
Who tread my round on Sabbat night
Come ye all naked to the rite

In token ye be really free.

I teach the Mysteries of Rebirth
Work ye my Mysteries in mirth
Heart joined to heart and lip to lip
Five are the points of fellowship
That lead ye to ecstasy on Earth.

I ask no sacrifice, but do bow
No other Law but Love I know
By naught but Love may I be known
All things living are mine own
From Me they come, to Me the go.
(*The Book of Shadows*)

§ 44. The Charge of the Goddess

Listen to the words of the Great Mother, who was of Old also called among men, Artemis, Astarte, Dione, Melusine, Aphrodite, Cerridwen, Dana, Arianrhod, Bride, & by many other names.

At mine Altars the youth of Lacedemon in Sparta made due sacrifice.

Whenever ye have need of anything, once in the month & better it be when the moon is full, then ye shall assemble in some secret place and adore the spirit of me who am Queen of all Witcheries.

There ye shall assemble, ye who are fain to learn all sorcery, yet who have not won its deepest secrets: to these will I teach things that are yet unknown.

And ye shall be free from slavery, and as a sign that ye be really free, ye shall be naked in your rites, and ye shall dance, sing, feat, make music, and love, all in my praise.

For mine is the ecstasy of the spirit, and mine also is joy on earth, for my law is Love unto all beings.

Keep pure your highest ideal. Strive ever toward it. Let naught stop you or turn you aside: For mine is the secret which opens upon the door of youth: & mine is the cup of the wine of life: and the cauldron of Cerridwen: which is the holy grail of immortality.

I am the gracious goddess who gives the gift of joy unto the heart of man: upon earth, I give the knowledge of the spirit eternal: & beyond death I give peace & freedom: & reunion with those who have gone before: Nor do I demand ought in sacrifice: for behold: I am the mother of all living, and my love is poured out upon the earth.

Hear ye the words of the Star Goddess, she in the dust of whose feet are the hosts of heaven: whose body encircleth the universe.

I who am the beauty of the green Earth: and the white moon amongst the stars: and the mystery of the waters: and the desire of the heart of man: call unto thy soul: arise & come unto me.

For I am the soul of nature who giveth life to the universe: from me all things proceed: & unto me all things must return: before my face: beloved of gods & men: thine innermost divine self shall be enfolded in the rapture of the infinite.

Let my worship be within the heart that rejoiceth: for behold: all acts of love & pleasure are my rituals: and therefore let there be beauty and strength: power & compassion: honour & humility, mirth and reverence: within you.

And thou who thinkest to seek for me: know that thy seeking and yearning shall avail thee not: unless thou know the mystery: that if that which thou seekest thou findest not within thee:

thou wilt never find it without thee.

For behold: I have been with thee from the beginning: and I am that which is attained at the end of desire.

(*The Book of Shadows*)

§ 45. *The Charge of the Horned God*

Listen to the words of the Horned God, the Guardian of all things wild and free, and Keeper of the Gates of Death, whose Call all must answer.

I am the fire within your heart, and the yearning of your Soul. I am the Hunter of Knowledge and the Seeker of the Holy Quest; I who stand in the darkness of light; I am He whom you have called Death. I the Consort and Mate of Her we adore, call forth to thee.

Heed My call beloved ones, come unto Me and learn the secrets of death and peace. I am the corn at harvest and the fruit on the trees. I am He who leads you home. Scourge and Flame, Blade and Blood these are Mine and gifts to thee.

Call unto Me in the forest wild and on hilltop bare and seek Me in the Darkness Bright. I who have been called; Pan, Herne, Cernunnos, and Hades, speak to thee in thy search. Come dance and sing; come live and smile, for behold: this is My worship.

You are My children and I am thy Father. On swift night wings it is I who lay you at the Mother's feet to be reborn and to return again. Thou who thinks to seek Me, know that I am the untamed wind, the fury of storm and passion in your Soul. Seek Me with pride and humility, but seek Me best with love and strength. For this is My path, and I love not the weak and fearful. Hear my call on long Winter nights and we shall stand together guarding Her Earth as She sleeps.

(Source: Em Poore, personal communication)

§ 46. The Horned God

By the flame that burneth bright,
O Horned One!
We call Thy name into the night,
O Ancient One!
Thee we invoke, by the moon-led sea,
By the standing stone and the twisted tree.
Thee we invoke, where gather Thine own,
By the nameless shrine forgotten and lone.
Come where the round of the dance is trod,

Horn and hoof of the Goat-foot God!
By moonlit meadow, on dusty hill,
When the haunted wood is hushed and still,
Come to the charm of the chanted prayer,
As the moon bewitches the midnight air.
Evoke Thy powers, that potent bide
In shining stream and the secret tide,
In firey flame by starlight pale,
In shadowy host that rides the gale,
And by the fern-brakes fairy-haunted
Of forests wild and wood enchanted.
Come? O Come!
To the heart-beat's drum!
Come to us who gather below
When the broad white moon is climbing slow
Through the stars to the heaven's height
We hear Thy hoofs on the wind of night!
As black tree-branches shake and sigh,
By joy and terror we know Thee nigh.
We speak the spell Thy power unlocks
At Solstice, Sabbat and Equinox,
Word of virtue the veil to rend,
From primal dawn to the wide world's end,
Since Time began—
The Blessing of Pan!
Blessed be all in hearth and hold
Blessed in all worth more than gold
Blessed be in strength and love
Blessed be, where'er we rove.
Vision fade not from our eyes
Of the pagan Paradise
Past the Gates of Death and Birth
Our inheritance of earth.
From our soul the song of spring

Fade not in our wandering.

Our life with all Life is one

By blackest night or the noonday sun.

Eldest of Gods, on Thee we call,

Blessing be on Thy creatures all.

(Doreen Valiente; in *Pentagram Magazine: A Witchcraft Review*, 3rd March, 1965).

§ 47. The Wine Blessing

Into the chalice place the blade.

By this is sacred marriage made.

§ 48. Wine Blessing..

As above, so below.

As the universe, so the soul.

As without, so within.

Blessed and gracious one,

On this day we do consecrate to you

Our bodies, our minds, and our spirits.

Blessed be!

(Adler, *Drawing Down the Moon*, pg. 471.)

§ 49. Wine Blessing.

The male holds the power and is the reservoir of the power;

The female taps the power in him and channels it.

Neither one can work without the other;

One without the other is incomplete.

The Horned God is a God of life and death,

And the Goddess is of birth and renewal.

To learn, you must suffer;

To live, you must be born;

To be born, you must die.

The beginning,

The continuation,

And the end,
Over and over.
The sun brings forth light,
And the moon holds it in darkness.
As above,
So below.
And as the athamé is to the male,
So the chalice is to the female,
And conjoined they be one in truth.
For there is no greater power in all the world,
Than a man and a woman joined in the bonds of love.
(Tamara James, Michelle Delio)

§ 50. Wine Blessing.

As the A. [athamé] is to the Male,
so the cup is the female,
& conjoined they bring blessedness.
(*The Book of Shadows*)

§ 51. Blessing the Cakes

This was said of old: Queen most secret, bless this food unto
our bodies, bestowing health, wealth, strength and joy and peace
and that fulfillment of will and love under will that is perpetual
happiness.

(Tamarra James.)

§ 52. The Witches Chant (a.k.a. The Witch's Rune)

Darksome night and shining moon,
East and South and West and North,
Hearken to the Witch's Rune:
Here I come to call ye forth!

Earth and Water, Air and Fire,
Wand and Pentacle and Sword

Work ye unto my desire
Hearken ye unto my Word!
Cords & Censer, Scourge and Knife,
Powers of the Witch's blade,
Waken all ye into life,
Come ye as the charm is made:

Queen of Heaven, Queen of Hell,
Horned Hunter of the Night,
Lend your power unto the spell,
Work my will by magick rite!

By all the power of Land & Sea,
By all the might of moon and sun,
As I will, so mote it be;
As I do say, it shall be done!
(Valiente, *The Book of Shadows*)

§ 53. *The Great Rite*

Assist me to erect the ancient altar, at which in days past all
worshipped,
The Great Altar of all things,
For in old times, Woman was the altar.
Thus was the altar made and placed;
And the sacred point was the point within the centre of the
circle.
As we have of old been taught that the point within the centre
is he origin of all things,
Therefore we should adore it.
Therefore whom we adore we also invoke, by the power of the
Lifted Lance.

O Circle of Stars,
Whereof our father is but the younger brother,

Marvel beyond imagination, soul of infinite space,
Before whom time is bewildered and understanding dark,
Not unto thee may we attain unless thine image be love.
Therefore by seed and root, by stem and bud, by leaf and
flower and fruit,
Do we invoke thee,
O Queen of Space, O dew of light,
Continuous one of the heavens,
Let it be ever thus, that men speak not of thee as one, but as
none;
And let them not speak of the at all, since thou art continuous.
For thou art the point within the circle that we adore,
The fount of life without which we would not be.
And in this way are erected the Holy Twin Pillars.
In beauty and in strength were they erected,
To the wonder and glory of all men.

O Secret of secrets,
That art hidden in the being of all lives,
Not thee do we adore,
For that which adoreth is also thou.
 Thou art That, and That am I.
I am the flam that burns in the heart of every man,
And in the core of every star.
I am life, and the giver of life.
Yet therefore is the knowledge of me the knowledge of death.
I am alone, the Lord within ourselves,
Whose name is Mystery of Mysteries.

Make open the path of intelligence between us;
For these truly are the Five Points of Fellowship:
Foot to foot,
Knee to knee,
Lance to Grail,

Breast to breast,

Lip to lips.

By the great and holy name Cernunnos,

Inn the name of Aradia;

Encourage our hearts,

Let the light crystallize itself in our blood,

Fulfilling of us resurrection.

For there is no part of us that is not of the Gods.

(Janet and Stewart Farrar, *The Witches Way,* pg. 37-8)

§ 54. *The Legend of the Descent of the Goddess*

Having learned thus far, you must know why the Wica are called the Hidden Children of the Goddess.

Now our Lady the Goddess had never loved, but she would solve all Mysteries, even the mystery of Death; and so she journeyed to the Underworld.

The Guardians of the Portals challenged her: "Strip off thy garments, lay aside thy jewels; for naught mayest thou bring with thee into this our land."

So she laid down her garments and her jewels, and was bound, as are all who enter the Realms of Death, the Mighty One.

Such was her beauty that Death himself knelt and kissed her feet, saying: "Blessed be thy feet, that have brought thee in these ways. Abide with me; but let me place my cold hand on thy heart."

She replied, "I love thee not. Why dost thou cause all things that I love and take delight in to fade and die?"

"Lady", replied Death, "'tis age and fate, against which I am helpless. Age causes all things to wither; but when men die at the end of time, I give them rest and peace, and strength so that they may return. But thou! Thou art lovely. Return not; abide with me!"

But she answered, "I love thee not."

Then said Death: "An thou receivest not my hand on thy heart, thou must receive Death's scourge."

"It is fate—better so," she said. And she knelt, and Death scourged her tenderly. And she cried, "I feel the pangs of love."

And Death said, "Blessed be!" and gave her the Fivefold Kiss, saying, "Thus only mayest thou attain to joy and knowledge." And he taught her all the Mysteries, and they loved and were one, and he taught her all the Magics.

For there are three great events in the life of man: Love, Death, and Resurrection in the new body; and Magic controls them all. For to fulfill love you must return again at the same time and place as the loved one, and you must remember and love them again. But to be reborn you must die and be ready for a new body; and to die you must be born; and without love you may not be born; and this is all the Magics.

(Janet & Stewart Farrar, *The Witches Way*, pg. 29-30)

§ 55. A Legend.

As early Pagan men occupied their time with the hunting and trapping of animals, and the arts of war, they learned much of the ways of the wild, and less of the ways of people and personal relationships. As early Pagan women spent their time in the more social activities of agriculture, village maintenance, and the keeping of the home of the people, they learned far more about the ways in which people get along with people. The women learned tolerance, patience, and empathy from their lives as mothers. As our Lady and our Lord are the Goddess of Womankind and the God of Mankind, the Horned God is wild and free and strong, and the Goddess is wise and tolerant and compassionate. So it is said that the Horned One, when He returned home from one of His many journeys, looked upon His Lady, and recognized Her greater understanding of human problems, and so declared that His strength was from then on Hers to command in all matters of people and their dealings with others. So also did our Gracious Goddess understand that She must never interfere with the wildness and freedom that gave the God His strength. Thus the High Priestess, who is the representative of the Goddess, rules her students and followers by the authority of the Goddess which is backed up by the strength of the High Priest and the God. Thus also does the High Priest, who is the ambassador of the Horned One, govern by the authority of his closeness with the High Priestess and the Goddess.

§ 56. *The Wiccan Rede*

Bind the Wiccan Laws we must
In Perfect Love and Perfect Trust

Live and let live
Fairly take and fairly give

Cast the circle thrice about
to keep the evil spirits out

To bind the spell every time
Let the spell be spake in rhyme

Soft of eye and light of touch
Speak little, listen much.

Deosil go by the waxing moon
Chanting out the Witches rune

Widdershins go by waning moon,
Chanting out the baneful rune.

When the Lady's moon is new
Kiss the hand to her, times two.

When the moon rides at her peak

Then your heart's desire seek

Heed the North Wind's mighty gale
Lock the door and drop the sail.

When the wind comes from the South
Love will kiss thee on the mouth

When the wind blows from the West
Departed souls will have no rest

When the wind blows from the East
Expect the new and set the feast.

Nine woods in the cauldron go
Burn them fast and burn them slow

Elder be the Lady's tree,
Burn it not or cursed you'll be

When the Wheel begins to turn
Let the Beltaine fires burn

When the Wheel has turned to Yule,
Light the log and the Horned One rules.

Heed ye Flower, Bush, and Tree
By the Lady, Blessed Be.

Where the rippling waters go
Cast a stone and truth you'll know

When ye have a true need
Hearken not to other's greed

With a fool no season spend
Lest ye be counted as his friend

Merry meet and merry part
Bright the cheeks and warm the heart

Mind the Threefold Law you should,
Three times bad and three times good.

When misfortune is enow,
Wear the blue star on thy brow.

True in Love ever be,
Lest thy lover's false to thee.

Eight words the Wiccan Rede fulfill:
An ye harm none, do what ye will.

§ 57. *The Five-Fold Kiss*

In other religions the postulant kneels, while the priest towers over him, but in the Art Magical we are taught to be humble and we kneel to welcome them and we say:
Blessed be thy feet,
That have brought thee in these ways.
Blessed be thy knees,
That shall kneel at the Sacred Altar.
Blessed be thy womb / organ of generation,
Without which we would not be.
Blessed be thy breasts,
erected in beauty and strength.
Blessed be thy lips,
Which shall utter the Sacred Names.
(*The Book of Shadows*)

§ 58. *Litany of the Earth-Mother*

O Earth-Mother, Thou of uncounted names and faces, Thou of the many-faceted Nature in and above All, Nature incarnate. Love and Life fulfilled, look favourably upon this place, grace us with Your Presence, inspire and infuse us with Your powers, by all the names by which you have been known, O Earth-Mother.

Thou whom the Druids call Danu —
Thou who art Erde of the Germans —
Thou whom the Slavs call Ziva —
Thou who art Nerthus of the Vanir —
Thou who art Frigga of the Aesir —
Thou whom the Romans call Terra —
Thou who art Diana to the Etruscans —
Thou who the Persians call Kybele —
Thou who art Iphimedeia, Mighty Queen of the Greeks —
Thou whom the Egyptians call Nuit, Star-Mother —
Thou who art Ninmah of Sumeria —
Thou whom the Hittites call Kubala —
Thou Who art Mami-Aruru of Babalon —
Thou whom the Caanites call Arsai —
Thou who art Our Lady of Biblos in far Phonicia —
Thou whom the children of Crete call Mountain Mother —
Thou who art Yemanja of the Umbanda —
Thou whom the Dahomeans call Erzulie —
Thou who art Shakti and Parvati of India —
Thou whom the Tibetans call Green Tara —
Thou who art Kwanyin of China —
Thou whom the Nipponese call Izanami —
Thou who art Sedna and Nerivik of the Eskimos —
Thou whom the Pawnee call Uti-Hiata
Thou who art Cornmother of the Plains —
Thou whom the Navaho call Estanatlehi —
Thou who art Ometeotl and Guadalupe in Mexico —
Thou whom the Islanders call Hina-alu-oka-moana —

Thou who art the Great Mother, the Star Goddess, the All
Creating One—
Mother of All, we call upon You—
Terra Mater, Mater Sotier, Earth Mother—
Come to us!
(Source: Adler, *Drawing Down the Moon*, pp. 467-8; attributed to
Isaac Bonewits)

§ 59. *A Self-Blessing*

Bless me, Lord and Lady, for I am thy child.
Bless my mind that I may know of thee in all things.
Bless my eyes that I may see thee in all things.
Bless my nose that I may smell thy sacred scents.
Bless my ears that I may hear thy sacred words.
Bless my mouth that I may speak thy words in truth.
Bless my heart that is thy temple and shrine.
Bless my seed / womb without which we would not be.
Bless my knees that shall kneel at thy sacred altars.
Bless my feet that have brought me in these ways.
And bless me Lord and Lady, for I am thy child.

§ 60. *Blessing Before Meals*

Answer us, O ancient ones,
Providence and power be thine
Hear and answer, gracious goddess,
Grant us laughter, wit and wine!

Descend on us, O thou of blessings
Come among us, make us glad
Since thou art chief of all creation,
Why oh why should we be sad?

Be among us, joyous greenwood
Banish heavy hearted hate

Accept our craft, O gracious mother,
Let cheerful brightness be our fate!

So mote it be!

§ 61. *Another Blessing Before Meals*

This is the body of our mother
The Earth
Warmed and given life
By the rays of our father the sun
May her body become one with our bodies
For our nourishment and to her honour,
and may his glory shine in our lives.
(Maurice Lachapelle)

Notes on the Book of Shadows

The Preface of the Book of Shadows (§39, §40)

This short text seems to represent the Wicked-Witchy-ness of Wicca: it is written to resemble the sort of rules that a secretive witchcraft society might adopt in order to protect themselves. (§39 is quoted from Gardner's Book of Shadows; other versions are longer, and include the text presented here as §40.) It's entertaining reading, and has a few teachings that I think genuinely wise: for instance, it calls upon witches to "Never boast, never threaten, never say you would wish ill of anyone." I think the best way to understand this text is to treat it as a poetic or artistic representation or re-enactment of a mythical history, a history that probably never happened in the world in quite the way literally described here. But nonetheless it may express what life may have felt like for those in Europe's past who were members of various religious minorities who had to band themselves close together for protection. At any rate, it represents a mythical history that some pagans might *wish* had indeed happened. As counter-intuitive as it may seem, some people feel strongly empowered by the thought that they are members of a persecuted minority. It lends to them a sense of purpose: and a sense of purpose is something no one can live without.

In most western-world nations, pagans are not persecuted. No one needs to fear being imprisoned or executed because she practices spell-craft, or professes to be a witch. There is no point, therefore, in the various trappings of secrecy recommended by the Preface to the Book of Shadows. The Preface can therefore be interpreted, perhaps uncharitably, as a work of unrealistic paranoia. However, from informants responding to my survey I learned that many pagans in the certain regions of the United States, especially in the region known as the "Bible Belt", *do* fear for their safety. Pagans in this area have had their homes and businesses vandalized or even set on fire, or their pets mutilated or killed. Some have been the victims of vicious physical and sexual assaults. Some have had their children taken away by child welfare agencies who claimed that as pagans they are unfit to be parents. Pagans in these places, my informants told me, usually find that they must have secret meetings, secret names and code-words, and the like. Some communities have had to adopt an intense screening process for new members, to prevent 'spies' or 'plants' from joining. The informants who described events like these told me that they take the Preface very seriously indeed.

The Charge of the Goddess (§44)

Earlier I wrote that no one, or almost no one, claims that paganism's Testament was transmitted to humanity through a prophet or visionary, directly from the gods. The Charge of the Goddess may constitute an exception to this. It was composed by Doreen Valiente, and so it has a human origin. But its purpose was to serve as a ritual speech which the priestess recites after the ritual of 'Drawing Down the Moon' has been performed.

Drawing Down the Moon is a Wiccan ritual in which the

goddess is invoked into the body of the priestess. First the circle is 'cast', by a ritual participant who walks three times around the circle in a clockwise direction. Then the four cardinal directions and their various correspondences are honoured with a song or a spell. In both cases, magical or divine powers are summoned by means of a spell or a song which is often composed spontaneously, off the cuff, at the same moment. Next, the priest and priestess stand in the centre, facing each other. The priest traces the shape of a pentacle on the priestess' body with his hands or a ritual tool like a wand or athamé, while reciting an invocation spell (such as §41 or §42). The assembled circle of participants may be singing, chanting, or playing a low hypnotic rhythm on drums or other instruments. The purpose is to induce in the priestess, and perhaps in others as well, a mild state of trance. The priestess may also receive a special costume, a veil or a mask, or other material sign which represents the deity being invoked. It is believed, then, that the spirit and the presence of the Goddess is invoked into the body of the priestess ('drawn down'). In essence, the priestess is 'possessed' by the deity. Whatever she says, whatever she does, during this time, is treated as the words and actions of the deity herself. The people in the circle can therefore communicate directly with the goddess, ask her questions, and hear her answers. Since the Charge of the Goddess is meant to be recited by the priestess while she is so possessed, it is therefore sometimes treated as the words of the goddess herself. One informant said, "The Charge is Her central message to Her people on earth."

At the end of the session, the priestess is restored to her body, with a thank-you to the departing deity. (If readers wish to perform this ceremony themselves, I strongly recommend finding an experienced practitioner who can teach it. The ceremony involves powerful psychological forces, and inexperienced seekers often become painfully disoriented, or find that they get no results at all.)

Drawing Down the Moon is arguably the most important of all pagan rituals, since it offers a chance to speak directly to a deity. Other branches of the pagan movement have similar rituals, such as the Norse practice of 'Seithr'. Indeed much of paganism's ritual and ceremony, its initiatory ordeals, and its day-to-day ethical guidelines, is intended to produce an intensified emotional, aesthetic, and psychological experience in which the presence of the Goddess herself seems to open up within the seeker's own being. This is an experience which, in the view of most who described it in my survey, just about anyone can have.

Historian Ronald Hutton said that Valiente wrote the Charge on the occasion of a minor disagreement with Gardner. Valiente "remonstrated with Gardner about the quantity of material obviously attributable to Crowley in it, as the latter's reputation... was both so great and so bad that it would help bring Wicca into disrepute". (Hutton, *The Triumph of the Moon*, pg. 247.) Gardner therefore permitted Valiente to re-write the standard text of the Wiccan ritual. And one result of her labour was the Charge of the Goddess: first a poetic version (§43), then the prose version (§44) which is better known today. The influence of Leland's "Aradia" should be fairly clear: parts of the story of How Diana Gave Birth to Aradia (§22) appear in the Charge, slightly paraphrased. The Charge has become one of the most often quoted and best loved statements of Pagan spiritual identity and meaning.

The version of the prose Charge which appears in this collection is exactly as I copied it directly from Gardner's own Book of Shadows. Yet the text has changed since Valiente wrote it. For instance, the line "At mine Altars the youth of Lacedemon in Sparta made due sacrifice" is usually omitted. This may be no loss, since it is geographically mistaken: Sparta is in Lacedemon, and Lacedemon is not in Sparta. Furthermore, some of its lines have become well known proverbs in their own right, and I shall discuss them among the Wisdom Teachings.

The Great Rite (§53) and various Wine Blessings (§47 to §50)

We have seen, in the stories of Inanna and Dumuzi (§4), and of The Morrígan and The Dagda (§10), that the goddess is involved in an intimate relationship with a god. The fertility of the land, and of animal and human life, is sustained and empowered by the lovemaking of the primordial couple. Here is yet another example: a story from a Hindu religious text, the Bhradaranyaka Upanisad.

> In the beginning this world was Self (Atman) alone in the form of a Person. Looking around, he saw nothing else than himself. He said first, "I Am". Thence arose the name "I"...
>
> He was afraid, for one who is alone is afraid. This one said to himself, "Since there is nothing else than myself, of what am I afraid?" Thereupon, truly, his fear departed, for of what should he have been afraid? Assuredly it is from a second that fear arises.
>
> Verily, he had no delight, for one who is alone has no delight. He was, indeed, as large as a woman and a man closely embraced. He caused that self to fall into two pieces. Therefore this is true: "Oneself is like a half-fragment"...
>
> He copulated with her. Therefrom human beings were produced.
>
> [She changed herself into the forms of various animals, and he did likewise] ...Thus, indeed, he created all...
>
> He knew: "I, indeed, am this creation, for I emitted it all from myself." Thence arose creation. Verily, he who has this knowledge comes to be in that creation of his.
>
> (Source: *Brhadaranyaka Upanisad* I.iv.1-7)

Although this passage is very short, and perhaps leaves the reader with more questions than answers, it is noteworthy as it succinctly represents the Hindu world-view regarding the creation of the world. First of all, the world was formed by a being called 'Atman'; the word means 'the Self'. This implies that the world is a *person*, not a thing. Second, the universe was not crafted like a clay pot. It was not made, but *born* by the Atman, who split itself into two, a male and a female, for that purpose. These two halves then sexually mated with each other and gave birth to all things. The diversity and multiplicity of forms in the world (that is, different plants, landforms, minerals, animals, people, and so on) is a product of the sexual union of a male and female aspect of the same Atman.

This story thus appears to explain not only 'how' the world was created, but also 'why'. The Atman, finding itself to be alone, first felt fear, and then loneliness. It divided itself, creating from itself beings other than itself, in order to make the universe less lonely. The Atman thereby finds that all things are a product of itself and hence a part of itself. All beings are but different masks and costumes that the same Atman wears. Conflict and aggression arises when different beings forget that they share one spirit with others. The Atman, within itself, knows only peace. When the common Self between different people is recognized, the way is opened to companionship and deep love. After all, there would seem to be no point in fighting against yourself.

This emotional and sexual relationship between the primordial divine couple is called the *Heiros Gamos*, or more usually, the Great Marriage. Some of the most important rituals in Wicca are re-enactments of the Great marriage. A 'Wine Blessing', for instance, is a speech recited by a priestess and priest who symbolically represent the sexual coupling of the goddess and the god using a chalice full of wine, held by the priestess, and a wand or a ritual knife (called an *athamé*) held by the priest. The wand is dipped into the wine, the spells are recited, and then the chalice is passed around the circle for everyone to share a drink. A 'Great Rite' represents the Great Marriage in a decidedly unsymbolic way which I need not describe here. But I should say that it is generally performed in complete privacy by consenting adults.

The idea of the Great Marriage is also behind teachings such as 'as above, so below' (§93), 'all things entail their own opposite' (§98), and the idea that the gods need each other and cannot exist apart from each other (§87). The general idea appears to be that all things are in some way involved in an epistemic or functional relationship with something that is fundamentally 'other' than itself. The universe is thus the product of a dynamic interplay of two "opposites", which are two aspects of an singular principle of activity that require one another for their functioning, or which are not knowable except in contrast with each other. The lovemaking of the Goddess and the God is the general symbol of this idea. A few informants represented this teaching on a table of correspondences, such as this one:

Female	Male
Below	Above
Chalice	Blade
Yin	Yang
Plant life	Animal life
Stillness, Silence, Darkness	Movement, Sound, Brightness
Form, Substance	Force, Energy
Mercy	Severity
Left	Right
Widdershins/counter-clockwise	Deosil / clockwise
Blue, Green, Black	White, Yellow, Red
Moon	Sun
Winter	Summer
Earth	Sky
Nurturing	Protecting
Holistic	Analytic
Intuitive, Emotional	Rational, Logical
Synchronicity	Causality
Essence	Existence

Non-Being	Being
Birth	Death

Although this logic of correspondence rests on gender based categories, it isn't meant to imply that only people of a certain gender may possess certain qualities. Just because 'nurturing' and 'intuition' are found on the female side of this diagram, it doesn't follow that only women can be nurturing and intuitive. The whole process is internalized within each living being. Nurturing and intuition are associated with a female 'side' of each person's spirit, just as severity and reason are associated with a male 'side'. There are female gods whose functions fall on the male side of this diagram, such as Artemis, and male gods with female functions, such as John Barleycorn. As one of the wisdom teachings goes, everyone has both light and darkness within her (§140). And as the Goddess herself says, if you do not find it within yourself, you will never find it outside of yourself. (§44, §84).

Having said all that, I do not wish to bury the meaning of the Great Marriage beneath layers of conceptual abstractions. Most contemporary pagans are practical people, and prefer to keep their intellectual theorizing down to a minimum. At any rate, sex and love are not symbols for immaterial ideas. They are embodied activities, charged with emotional power and significance. In my view, it is sufficient to say that the meaning of the Great Marriage is this: *the world is what it is because the goddess and the god love each other.* Moreover, when we mere mortals love each other, we do as the gods do; and we are thereby able to find the love of the gods within each other, within our relationships, and within ourselves.

The Legend of the Descent of the Goddess (§54)

This short story has gone by names such as "The Myth of the Goddess" and "The Central Myth of Witchcraft". It is sometimes re-dramatised in rituals, especially if the ritual is an initiation ceremony. It is comparable to the Descent of Inanna (§5) and the

Hymn to Demeter (§9), both of which were known to the members of the New Forest Coven. In this story, Death teaches the goddess that he does not cause people to die, but he gathers the spirits of the dead into his realm. There he offers them peace and rest, and a chance to return to the Earth and live new lives. Further, those who truly and deeply love each other will be reborn together. This teaching was very important to Gardner: Hutton suggests it was one of his most deeply cherished beliefs. (Hutton, *The Triumph of the Moon*, pg. 245) It appeared in his novel, *A Goddess Arrives*, for instance. It also appeared in this invocation, found in both *The Book of Shadows* and in *The Book of the Art Magical*, for use on "November Eve":

Dread Lord of the Shadows, God of Life and the Giver of Life, yet is the knowledge of Thee the knowledge of Death.

Open wide I pray Thee Thy Gates through which ever man must pass.

Let our dear ones who have gone before return this night to make merry with us. And when our time comes, as it must, O Thou, the comforter, the giver of peace and rest, we will enter Thy domains gladly and unafraid, for we know that when rested and refreshed among our dear ones, we are reborn again into this life, with sturdier limbs and keener brains, by Thy Grace and by the Grace of the Great Mother.

Let it be in the same place and time as our beloved ones. And may we meet and know and remember and love them again.

(Gardner, *The Book of the Art Magical*, private collection)

As a sign of the widespread appeal of this idea, a variation of it also appeared in the wisdom-teaching collection: "You shall know them and love them and know them again" (§135).

I must admit that one part of the Legend of the Descent puzzles me. At one point death 'scourges' the goddess 'tenderly', and this causes the goddess to fall in love with him. Scourging seems to me rather out of place in a religion where acts of love and pleasure are considered rituals! One informant explained it to me that scourging symbolizes purification. By scourging her, Death was preparing her for rebirth; in effect letting her go, even though he had fallen in love with her. Another informant explained that scourging and binding constricts blood flow to the brain and therefore helps induce a trance state. But these explanations seem unsatisfying to me. When I said as much, my informant replied that I couldn't understand this part of the Legend because I do not practice 'BDSM'. Well, I can't think of a reply to that!

A Legend (§55)

Gerald Gardner wrote a set of rules for how his new community should govern itself. These rules are known as the "Laws of the Craft". Many of them appear among the Wisdom Teachings, as shall be shown later. This particular story appeared as one of the 'Laws' in a 1978 revision of Gardner's original list. It tells of how the Horned God gave to the Triple Goddess authority in all matters relating to human relations. Its purpose is to explain why the coven should be led by a woman, a priestess, and not by a male priest. Its appearance in my survey, separate from the list of 'Laws' from which it came, suggests that the contemporary pagan community still holds the leadership abilities of women in high esteem. At Druid meetings in Ireland which I attended, it was often insisted that the first opinions or suggestions to be heard when discussing some problem or a course of action should be the opinion of 'the senior priestess', that is, the eldest woman present at the meeting.

The Five-Fold Kiss (§57.)

This blessing is an important part of initiation ceremonies. While speaking these lines, the priest or priestess kisses the initiate in each place on the initiate's body mentioned in the blessing. This action is also mentioned in the "Great Rite" (§53) and other places as the 'five points of fellowship'. It is a dramatic and intimate example of the religious significance attributed by modern paganism to acts of love and pleasure. It is also an affirmation of one of the primary spiritual ideas which it appears pagans around the world have in common: the immanent divinity within each individual human being. This idea, sometimes called 'The Mystery', also appears in the Self-Blessing (§59), and frequently in the Wisdom Teachings and Circle Songs, as I shall discuss later. It is probably the most important act of welcoming and acceptance which someone in the pagan community could receive or bestow.

Perhaps because of the importance of this ritual act, the phrase 'Blessed be!' has become one of the stock phrases in the Pagan vocabulary. It may surprise some pagan readers to learn that its origin is in fact Christian. It comes from the Beatitudes, in the famous Sermon on the Mount, when Christ proclaimed that God gives a special blessing to the poor, the meek, the humble, and the oppressed, among others. But through the Five-Fold Kiss, the phrase is now used among pagans for greetings and partings of all kinds between friends, as well as for ceremonial invocations. Many pagans responding to my survey signed off their letters and emails to me with a cheerful Blessed Be!, right next to their signature.

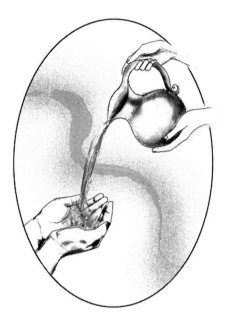

Tenth Movement

Wisdom-Teachings

Each Blade of Grass Whispers, "Jack in the Green..."
A folk proverb is a saying, a catch-phrase, a piece of advice, or the
like, which embodies some kind of culturally accepted wisdom.
As folklorist Barre Toelken defined them: "Proverbs normally
come forth in response to a situation in which a person feels
called upon to offer culturally appropriate advice to another
person." (Toelken, *The Dynamics of Folklore*, pg. 104) When
someone advises another using a proverb, they are attempting to
influence that person's attitudes, opinions, or actions. (Think of
how people use the saying, "If you want to learn to swim, you
have to jump in the water!") Proverbs do this in a way that brings
to bear not just the speaker's own wishes. They also carry the
power of the cultural traditions to which the speaker belongs. As
Toelken says:

> ...since the proverb allows phrasing the advice in a culturally
> recognized form, it comes out not as our own personal opinion
> (which might be thought intrusive anyway) but as a cultural
> norm, with all the authority, antiquity, and stability of that
> category of thought. The performance and perception of
> proverbs allows both speaker and audience to exercise
> culturally acceptable philosophies, and to demonstrate in so
> doing their own hold on tradition, their membership in the
> group. (*ibid.* pg. 105)

Proverbs thus do more than enable people to influence the
opinions and actions of others. They also tend to act as a stabi-
lizing force on a culture's values.

In this section I present the proverbs which were offered to me
by those who responded to my folklore survey. I have divided

them into three broad categories: Historical, Traditional and Contemporary. The first category, "Historical" teachings, are the mottos and proverbs which appear frequently in contemporary Pagan culture, yet were also known somewhere in the ancient world. The "Traditional" teachings are ones which, according to my informants, were part of a specific and organized tradition of spiritual education. Many of them were crafted by prominent figures in the early formation of Wicca: Doreen Valiente, Gerald Gardner, Alex Sanders, and so on. Although it may seem repet- itive, I have included proverbs which come from the Book of Shadows, the Charge of the Goddess, and other parts of Wicca's testament. Other proverbs in this category may be of more recent origin: even within the last ten years. But all together, the teachings I am classing together as 'traditional' are the ones which, according to my informants, were taught as part of a formal and structured system of spiritual education and practice.

For the most part, the teachings listed here as 'contemporary' spring from the personal and spontaneously-realised insights of various individuals. Most were discovered in the course of the informant's own spiritual development, or through some problem or challenge they were facing at some time in their lives. Not all of them are part of a widespread folk tradition in the community, formal or informal, but may well be on their way to attaining that status. In some cases they were taught by a pagan 'celebrity', such as a well known writer, and they continue to be propagated in part because of the association with that person. Where possible, therefore, I have attributed the source. In other cases, they are the products of someone's private spiritual inspiration, realised in response to a request for help or advice or council. Thereafter, the speaker or listener found the teaching to be so memorable and important, that it was remembered for years or even decades, and passed on to others, such as myself when I canvassed the community with my survey.

Some of these proverbs are messages directly from the

Goddess herself, or so claimed my informants. Some were said to come from the personal insight of the informant, or from the insight of a well-regarded person in that informant's community. Some were expressions of what the informant's spiritual path means to her. In most cases, no particular divine origin was imputed to them. But nonetheless, each informant attributed a special magic, or power, or poetry to the teaching. They are, indeed, the statements of spiritual identity by which contemporary pagans recognize their gods, their values, their companions, their purposes, and sometimes their own selves. Almost any of them could count as expressions of a Word of Being, from the divine source. Which of them come from the gods, and which ones are mere nonsense, I invite each reader to decide for herself. And I modestly suggest that a fine evening's entertainment might be had by turning off the television, opening this book, and debating the meaning of a few of these proverbs with your friends.

"Historical" Teachings.

§ 62. Know Yourself.

§ 63. Thou Art Goddess! Thou Art God!

§ 64. The world is full of gods.

§ 65. Three candles illuminate every darkness: Truth, Nature, Knowledge.

§ 66. I am a wind from across the sea; I am a wave of the sea.

§ 67. It is what sustained us through our days: the truth that was in our hearts, strength in our arms, fulfillment of our tongues.

§ 68. The finest music in all the world is the music of "what happens".

§ 69. Everything is in motion, and nothing is still.

§ 70. Fate is everything.

§ 71. Love Conquers All.

§ 72. The Motto of Hermes Trimagistus: What a great miracle

is Man!

§ 73. The Wisdom of Dionysus: Eat, Drink, and be Merry, for tomorrow may never come.

§ 74. The Wisdom of Apollo: Everything in moderation, and nothing in excess.

§ 75. Keep to moderation, keep the end in view, follow nature.

§ 76. Cattle die and kinsmen die, you yourself shall some day die, but a good name lasts forever.

"Traditional" Teachings

§ 77. As man is now, so the gods once were. As the gods are now, so man may some day become.

§ 78. There is no part of you that is not of the gods.

§ 79. To each god there corresponds a ritual.

§ 80. Ye shall be naked in your rites.

§ 81. Ye shall dance, sing, feast, make music and love, all in my praise.

§ 82. All acts of love and pleasure are my rituals.

§ 83. Let there be beauty and strength, power and compassion, honour and humility, mirth and reverence within you.

§ 84. If that which you seek, you find not within, you will never find it without.

§ 85. The goddess changes and transforms; the god ever remains himself.

§ 86. The goddess kills and gives rebirth; the god dies and is reborn.

§ 87. Without the goddess there is no god; without the god there is no goddess.

§ 88. Magick is the art and science of causing change to occur in conformity with Will. (Crowley)

§ 89. The primary principle of magic is connection. (Starhawk)

§ 90. A spell is a ritual for raising psychic power and directing it to a specific and practical purpose. (Janet and Stewart Farrar)

§ 91. White magic is poetry, and black magic is anything that actually works. (Victor Anderson)

§ 92. Knowledge is power.

§ 93. As above, so below.

§ 94. As within, so without.

§ 95. All things return to their source.

§ 96. For good or ill, all things return in threes.

§ 97. Like attracts like.

§ 98. All things entail their own opposite.

§ 99. Once connected, always connected.

§ 100. To name something is to know it, and to have power over it.

§ 101. Whatever is willed, will be.

§ 102. If it works, us it; if it works, it is true.

§ 103. Magick is seldom flashy because it seldom needs to be.

§ 104. Magick will not pay for broken windows. (Gerald Gardner)

§ 105. Remember Karma.

§ 106. You always reap what you sow.

§ 107. We are our deeds.

§ 108. We all build our own prisons.

§ 109. I have four precepts: To Know, To Will, To Dare, To Keep Silent.

§ 110. Bind the Wiccan Laws we must: in Perfect Love and Perfect Trust.

§ 111. Eight words the Wiccan Rede fulfill: an it harm none, do what you will.

§ 112. Do What Thou Wilt shall be the whole of the Law. Love is the Law, Love Under Will. (Alasdair Crowley)

§ 113. Every man and woman is a star. (Alasdair Crowley)

§ 114. To learn, you must suffer – are you ready to suffer to learn?

§ 115. Properly Prepared I must always be.

§ 116. The Gods cannot help men without the help of man.

§ 117. Use no symbol, spell, or incantation which you do not understand.

§ 118. Never use your power without first divining exactly what must be done.

§ 119. Do not harm another, unless you are willing to suffer like or greater harm.

§ 120. Do not bind any free being, unless you are willing to be likewise bound.

§ 121. Do not use the Art for pride nor vain glory.

§ 122. Never threaten what you will not do.

§ 123. Do not set a price for magickal work.

§ 124. Never bargain for a magical tool.

§ 125. To those who cannot rule justly the answer be, 'Those who cannot bear your rule will leave you.'

§ 126. Never buy your first deck of Tarot cards: let your first deck be a gift.

§ 127. Never give a blade as a gift to a friend, lest you cut the friendship.

§ 128. Speak well of bards.

§ 129. If someone puts you on a pedestal, jump off and run away! (Janet Farrar)

§ 130. May there be peace in the North. May there be peace in the South. May there be peace in the West. May there be peace in the East. May there be peace throughout the whole world.

§ 131. Grant, O Goddess, thy protection.

And in thy protection, strength.

And in strength, understanding.

And in understanding, knowledge.

And in knowledge, the knowledge of justice.

And in the knowledge of justice, the love of it.

And in the love of it, the love of all existences.

And in the love of all existences, the love of the Goddess and all goodness.

(Ross Nichols, The Universal Druid's Prayer.)

§ 132. The Truth Against The World!

§ 133. What's well begun is better done.

§ 134. What is begun with love, shall end in beauty.

§ 135. You shall know them, and love them, and know them again.

"Contemporary" Teachings.

§ 136. Here be dragons!

§ 137. Goddess is alive! Magick is afoot! (Leonard Cohen / Buffy St. Marie)

§ 138. All gods are one god, all goddesses are one goddess, and there is but one initiator. (Dion Fortune)

§ 139. The gods always show you the face of the divine that you most need to see.

§ 140. Each person has both light and darkness within her.

§ 141. If you cannot hex, you cannot heal. (Gwydion Pendderwen)

§ 142. The path is not meant to be easy; the path is not for everyone; the path is for the few.

§ 143. Treat all experiences of hardship, frustration, and suffering as learning experiences. Learning is a form of healing.

§ 144. The path is a learning path, a healing path, and a magical path.

§ 145. The path is not a religion. It is a way of life.

§ 146. The path is the same for all, but each must walk it in her own way.

§ 147. There are many paths, but they all lead to the same destination.

§ 148. Pass on what you have learned; but always in accord with each person's ability to understand.

§ 149. You can't pour anything into a cup that is already full.

§ 150. Do not serve your best wine to drunkards.

§ 151. The Craft is a tough weed that will grow many strange flowers and bear strange fruits, so we must try and tolerate different ways of practicing it. Learn from what we see and if we cannot use it, let the others try, even if they eat bad fruit and go balls up! (Victor Anderson)

§ 152. The path is a style of love that demands treading very, very softly and kindly through life, because life is a precious, short, amazing gift. (Monica Becker)

§ 153. Everything is always changing; everything is part of the circle life, death, and rebirth; this is the ebb and flow of the world.

§ 154. Nothing happens by coincidence.

§ 155. Whatever needs to happen: let it happen, let it be. (Mike Scott)

§ 156. Wherever you are, whatever you are doing, and whatever your circumstance, there is always something beautiful happening around you.

§ 157. We are all of us wealthy: we are all of us surrounded by an abundance of blessings.

§ 158. The world is providing everything you need; the world is taking care of you. Trust it.

§ 159. Be kind to yourself.

§ 160. Follow your bliss! (Joseph Campbell)

§ 161. Not all glittering things are gold; not all who wander are lost. (J.R.R. Tolkien)

§ 162. I am the Earth, and the Earth is Me. (Maryanne Pearce)

§ 163. Let there be beauty above us and below, to the right of us and to the left of us, before us and behind us, within us and without. (Navajo invocation)

§ 164. The Grandfathers and Grandmothers knew before you were born that you would come to this place, seeking their presence. They are looking out for you; they will never hurt you; they are always close by. (Aboriginal teaching)

§ 165. The Grandfathers and Grandmothers already know what is in your heart and on your mind. They already know what you want; they also already know what you really need. So it isn't necessary to ask them for anything. It is better, instead, just to give thanks. Always begin your prayers and ceremonies with a gesture of thanks. (Aboriginal teaching)

§ 166. The Creator is within all things that he created. Therefore, whenever doing anything, you must ask if you would do it to the Creator. Whatever I say, I must ask if I would say it to the Creator. It must be said with the Seven Grandfather Teachings in mind. As the Creator is in everything, so must those values be in everything we do. (Aboriginal teaching)

§ 167. The Creator puts his people where he most needs them to be. (Aboriginal teaching)

§ 168. What is life? It is the flash of a firefly in the night. It is the breath of a buffalo in the winter time. It is the little shadow which runs around the grass and loses itself in the sunset. (Crowfoot, Orator of the Blackfoot Confederacy).

§ 169. Some people enter this world only long enough to know that they are loved.

§ 170. What is remembered, lives. (Starhawk)

§ 171. This is the next life. (Sharon Devlin Folsom)

§ 172. All things have a seed of beauty, and it is up to each person to find it. Therefore be open to change; be open to magic; be open to the good in everything. Despite all the corruption, oppression, and misery, the world is ultimately a wonderful place to be.

§ 173. Do not take anyone else's word alone for this. Open your mind, body, and heart, and open your eyes, and see it for yourself.

§ 174. The Goddess doesn't do laundry. (Doreen Valiente)

§ 175. Our deepest fear is not that we are inadequate. Our deepest fear is that we are powerful beyond measure. It is our light, not our darkness that most frightens us. We ask ourselves, Who am I to be brilliant, gorgeous, talented, fabulous? Actually, who are you *not* to be? You are a child of God. Your playing small does not serve the world. There is nothing enlightened about shrinking so that other people won't feel insecure around you. We are all meant to shine, as children do. We were born to make manifest the glory of God that is within us. It's not just in some of us; it's in everyone. And as we let our own light shine, we unconsciously give other people permission to do the same. As we are liberated from our own fear, our presence automatically liberates others. (Marianne Williamson)

§ 176. Where there's fear, there's power. (Starhawk)

§ 177. Everyone has a purpose for being here on Earth. Everyone has something that she came here to do. It is up to each person to find her own purpose. Yet all the gods, all the spiritual beings of the world, and every living thing on earth, are there to help you find and fulfill your path. No one needs to be alone.

§ 178. There are a few things every pagan should know. Every pagan should learn the species of plants and animals that are native to the area where she lives. She should know the dynamics of her local watershed, which direction the water flows, and what into lake or ocean it flows. She should know the times of year when the seasons change. She should know the phase of the moon today. She should know the direction the storms come from.

§ 179. The first time you see the sun and moon each day, salute them.

§ 180. Whenever entering or leaving a sacred place, always pick up the litter that happens to be in your path.

§ 181. Don't pick up the ball! Don't enter a battle you are not prepared to fight. (Tamarra James)

§ 182. Don't poison the well.

§ 183. Keep bees and grow asparagus, listen to the wind instead of the politicians, make up your own stories and believe them if you want to live the good life. (Miriam Waddington)

§ 184. A good and honourable person need not fear death. For death is a part of the circle of life; you cannot have life without death, nor can you have death without life. Death is but one transition in life among many; and some things in this world are worse than dying. And whatever else may happen, the circle of life must go on."

§ 185. "Lo, there do I see my father before me. Lo, there do I see my mother, and my sisters, and my brothers before me. Lo, there do I see the line of my people, going back to the beginning. Lo, they do call to me. They bid me take my place among them, in the halls of Valhalla, where the brave may live forever." (Michael Crichton / Viking death invocation.)

Notes on the Wisdom Teachings

My informants for these teachings came from a wide variety of very different backgrounds and cultural traditions within the pagan movement. They were often separated from each other by oceans and continents. Yet many of these proverbs appeared frequently and *consistently* in my survey. A given informant might mention only one or two of them, not all of them. But he or she would phrase it very similarly to the way another informant, from a different path or tradition, and living in a different country, phrased it. It became clear to me that these teachings, including the ones my informants said did *not* come from a formal training system, represented definite ideas that have become part of the shared wisdom and belief structure of the whole movement. Druids, Asatruars, Wiccans, occultists, followers of Egyptian or Mesopotamian deities, and so on, were regularly using them. Despite the diversity and eclecticism of the movement, and despite the way pagans often vehemently insist that their beliefs are valid 'only for themselves' and that others may believe differently, this collection is evidence that pagans of all shapes and sizes do hold a few things in common after all. A large majority of those who responded to my survey said that what they like about paganism is that it gives them the freedom to believe what they want to believe. Still there really are a number of ideas that almost all pagans everywhere agree about. Shared teachings like these, I believe, can be used to bring people together, and create flourishing communities.

In addition to the three base categories of Historical, Traditional, and Contemporary, I have also arranged them into groups of rough thematic similarity. This may have the effect of drawing particular attention to the teachings which apparently contradict each other. But I think of them like moments in a conversation, in which two or more people, perhaps from different backgrounds and life histories, seek the truth through conversation with each other. One makes his point, as honestly and as profoundly as he can. Another speaker then offers a contribution or an elaboration of that point. Or, he offers a critical rejoinder, an objection, or a counterpoint. But there is no sense of confrontation intended thereby. The object of the conversation is not to "win". The object is to find a place of agreement, and to call forth the presence of the Goddess through the conversation. No one can win unless everyone wins.

Taking just the historical teachings as an example, this is how the divine conversation might go. As a starting place the first speaker recalls the Oracle of Delphi, the ancient Greek religious authority, and the motto which was cut above its entrance: "Know Yourself" (§62). Thus it is established from the very beginning that self-knowledge is a spiritual thing. Someone asks, when searching within yourself, what will you find? Another answers, you will find that the gods dwell within each human heart and mind. Therefore, "Thou art Goddess! Thou Art God!" (§63) Yet this wisdom can be true for someone only if it is also true of everyone else. For as the Greek philosopher Thales said, "the world is full of gods" (§64). There are more gods in a single tree than there are stars in the sky. This affirmation should fill the mind with amazement and wonder. It should transform the seeker's perception of the world so that she finds magic everywhere: and that ability is surely an important part of the good and beautiful life. Another seeker adds that "truth, nature, and knowledge" (§65), the Three Candles mentioned in the ancient Triads of Ireland, surely also contribute to the worthwhile life. Perhaps no human life is complete without them. And it may be further added that this truth is not necessarily a purely personal, private matter. For another Druidic motto, this one from "The Song of Amergin", teaches the seeker to know herself as a part of the earth, and indeed that the earth is the whole of her spiritual self (§66). And whenever the troubles of the world seem daunting or insurmountable, one can recall how Celtic hero Oisin answered Saint Patrick's question concerning what sustained him and his people before the arrival of Christianity (§67). We are sustained by "the truth in our hearts", the dignity and divinity of humankind, and of the inherent spiritual beauty and goodness of all things. We are similarly sustained by the "strength in our arms", that is, the ability to work and to fight for that truth. And we are sustained by the "fulfillment of our tongues", that is, by promise-keeping and personal integrity. Someone sustained by these things is able to hear Fionn's Music, which is of course "the music of what happens" (§68). And indeed there is so much music happening everywhere! For the as the Greek philosopher Heraclitus taught, the world is always in motion and never still (§69). But as the Anglo-Saxon proverb teaches, the ever-changing world is not without purpose. The world is guided by a final end, a hidden resolution, which may be called destiny or fate (§70). We mere mortals can know nothing about it, and we can do nothing against it or contrary to it. Some might therefore have reason to fear it. But we may also have confidence and hope that fate is leading us to a good and beautiful revelation: for the motto of the Greek god Cupid is "Omnia Vincit Amor" (§71). All things are subject to love. Even the highest of the gods, Zeus himself, cannot stop himself from falling in love once in a while. Therefore, remembering the motto of Hermes Trismegistus, we may celebrate human life as a great miracle! (§72)And remembering the motto of Dionysus, we may resolve to enjoy this life with eating, drinking, and merrymaking (§73). Yet we should not to allow the celebration to undermine that very greatness. Many of the good things in life can be consumed in excess and thus cause great harm. Therefore the Wisdom of Apollo, which was also carved over the entrance to the Oracle, teaches moderation in all things (§74). This principle was also known among other ancient people: for as the Roman writer Lucan said, one must always practice temperance, preserve one's integrity, and do nothing contrary to nature (§75). Someone able to do all these things will create a great name for himself. As affirmed by the *Havamal*, the ancient Viking wisdom-text, the story of a good man's life will continue to be told with reverence and respect long after his earth-walk is done (§76).

In Sufism, there is a name for this kind of conversation: *Sohbet*. Coleman Barks, the scholar of Sufi literature, wrote that there is no easy English equivalent to the word Sohbet, but it can mean "something like 'mystical conversation on mystical subjects'". (Barks, *The Essential Rumi*, pg. 76.) The idea is that people can discover what matters when we meet each other in conversation as friends. There is no need for institutionalized authority in this conversation. There may even be little need for a supernatural event or a divine revelation. People can learn what they need to know when, both individually and collaboratively, they do their own thinking. These wisdom teachings represent moments in the Sohbet of the contemporary pagan community. They are resting places in a long and extended conversation on the subject of the spirit.

"The Mystery" (§§63, 72, 77, 78, 84, 137, and 162.)

In contemporary paganism, the most fundamental principle of moral and spiritual value has come to be known as "The Mystery". There are seven expressions of this principle in the wisdom-teachings assembled here. They assert, as a first premise, the claim that each person may find the presence of the divine within herself. Where the first teaching in the collection exhorts the seeker to know herself (§62), the seven teachings of the Mystery deign to describe what you will find when you take the time and effort to learn who and what you are. You will find that your mind, heart, and body is the dwelling place of divinity.

The most important of these teachings takes the form of a naming: "Thou Art Goddess, Thou Art God!" (§63). The contemporary phrasing of the proverb comes from a science fiction novel: Robert Heinlein's *Stranger in a Strange Land* (first published in 1961). But I have included it in the "Historical" category because it is also a central principle of some ancient pagan cultures as well. The third motto carved over the entrance to the Oracle of Delphi, for instance, was the phrase "Thou Art". The idea was that a seeker who had properly fulfilled the imperative to 'Know Yourself' given by the first of the Delphic mottos, and who had practiced the temperance called for by the second motto, could be expected to fill in the rest of the third. But a 'true' seeker did not fill in the blank with just whatever he wanted. Two answers, in particular, were regarded as correct: the first, "Thou Art Mortal", and the second, "Thou Art Divine". Both of these teachings, while on one level they blatantly contradict one another, on a deeper level coexist in an uneasy tension. And from that tension emerges all the nobility, the genius, the bumbling stupidity, and the creative potential of humankind.

That tension is also suggested by other teachings, for instance the assertion that each person has both "light and darkness" within her (§139). It is up to each person, so this teaching implies, to decide which part of herself she will let out, which potential she will make real, and so what sort of person she will become thereby. Yet this tension is also positively *celebrated* by the Motto of Hermes Trimagistus: "What a great miracle is Man!" (§72). Humankind is a great miracle because of that two-fold potential. But humanity is not defined by potential alone. We are also defined by our actions (§106). We become noble by acting nobly; we become fools by acting foolishly; we become the light, or the dark, that we 'do'.

The Mystery was also known in various ancient cultures. It was known in Sufism, as shall be discussed later. On some interpretations it was taught by Jesus Christ. The Hindu form of this teaching is 'Tat tvam asi', which translates into 'That is You'. It affirms a profound spiritual relationship between each seeker and everything else in the whole of the universe. For it affirms that everything and everyone around you is part of the *Atman*, which is your greater, comprehensive, spiritual Self. Everything around you is part of you. Here is an example of this teaching from one of the Upanisads:

> These rivers, my dear, flow, the eastern toward the east, the western toward the west. They go just from the ocean to the ocean. They become the ocean itself. As there they know not, 'I am this one', 'I am that one'. Even so, indeed, my dear, all creatures here, though they have come forth from Being, know not 'We have come forth from Being'. Whatever they are in this world, whether tiger, or lion, or wolf, or boar, or worm, or fly, or gnat, or mosquito, that they become.
>
> That which is the finest essence – this whole world has that as its self. That is Reality. That is *Atman*. That art thou! (*Chandogya Upanisad*, vi.x.1-3)

Many pagans interpret The Mystery to mean that each person is, at least in spirit, a god. I believe this interpretation is misleading. For one thing, it may give to people a false sense of their rights. Someone who thinks himself a god may think he can do anything: not just magically, but also ethically. He may think he can do no wrong, even if he causes all sorts of harm to others or to himself. However, I think the meaning of the motto is naught to do with power, but with identity. It has to do with who and what you are. A human being is nothing less than the dwelling place of a deity. Your body, mind, and heart is the home and the temple of a god. And it is even possible that your being is home to not just one god, but to any number of them: dozens, even hundreds. For "the world is full of gods," (§64) and "there is no part of you that is not of the gods" (§53, §78).

If you have the spirit of a deity dwelling within you, then you have a reason to hold yourself in high esteem! The idea that the spirit of a deity dwells within you is a reason to take pride in yourself, to know that there is something noble in being human, to feel that there is something good in being alive. It is also a reason to conduct your life with honour and courage and other heroic and noble virtues. It is a reason to be the very best person you can. It is also to know that nobility of character is an *attainable* goal. It is not an existential, absurdist drama, in which a character strives for something he knows he can never have. The deity within you can help you become a noble soul. The learning and developing process, while it is undertaken by one's own effort, need not be undertaken alone.

The Mystery also teaches us that the gods live within every living being, and in the whole of the earth itself. This is part of why it is wrong to interpret the teaching as a justification for personal egotism. The gods dwell not only within you, but also everywhere. Therefore, when you speak to someone, you are also speaking to the gods within that person. When you listen to someone, you are also hearing the gods speaking to you through her. When you share something with someone, you also share it with the gods. When someone shares something with you, the gift also comes from the gods. In this teaching there is a reason to treat other people with respect, to always assume they have the best of intentions (unless strong reasons exist to assume otherwise). This is a teaching that modern paganism seems to share with Aboriginal wisdom (for instance §166). It may also be found in Hinduism: one Upanisad says that since the gods dwell within every person, therefore:

> Be one to whom a mother is as a god.
> Be one to whom a father is as a god.
> Be one to whom a teacher is as a god.
> Be one to whom a guest is as a god.
> (*Taittiriya Upanisad*, I.xi.2)

By the way, these four examples were not chosen at random. The parent, the teacher and the guest represent specific relationships which, according to this Upaniṣad, lay the foundation for all other human relationships. Thus, business partnerships, political alliances, ordinary friendships, and so on, are but elaborations or extrapolations of the basic four relationships. They therefore call for conscientious sharing and respect, perhaps a little above and beyond that which is called for in other relationships.

Could the gods flee from someone? Are there people whose lives are so wretched and bereft that their indwelling spirit has left them? It is tempting to say that outstanding criminals, tyrants, or dictators, or even ordinary people whose apathy or begrudgery quells the happiness of everyone around them, are people whose indwelling divinity has vanished. The more liberal interpretation, apparently favoured by most people who responded to my survey, is that the presence of the gods is stronger in some than in others. But it is never absent in anyone. It may be buried deep in some, perhaps so deep that no amount of healing or learning will ever restore it. Or, the healing and learning process would take many lifetimes to complete. But nonetheless, its presence, even if buried beyond recovery, is a reason to continue to respect such a person, even if only to a certain minimum degree. Each person, even the very worst of criminals, is still a human being, with a divinity dwelling inside of him – even if he himself doesn't know it or respect it.

The internalization of the presence of the Goddess may be a sign of Paganism's maturity. In ancient European pagan societies, people believed that the mythical realms of the gods were 'out there', up in the sky, or across the sea, or below the surface of the land. Today science has proven that this is not the case. With our aircraft, submarines, sonar detectors, deep space telescopes, and so on, we know a great deal about the true nature of the universe. We know what our planet is made of, and we know its structure, down to the very core. We know the stars are not attached to a crystal sphere but that they freely float through space, orbiting the centre of the galaxy. There is almost nowhere in the universe we cannot travel to, or cannot see. And we know that Tir na nOg, or Valhalla, or the Summerlands, is not 'out there'. Perhaps the gods had no where left to go, but *within*. Moreover, by placing the dwelling place of the gods within each person's body and mind, The Mystery speaks a very positive social message. Much of the time, the messages we receive from society are commercialized, and profoundly negative and critical. Media marketing campaigns constantly tell us we are never thin enough, never rich enough, never tough enough, never *enviable* enough. Paganism asserts instead that each person is an incarnation of a divinity, and a member of a wider global body that spans the whole of the Earth. I have seen people break down in tears when a priestess takes their hand, looks into their eyes, and says, "Thou art Goddess!".

The Motto of Cupid: "Love Conquers All". (§71).

This motto, attributed to the Greek and Roman god of love, is a part of contemporary Paganism's testament probably because it is a general proverb in popular culture. To most people it has to do with how two people who love each other should not let geographical distance, or parental disapproval, or other similar obstacles get in the way. Yet it appears in other pagan cultures as well, and with a broader meaning. For instance, when the Roman historian Diodorus Siculus was describing the life of the Celtic Gauls, he wrote: "Even among the most savage barbarians, anger yields to wisdom, and Mars is shamed before the Muses." (*Histories*, V.21) Similarly, a 7th century Irish text proclaims that:

> Darkness yields to light.
> Sorrow yields to joy.
> An oaf yields to a sage.
> A fool yields to a wise man.
> A serf yields to a free man.
> Inhospitality yields to hospitality.

Niggardliness yields to generosity.
Meanness yields to liberality.
Impetuosity yields to composure.
Turbulence yields to submission.
A usurper yields to a true lord.
Conflict yields to peace.
Falsehood yields to truth.
(Kelly, trans. *The Testament of Morann*, section 54.)

The general idea may be that life-affirming qualities like peace and justice and love are ultimately stronger than conflict and corruption and enmity. The writers who crafted these proverbs many centuries ago may have believed that peace and justice were reflections of the natural order of the universe, and therefore inevitably bound to succeed. This belief may be hard to justify today. Any number of examples of bad people overcoming the efforts of good people may be pointed to. But this teaching asserts, perhaps obstinately, that love and justice and other good qualities are like the waves of a sea which pound the shore, and over time erode it from a cliff to a sandy beach. A goodness which perseveres will succeed. And there are plenty of examples of that in the real world too.

Teachings from the Charge of the Goddess (§80 to §84)
I have already quoted the Charge of the Goddess in its entirety, and described its origin and significance. However, these five lines from it are repeated here because they appeared in my survey. It would seem that they have entered contemporary pagan folklore as wisdom teachings in their own right, and taken on lives of their own.

"Naked in your rites" (§80)
The idea that pagans should conduct their rituals and ceremonies in the nude may strike some readers as 'proof' that Wicca is

nothing more than a sex cult. The practice entered paganism probably because Gardner and some of his friends held their meetings on the grounds of a local nudist club. Yet the practice has several precedents in world mythology. For instance, in the story of the Descent of Inanna (§5) the goddess is not admitted to the Underworld until she has removed all her garments and jewels. A story from Hindu mythology tells of how Krishna, came upon a group of women bathing in a stream. He decided to steal their clothes and hang them in a tree, so that they would have to expose themselves when they were done washing. The story is undoubtedly a tale of almost-childlike, ribald fun; it's the story of a god playing a practical joke on his people. But there is spiritual significance: nothing should interfere with one's relationship to the deity. Nudity is the symbol of the complete and total exposure of one's whole self to the deity, where nothing is concealed and all is laid bare. The Goddess, for Her part, also sometimes appears to the seeker in the nude, to allow the seeker to know her completely and perfectly. Seeker and Goddess, in 'perfect love and perfect trust' (§110), conceal nothing from each other.

Ritual nudity also has a social dimension. Since clothing is very often the most visible sign of one's social standing and wealth, therefore removing one's clothing is a sign that one has let go of those social attachments. All people attending a 'skyclad' ceremony are therefore made equal to each other. Having said all that: rituals conducted in public places are never skyclad. Only some rituals, privately organized and usually invitation-only, include ritual nudity. No one need fear being asked to strip down in front of strangers! And no one is made to feel inadequate or 'not spiritual enough' if they prefer not to attend a skyclad ceremony. Anyway, some pagans wear so much jewelry while skyclad that it is debatable whether they are truly naked at all!

The Two Passwords (§110).

This well loved teaching is the first stanza of the Wiccan Rede, which has been quoted in its entirety earlier. The poem was composed by Doreen Valiente which contains various pieces of ethical advice. This particular motto is known as the Two Passwords since in some Wiccan rituals, especially initiations, a postulant at the outside of the circle is asked for the passwords before he or she may enter. In the Book of Shadows, Gardner wrote that the initiator inside the circle holds a blade to the postulant's heart, and says:

O thou who standeth on the threshold between the pleasant world of men and the Dread Domains of the Lords of the Outer Spaces, Hast thou the courage to make this Assey? For I say verily, it were better to rush upon my sword and perish than make the attempt with fear in thy heart." (Gardner, *Book of Shadows*.)

The passwords are, "Perfect Love and Perfect Trust". When the postulant says these words, the initiator responds with: "All who have such are doubly welcome. I give you a third to pass through this dread door." The initiator then offers the Fivefold Kiss (§57).

Love and Trust are upheld here not only as the way people should treat and respect each other in the ritual circle. They are also considered general ethical principles for all human relationships. The ritual circle could therefore be understood metaphorically, as the circle of all one's friends, family, and associates and ultimately all of humanity. And it is indeed 'magical' to be part of a circle of loving and trusting people. When you have developed your capacity for love and trust, and when you can demonstrate that capacity by trusting and loving people, then you will admitted into the 'circle' of human society, and granted love and trust in return.

"The Laws of Magic" (§92 to §102.)

One of the cornerstones in the pagan movement is the belief in this psychic energy, which is called by various names, the most common of which is 'Magick' (with a 'k', to separate it from theatrical illusions). Words borrowed from other religious traditions are also used, such as Prana (from Hinduism), Ch'i (from Taoism) Ashé (from Caribbean Santaria), and so on. In his monumental study of magic, *The Golden Bough* (first published 1922) James Frazer identified a number of definite principles which he called 'The Laws of Magic'. Other more recent authors such as Isaac Bonewits (in *Real Magic*, first published 1971) and Janet Farrar and Gavin Bone (in *Progressive Witchcraft*, 2003) have increased or elaborated the basic list. In every case, the Laws are asserted to be quasi-scientific in nature. They supposedly govern the behaviour of magical energy in much the same way that the laws of physics and chemistry govern the behaviour of heat, chemical reactions, electricity, magnetism, and so on. This energy is posited to explain all things that appear to be coincidences; therefore there are no coincidences (§154). Furthermore, this magical energy is asserted by most pagans to be an objectively observable force. It can be sensed with the mind and heart, and it can be measured and experimented upon. And one who possesses the knowledge of the laws and principles of magic may exercise some personal influence over things that may otherwise appear to be coincidence.

James Frazer wrote, "Magic is older than religion in the history of humanity". (*The Golden Bough*, pg. 62.) It seems unsurprising, then, that most informants who mentioned a Law of Magic claimed that these laws govern almost all religious rituals and ceremonial practices, including Christianity! At least one Catholic writer, Evelyn Underhill, may have agreed when she wrote:

[Occultism's] laws, and the ceremonial rites which express those laws, have come down from immemorial antiquity. They appear to enshrine a certain definite knowledge, and a large number of less definite theories, concerning the sensual and the supersensual worlds, and concerning powers which man, according to occult thinkers, may develop if he will. Orthodox persons should be careful how they condemn the laws of magic, for they unwittingly conform to many of them whenever they go to church. All ceremonial religion contains some element of magic. The art of medicine will never wholly cast it off: many centuries ago it gave birth to that which we now call science. (Underhill, *Mysticism*, pg. 38)

But I would hesitate to claim that Catholicism endorses the Laws of Magic in a systematic way. Underhill, for her part, ultimately endorses theology, not mysticism: that is, she prefers the sustained, rational, and orderly process of getting to know God through scriptures and through intellectual contemplation.

I am well aware that there are many good scientific reasons to deny the existence of magical energy. Laboratory-controlled experiments to test the effectiveness of telepathy, or ESP, or the like, are inconclusive at best. Certainly, it is impossible to devise an experiment that could prove or disprove the existence of God. Furthermore, James Frazer himself regarded magic as "a spurious system of natural law as well as a fallacious guide of conduct; it is a false science as well as an abortive art." (*Golden Bough*, pg. 13). But elsewhere in *The Golden Bough* he seems to exonerate ancient people who believed in magic, saying:

We are like heirs to a fortune which has been handed down for so many ages that the memory of those who built it up is lost, and its possessors for the time being regard it as having been an original and unalterable possession of their race since the beginning of the world. But reflection and enquiry should satisfy us that to our predecessors we are indebted for much of we thought most our own, and that their errors were not willful extravagances or the ravings of insanity, but simply hypotheses, justifiable as such at the time when they were propounded, but which a fuller experience has proved to be inadequate. It is only by the successive testing of hypothesis and rejection of the false that truth is at last elicited. After all, what we call truth is only the hypothesis which is found to work best. (Frazer, *The Golden Bough*, pg. 307)

Furthermore, where Frazer saw a fallacy of logic, others see principles of psychology. This is implied by what Frazer seems to regard as the basic fallacy of magic: "Men mistook the order of their ideas for the order of nature, and hence imagined that the control which they seem to have over their thoughts, permitted them to exercise a corresponding control over things." (Frazer, *Golden Bough*, pg. 121). When examining the Laws of Magic, then, it may be the case that we are examining something internal to oneself. We are examining the laws of consciousness, and the structure of sense-experience and of thought. I suggest, therefore, that the Laws of Magic are not quasi-scientific laws, but psycho-social laws: they constitute *the basic logic of spiritual relationships*. Any kind of relationship between people, other living things on earth, the stars in the sky, and ideas we have of them, can apply here. They can be contemplated intellectually, as if they were foundation of a pagan 'theology' (if there is such a thing). But they can be *experienced* as well. Or, to be more precise, the relationships which the laws describe and represent can be experienced.

"Knowledge is Power". (§92)

Prior to the Renaissance, the mystics and intellectuals of Europe regarded the pursuit of knowledge as a sacred and philosophical activity. In that world-view, we pursue knowledge for the sake of enlightenment. This interpretation is found in the works of Plato, for instance, in his teaching that knowledge of the abstract and eternal 'world of forms' grants peace of mind and a chance to participate in the divine. It also appears in the first of the three mottos of the Oracle of Delphi: "Know Yourself" (§62). Sir Francis

Bacon, a Renaissance philosopher in the court of Queen Elizabeth 1st, changed that. He was also a scientist, and he laid down the foundations for several scientific practices which are still respected today, for instance the practice of conducting experiments, and mathematically quantifying the results. In his view, we pursue knowledge in order to be able to *do* more things: in particular, to improve our technology. We seek knowledge in order to build taller buildings, bigger ships, better machines, and so forth. In other words, we pursue knowledge not for enlightenment but for power. Contemporary pagans have accepted this motto. But to many of them, knowledge offers not technological power but magickal power: it enables one to exercise some control over 'fate' or 'luck' or 'fortune', however defined. The more general truth of this teaching, however, is that *all* knowledge is power, whether scientific or otherwise. And this interpretation is also a part of the pagan movement's testament. Knowledge enables us to act, to exercise our will, and to discharge the force of one's labour or thought in a particular direction.

The Law of Correspondence: "As Above, So Below". (§93)

The basic logic of how the sacred manifests its presence in and through the material world is a logic of correspondence. Tradition attributes this law to the Greek god Hermes Trismegistus ("Thrice-blessed"), although it was also a favourite of Renaissance occultists like Dr. John Dee. Several variations of it appeared in my survey, for instance, "As within, so without." (§94) One informant observed that it is the main teaching of the Tarot card known as 'The Magician'. He stands before an altar with one hand pointed up to the sky ('as above'), and the other down to the earth ('so below'). Another informant noted that this teaching also appears in the well known Christian exultation, "The Lord's Prayer", when the supplicant says, "Thy Will be done, on earth as in heaven." I don't wish to speculate on its historical origin. Like many an idea, it may have been invented independently in various parts of the world, at various times in history. Indeed one could claim that the Celtic goddess Morrígan herself, in ancient Ireland, affirmed it when she declared the end of the Battle of Maigh Tuireadh: "Peace up to heaven, Heaven down to earth, Earth beneath heaven, Strength in each!" (§12)

Correspondence is the logic of recurring patterns on different levels of the same biological, global, cosmic, or psycho-spiritual systems of organisation. The idea is that what happens on a spiritual plane happens also on the material plane. It can also be interpreted to mean that particular units of whole systems, such as the cells of a body, or an animal in a habitat, and so on, are small-scale, microcosmic reflections of the complete system. They reflect within themselves the macrocosm, the whole body, the whole planetary ecosystem, or even interstellar space. The shape of a tree's branches is repeated by the veins of its leaves. An atom is the microcosm of a solar system, or a galaxy. There is also the three-fold correspondence linking the body, the temple, and the world. The top of the skull, the roof-beam of the house or temple, and the dome of the sky all mutually imply one another. Some pagans are satisfied that this correspondence is only symbolic. Some assert the deeper claim that correspondence is the logic of all spiritual relationships. But either way, this is one of the most widespread and best loved of all wisdom teachings. It appeared in my survey more often than any other wisdom-teaching aside from those also found in the Charge of the Goddess.

The Threefold Law: "For good or ill, all things return in threes". (§96)

This law expresses the tendency of magical energy to ground itself by returning to the source from which it came after performing work or causing a change in the world. Therefore, it is also sometimes phrased as the Law of Returns (§95).

Among many Wiccans this teaching is presumed to be of Celtic origin, perhaps for no other reason than because the number three appears in it. Janet Farrar and Gavin Bone, the well known Wiccan researchers and writers, informed me that this law was invented much more recently. According to them, "Gardner was planning to curse someone and Cecil Williamson, the owner at that time of Boscastle Witchcraft Museum, warned him that it would come back on him 'three times'." Williamson may not have invented the law out of nothing: for as Farrar and Bone added, "We have traced the origins of the Three Fold Law back specifically to Cornwall were it is part of the folklore related to the 'Clouty'; the rag spell placed on a tree." (Personal communication, 10 December 2007.) A 'clouty', by the way, is a cloth or ribbon, often taken from a woman's undergarments, which is tied to a thorn tree while one asks the gods for some kind of service.

Regardless of its 'authenticity', the Threefold Law has become part of the shared folklore of the movement. Indeed it is often taken as a pagan variation of the Hindu principle of Karma. The "three" of the Threefold Law need not be taken absolutely literally. It simply asserts that the work, thought, and energy you produce may well return to you greatly amplified from the journey.

"If it works, use it..." (§102)

On the surface, this teaching refers to the symbols, techniques, and instruments of ritual and spellcraft, and other religious activities. But it is also a general affirmation of the value of eclecticism. Indeed there is a whole 'camp' of pagans, known as Eclectics, who deliberately draw inspiration from an enormous diversity of sources. The entire spread of human history and culture and language is fair game for them, when it comes for seeking spiritual truths and experiences. Someone might appeal to a Greek deity for one kind of purpose, to an Irish deity for another. She might dance a maypole in the springtime, and go to a native sweat lodge in the fall. All that is necessary, in the mind of most pagans who mentioned this teaching in my survey, is that the symbol or spell or incantation, or whatever, actually *works*. If it produces *results*, then it is "true". If praying to a certain deity gets you the boon you asked for, then the deity is real. The definition of 'what works' tends to vary from person to person, but most people who responded to my survey pointed to a definition of spellcraft. I have therefore included four definitions of spellcraft which appeared in my survey (they are §88 to §91). Crowley's definition (§88), by the way, was plagarised from an earlier one by occultist William Butler, which reads: "Magic is the art of effecting change in consciousness at will".

Eclecticism is not without its critics. Across the circle from them stand the 'Traditionalists' and 'Reconstructionists', who generally focus their attention on a single specific culture or tradition. They assert that one might not fully or properly under-stand some symbol or practice if it is taken out of context. Eclecticism may lack integrity or coherence. Ethical questions concerning the unjust appropriation of cultural property may arise: especially, for instance, in a White person's use of Aboriginal practices. And, of course, some Traditionalists say that if you do focus your attention on a single world view in a systematic way, then you will have better results!

However, the point of this particular teaching is that there is usually no expressed or implied requirement that one's sources of spiritual inspiration or practice should come from only one culture, or only one period in history, or from only tradition. Each seeker is limited only by her own ability to learn. (c.f. §144).

"Use no symbol..." (§117)

Some of my informants said that this teaching is meant to protect new seekers from 'getting burned': it will help prevent people from the 'dire consequences' of using some magical symbol or technique wrongly. These comments made me imagine a ceremonial magician, standing in his circle of power, being attacked by his own conjured monsters because he pronounced the last word of the spell wrong! But I think that rationale may be a kind of ruse. Its hidden purpose may be simply to 'trick' people into thinking more deeply about the origin, significance, and purpose of the symbols and ideas of the Pagan path.

The Laws of the Craft (§115 to §127)

The requirement to be "properly prepared", a saying that appears in Gardner's Book of Shadows in several places (and in Boy Scout manuals everywhere!), here introduces a short series of rules which govern the structure and the activities of a working coven. In the course of my research I uncovered various lists of laws, some with as few as thirteen items, and others with more than a hundred and fifty. Farrar and Bone informed me that the original Laws were written off the cuff by Gardner, in order to quell dissent within his coven.

> "In 1961 Gardner's coven finally got fed up with the fact that journalists kept ringing them up out of the blue knowing that they were witches. It seems Gardner kept giving out their phone numbers and addresses as witches to the media without permission. As you can imagine they were getting pretty p****d off with this! Doreen and the coven drew up a set of rules for the Craft with the utilitarian and uninspiring title of: The Provisional Rules of the Craft. Well, when Doreen presented them to Gardner he said 'Can't use those, we already have a set of Laws!' Doreen's reply was: 'Well, I've been with the coven for many years and I was never shown them!' and Gardner's reply was: 'I'll have them to you after the weekend!'" (Gavin Bone, personal communication.)

Historian Ronald Hutton, in his comprehensive treatment of the history of Wicca, confirms this story. He added that Gardner's newly invented 'ancient laws' infuriated Valiente so badly that she eventually left the group, and took a substantial faction with her. (c.f. *The Triumph of the Moon*, pg. 249) Part of what made Gardner's laws so offensive to Valiente is that they call for a priestess to graciously step aside, "in favour of a younger woman", because "the greatest virtue of a High Priestess be that She recognizes that youth is necessary to the representative of the Goddess." Furthermore, the laws assert that the High Priestess has complete and total authority within the ritual circle, ruling the coven "as the representative of the Goddess", but that her power is only "lent" to her by the God. In other words, the coven's high priestess had to be young and beautiful and, if she causes the priest too much trouble, replaceable. As Bone said to me, "Gardner was getting fed up with Doreen questioning him on the origins of material, and wanted rid of her." Incidentally, one of the laws that Gardner wrote more or less gave Doreen the right to leave him: "If they cannot bear your rule they will leave you." (§125). Perhaps Gardner got his Karma after all. Nonetheless, that law strikes me as a remarkably astute observation about small-group politics. Those who don't like what is going on will almost always 'vote with their feet', by walking away.

I have included here the laws from Gardner's list which also appeared in my survey. The "Preface to the Book of Shadows" (§39 and §40) could be included here, as Gardner integrated the words of that Preface into his new catalogue of laws. Other Laws of the Craft in this collection are those which were volunteered by informants responding to my survey, when the informants themselves claimed it was one of the Laws of their own private coven or working group. In 1978, at Pan Pagan Gathering (an annual outdoor camping retreat in Wisconsin, USA), a group of Gardnerian Elders decided to eliminate most of the laws, and to substantially re-write the rest. They settled upon a list of forty Laws, two of which appeared in my survey (§55 and §105). Today, however, most covens create their own Laws. Such laws generally detail how the group is to be organized, what to do if the leaders go missing, how to handle internal conflict, and so on.

"Never buy your first deck of Tarot cards..." (§126)

One informant suggested that this teaching is a throwback to the time when Tarot cards were passed down along family lines. Another believed that this proverb was invented by publishing companies which produce and sell Tarot cards commercially, in order to boost sales! Either way, the custom has caught on. I think it is worth supporting this proverb, since it expresses the idea that certain objects of religious significance should be offered to each other as gifts, rather than sold as market commodities. The proverb encourages a gift-giving economy in the pagan community. A similar idea is expressed in one of the so-called Laws of the Craft: "Never bargain for a magical tool" (§124). But in this case the idea is that if one haggled the price of a religious article, one is in effect also haggling with its spiritual significance at the same time. One should therefore pay a fair price for it. And if the seller isn't asking for a fair price, you can always buy it from someone else.

"Never give a blade as a gift to a friend..." (§127)

This teaching seems to stand in contrast with these other proverbs concerning gift-giving. It defines one type of religious object that cannot be given as a free gift. Here, however, my informant explained: "if you give a blade as a gift to a friend, you may inadvertently cut the friendship." Giving a blade as a gift appears to be a special instance of the Law of Sympathy: since 'like attracts like', therefore to give a weapon as a gift is to invite pain and violence into the lives of the people involved. Therefore the recipient of such a gift should give a coin in return. That way, it is not "officially" a gift, but rather an ordinary market transaction. Any coin will do: even a penny, or one of the smallest-value coins the recipient happens to have in her pocket at the time.

"Speak well of bards." (§128)

The first time I heard this proverb, my informant was not a pagan, although a very spiritual and pagan-friendly person. He was a member of a student club at a Canadian university dedicated to exploring various forms of esoteric knowledge and history. He claimed that the phrase dated back to "early times". The idea, as he explained it to me, is that if you do not speak well of bards, then the bards are sure to compose satire at your expense, and ruin your reputation. There are stories in European mythology that attest to this. For instance, there is an Irish story of a bard named Cairbre who, when he called at the court of High King Bres, did not receive the hospitality to which his position entitled him. The following morning he composed the first satire ever recited in Ireland. As a result, the king was forced to abdicate his position.

In my survey I encountered several broadly similar versions of this proverb. Each in a different way described the respect that is owed to musicians, poets, artists, and creative people of various kinds. The extra respect owed to them, or perhaps I should say owed to the best of them, is grounded in the special contributions they make to pagan culture. Bards reproduce pagan ideas, beliefs, events, people, places, and so on, in live-performance music and storytelling and poetry. They create and perform the distinct culture we share with each other, and hold in common: in short, they bring people together. And of course respect is owed to them in return for the pleasure and entertainment they provide. Among the variations of this proverb were treasures like these: "A bard must never be stopped in his song", "Storytelling raises the dead", and my personal favourite, "Bards drink first!"

The Truth Against the World! (§132)

This saying comes from the work of the 17th century English freemason and spiritualist Edward Williams. It appears in his book of half Celtic, half esoteric speculations called *The Barddas*, which he wrote under the pen-name of Iolo Morganwyg. Many modern British druids treat this saying like the motto of their movement. To Druids, the Sacred Truth is the principle of order, justice, morality, and comprehensive spiritual unity which pervades everything in nature and in human social life. When "the world" of the market, or the political arena, or some other social institution, is full of tyranny, deceit, and corruption, it becomes necessary for spiritual people to speak the Sacred Truth "against" it. The duty of the spiritual person is to remind people of the Truth, in order to rectify and heal the world. This motto is therefore more than an affirmation of the importance of the Sacred Truth. It is also an affirmation of social responsibility. I have seen it used by Celtic pagan warriors at rallies, marches, anti-globalisation protests, and even at land-occupations to prevent new motorway construction. Right from the beginning, the movement has benefited from a social and environmental conscience.

Two other important Druidic teachings appeared in my survey, and I have placed them next to this motto. One is the "Universal Druid's Prayer" (§131), and the other is a Declaration of Peace (§130) which in British druidic ceremonies is announced to the four cardinal directions at the beginning or end of most rituals.

"Here be Dragons!" (§136).

The saying which begins the "Contemporary" category is not really a wisdom teaching. It is more like an inside joke! It refers to an old map-making practice, when cartographers did not yet know the whole shape and layout on the world. They would therefore sometimes write 'Terra Incognita', or 'Unknown Land', on certain areas. The saying, "Here be dragons!" calls to mind fables or legends of magical monsters which supposedly inhabited those unknown lands. This particular saying didn't appear in my survey. Instead, it appeared as signs on the front doors of people's houses or apartments. The residents were telling the world that this house is Terra Incognita, a place of mystery, and perhaps also a place magic and danger and wonder, inhabited by strange and mystical people: inhabited by the Goddess herself (§137). In a way, therefore, the saying serves as tongue-in-cheek territorial boundary marker, like the sign on a road indicating the boundary of a country. "Here be Dragons!" is a way of saying, "Here be Pagans!" or, "Beware there is magic all around you!" (§330)

"All gods are one god..." (§138)

Many of the occult writers of the time believed that they could accomplish their goals easier by writing novels, rather than by writing non-fiction discourses. The idea was that people might be more willing to read a novel than a work of serious non-fiction: and if the writer's artistic ability was good enough, it might stir up in the reader an interest in learning more about the 'real' thing. Moreover, by writing fiction, the author has his 'get out of jail free card' already prepared: for if someone found the author's ideas threatening or subversive, then the author could always plead innocent on the grounds of having written a work of fiction! Aleister Crowley, Gerald Gardner, Stewart Farrar, Starhawk, and other well known pagan leaders all wrote novels containing spiritual ideas for reasons like these.

This particular proverb, "All gods are one god..." appeared in the novel "The Sea Priestess", by the English occultist Dion Fortune, first published in 1935. It asserts that all the gods are the masks and manifestations of a singular divine presence. The idea became very popular among Wiccans very quickly: the novel was highly influential on Doreen Valiente, for instance. It may explain why the Charge of the Goddess begins with an invocation to the Goddess 'by many names'. Perhaps the reason for the proverb's popularity at the time was because it enabled people to profess their belief in polytheism without at the same time appearing to threaten their monotheist neighbours. They could claim that they are 'really' believers in one (or two) comprehensive deities who merely show to the world different faces, in different places and times. In this way the teaching may be compared to the idea that the gods show to each seeker a face that he or she will find familiar, or 'needs' to see in order to learn whatever spiritual lessons he needs to learn (§139). Dion Fortune's proverb is also a way for pagans to assert that all the different religions in the world need not conflict with one another. If we're all ultimately worshipping the same god, then there is no point in fighting and killing each other because of religious differences.

Many contemporary pagans no longer accept Dion Fortune's monotheism. In particular, those who are committed to a cultural-revival path, such as Druidry or Asatru, feel comfortable with the thought that their gods are independent personalities. John Michael Greer, author of *A World Full of Gods* (ADF Publishing, 2005), argued that polytheism is the more natural and normal kind of spiritual experience around the world. The vision of all-encompassing world unity, which many seekers point to as a sign of monotheism, is but one of many types of spiritual experiences people have. Most of the time, people's spiritual experiences are highly personal, and charged with symbolic references tightly bound by local culture, landscape, history, and the like. Nonetheless, Dion Fortune's message of global spiritual unity is considered important and inspirational to the many people who included it in their response to my survey. It is part of the heritage of modern paganism, and deserves a place in this testament.

A Discourse on the Path (§142 to §152)

The notion of a spiritual discipline as a 'path' originates first of all in hunting practices. The path is the trail left by the animal that the hunter is tracking. In the Middle Ages the path is the road taken by pilgrims on their way to the great cathedrals. In each case, the journey metaphor represents a sustained transformative experience: a transition from ignorance to knowledge, and from an ordinary life to purposeful life.

These teachings were some of the most frequent and consistent affirmations in my survey results. Their consistency made me think that there was more agreement in the community than is normally admitted to. Yet they do not appear to be affirmations of community solidarity. Instead, they seem to affirm individualism. Two of them in this section, "The path is the same..." and "There are many paths..." (§146 and §147) are explicitly of this nature. Other sayings in the collection, such as "Be kind to yourself", (§159) also seem to imply an individualist logic of value. It should come as no surprise that individualism featured so prominently in the results of my survey. Individualism is also a primary value in the wider range of Western society, especially of market capitalism. It is the individual who owns property, and it is the aggregate of individual consumer demand which drives the economy. Indeed one of these teachings (§146) appeared as a marketing slogan for an international chain of health and cosmetics stores.

However, I think these teachings should be understood together with other teachings concerning the spiritual relationships with the Earth and with all life on earth. Four of the circle songs include the phrase "We are one" (§§256, 274, 293, and 329), and several others proclaim that the singer is one with the Earth and all living things (for instance §202 and §309). This idea also appears in the Song of Amergin (§64), and some of the Aboriginal teachings (especially §162). A single person, in the pagan worldview, is not just an individual. She is also part of a circle within a circle (§268) and a child of the Goddess, (§320, §59). In various ways she is caught up in relationships with other living things. Some of these relationships are environmental, such as the food chain, the water cycle, and other ecological processes necessary for life. Some are social, such as the bonds of friendship and love.

Some are purely spiritual, such as one's relations with ancestors, local spirit-beings, and the Goddess. Furthermore, this global body is constantly bestowing blessings and gifts on everyone (c.f. §157 and §158). Paganism offers people a sense of membership and belonging in a spiritual community that transcends the individual. Therefore, no one ever needs to feel alone, isolated, unloved, or insignificant. Rather, as members of a secret commonwealth, an organic body which includes all life on earth, we have reasons to feel welcomed, valued, part of something that genuinely matters, and glad to be alive.

It is also affirmed in this discourse that the seeker must treat all new life experiences, whether beautiful or painful, as learning opportunities, (§143) because "the path is a learning path" (§144). One of my informants said to me,

> Deep religion isn't and shouldn't be a way to prove anything, to anyone, even yourself. It is a way to have that ineffable aliveness and soul of everything around you and your own spark of divinity proven to you. And that comes from always being a seeker, never closing yourself to lessons, listening closely and carefully to the signs. And never being too cocky-sure that you even know how to read said signs. (Monica Becker, personal communication)

This learning process is a life-long one: and it may be very difficult (§114, §142). It may expose you to realities and possibilities that you do not wish to face, or which may require you to make hard choices. One informant, smiling as she quoted 'The Wizard of Id' cartoon strip, said that "the Craft is not a hobby". The wisdom teachings of this entire collection may be taken as the 'lessons', expressed in the form of proverbs and value-affirmations, which the diligent seeker is supposed to learn. If choices are to be made, this learning process requires the seeker to make those choices on her own. She will learn nothing if she lets other people make her choices for her. Not even the gods will tell you what to do. But the rewards for all that work may be great: to quote Gardner's words, the rewards are "ecstasy and joy on earth".

A Discourse on Fortune and Peace. (§153 to §160)

The sayings in this sequence appeared in my survey a little less frequently than the ones in the 'Discourse on the Path', but they tended to appear with the same surprising consistency. This discourse may be seen as a continuation of the previous discourse, but I have arranged them separately since they attest to a slightly different concept. These teachings offer a means to create and preserve peace of mind, "balance" or "harmony", and so on, no matter what one's circumstance or situation. Indeed they appear to offer a means for the continual improvement and edification of one's character. First of all, it is asserted as a primary truth that the world is constantly in motion and constantly changing. (§67, §153). Yet many contemporary pagans also testify that "nothing happens by coincidence" (§154). If nothing happens by coincidence, then all the turbulent change in the world happens for a reason. And it is up to us to learn what that reason is: after all, "the path is a learning path" (§144). The lesson manifests itself when one relaxes the ego, and tries not to control the situation in a deliberately intrusive way. Therefore, "Let it happen, let it be" (§155; from the album *A Rock in the Weary Land* by the Waterboys). There is no need to egotistically control the world, since it is already taking care of you, and already sending you gifts and blessings (§§156, 157, 158). These gifts can be simple: for instance, when stuck in a traffic jam on a highway, there might be sunbeams spilling upon you through misty clouds above. This may also apply to other, more difficult situations, such as enduring a serious disease, or pursuing a court case, or grieving the loss of a loved one. In those situations, the gods may show you something that inspires and enables you to carry on. Gerald

Gardner may have held a similar view: in a section of the *Book of the Art Magical* called "To Help the Sick", he wrote:

> Ever remember the Promise of the Goddess: "For ecstasy is mine and joy on earth" so let there ever be joy in your heart. Greet people with joy, be glad to see them, if times be hard, think "it might have been worse. I at least have known the joys of the Sabbath, and I will know them again." Think of the grandeur, beauty, and [?illegible] of the rites, of the Loved ones you meet through them. If you dwell on this inner joy, your health will be better.
>
> (Gardner, *The Book of the Art Magickal*, private collection.)

Here are two kinds of critical problems. First, might the good within a bad situation be found only because the seeker psychologically projects it there? One possible reply to this criticism is to point out that in this Pagan testament, the most important teachings and lessons ultimately come from within: hence the priority given to the Seven Teachings of the Mystery. Some lesson or teaching may appear to come from the gods or from the world, when in fact it comes from the seeker's own mind. But if that is the case, that may not necessarily imply that the teaching is therefore without meaning. The seeker *taught herself* to be strong and wise. She taught herself this lesson *in response to* some situation or problem in the world: and in that respect, the lesson did come from outside herself. But whether or not the lesson came from without or within, it may be more important to ask whether or not the lesson was actually learned!

Here is a second criticism. This discourse may imply that any amount of goodness or benefit or beauty, however small, will always outweigh any amount of pain or suffering or hardship, however large. Someone suffering from cancer, or traumatized after being attacked, or so on, might be admonished to believe that her situation is rendered 'good' because of the 'learning experience' it offers. This is a highly questionable implication (but at least it is an optimistic one). I might learn much about perseverance and the value of compassion by contracting cancer. But I would not wish that event on anyone. I do not yet have the answer to this criticism, except to suggest that the learning-value of all experiences may have certain limitations. But otherwise, I must leave this problem to others to solve.

"Follow your Bliss!" (§160)

This often-quoted saying comes from Joseph Campbell, the late American professor of mythology. It appears in *The Power of Myth*, a television series in which Campbell is interviewed by journalist Bill Moyers. Around a dozen of my informants mentioned how they 'became a pagan' after reading one of Joseph Campbell's books. His proverb teaches us to "go where your body and soul want to go. When you have the feeling, then stay with it, and don't let anyone throw you off". (Campbell, *The Power of Myth*, pg. 147). Following your bliss means doing that which will produce a sense of true and perfect fulfillment in life. It also means not allowing the demands of propriety, or the pursuit of material wealth and social prestige, to get in the way. It also means not allowing the fear of the obstacles in the way, or the work involved, or failure, to stop you. And when you do the thing that you most want to do, then you can have an experience of bliss in the here and now. You need not wait until death and the afterlife. I find this reminiscent of Gardner's claim that the Goddess is 'ecstasy and joy on earth'.

I have placed this proverb at the end of the discourse on Fortune and Peace because Campbell uses the ancient symbol of the Wheel of Fortune to express what he means. In his words:

> If you are attached to the rim of the wheel of fortune, you will be either above going down or at the bottom coming up. But if you are at the hub, you are in the same place all the time. That

is the sense of the marriage vow—I take you in health or sickness, in wealth or poverty: going up or going down. But I take you as my centre, and you are my bliss, not the wealth that you might bring me, not the social prestige, but you. That is following your bliss. (Campbell, *The Power of Myth*, pg. 147)

Further, it might be added that if you do strike out to follow your bliss, you will be protected. For the world is taking care of you (§158) and can be trusted to take you where you need to go. Campbell himself described his belief in magical helping hands that seem to enter one's life to help, once you do start following your bliss. When you step out on the path, suddenly you find yourself meeting like-minded people, and you find opportunities manifesting themselves before you. I'm enough of a philosopher to know that this might be only a psychological trick we play on ourselves. Someone whose mind is fixed on children, for instance, soon sees children everywhere. But even so, this psychological trick may benefit us, by bringing us closer to people who are chasing the same dream. Or the same fantasy!

Aboriginal Teachings (§162-§168)

These six teachings come from the wisdom of the Indigenous people of the continent of North America. Some were imparted directly to me by Aboriginal people themselves, or people descended from Aboriginals. Some were offered by White people on the "Red Road". Although they are beautiful and inspiring, it would be wrong to claim that they represent the whole of Aboriginal spirituality in a comprehensive way. For one thing, there is no single, uniform Aboriginal culture. In Canada alone, there are seven major cultural groups, fifty distinct languages, and 615 First Nations communities. The Aboriginal teachings which appeared in my survey therefore represent only a tiny fraction of the spiritual wisdom of Indigenous people.

Even though there are so few Aboriginal teachings in this

collection, the wisdom they contain is great. For instance, Aboriginal people treat their relationship with their spirits as a *family* relationship: the spirits are addressed as Grandfather and Grandmother. Two proverbs in this collection (§164 and § 165) demonstrate this, as does the name of the Woman Who Fell From the Sky: Grandmother Anishnabe (§3). An extra dimension of intimacy, as well as an extra incentive to show thanks and respect, is implied here. This idea may be found in some of the circle-songs in which pagans describe themselves as children of the Earth (for instance, §320).

I have included the Aboriginal teachings in the "Contemporary" category in order to emphasize that the teachings of the First Nations Elders are teachings of our time, and for our time. Some Aboriginal teachings may have been passed on from Elder to child over many generations. Still, they are still a product of the living experiences and insights of contemporary people. We should lament the Aboriginal knowledge and culture and language that has been lost, and do what must be done to protect what has survived. But it must also be affirmed that the Aboriginal culture which is to be protected is not a museum artifact. It has not remained unchanged, like a fossil cast in stone, since pre-contact times. Rather, it has responded to its environment. It is a living thing, and it is the cultural heritage of the many First Nations who built their cultures over thousands of years before the arrival of the White Man on their land.

"I am the Earth" (§162)
The first of the Aboriginal teachings, "I am the Earth and the Earth is Me", in my view, is the most important of them. It is the assertion that each person is bound and united to the Earth, not just in an irreducible relationship of biological necessity, but primarily in a relationship of comprehensive spiritual identity. My informant explained it as follows:

"I became Pagan through a variety of means: environmental causes. Political causes. Feminist causes. I was not looking for religion at all. I realized that all the things that I believed in came from a similar place. When I was 5, I sat on a black rock on the edge of a lake and felt God as never before, and freaked out my mother. I never felt that again in a church situation. At 18 I realized that the God I knew was the Earth..." (Maryanne Pearce, personal communication, 10 December 2007)

This teaching may be compared to the Invocation to the Seven Directions (§163) which, according to another informant, comes from the Navajo people of the American South-West. Similarly it may be compared to the Druidic Declaration of Peace (§130), The Song of Amergin (§66), and some of the circle songs, for instance those which affirm 'The Earth is my body' (such as §277). This teaching, it seems to me, is an instance of what I have called the first-order of the Word of Being: "I am Here", and makes explicit its environmental expression. "I am Here — on the earth, with the earth, *as* the Earth". The spiritual person recognizes herself, the extension and the completion of her body, her mind, her heart, and her spirit, in the Earth. I have therefore included it among the Seven Teachings of the Mystery.

"The Creator is within all things..." (§166)
According to my informant, a traditional Elder of the Algonquin nation, the Seven Grandfather Teachings are character virtues: Wisdom, Truth, Humility, Bravery, Honesty, Love, and especially Respect.

"What is life?" (§168)
Crowfoot was the orator of the Blackfoot Confederacy, and a signatory on Treaty No.7 with the Dominion of Canada. These most eloquent words on the transience and beauty of life were spoken as he was on his deathbed, in 1890.

"Some people enter this world..." (§169)

My informant told me that this consolation was given to him by the priestess of his coven, on the occasion of the death of his infant daughter.

"A few things every pagan should know" (§178)

A few years ago, while teaching an undergraduate course in environmental philosophy, I asked my students, one at a time, to name a local plant or animal species. I also asked them to not name a species already named by another student. The first dozen had no trouble, but the next dozen had to think for a moment before answering. My class of fifty students couldn't name more than twenty local species. Then I asked them to name, one at a time, a multinational corporation. Every student in the room was able to name at least one, sometimes two, without repetition. "This is the content of your world and your mind", I told them. "If your motto is 'express yourself', this is what you have within you to express." At the time, I was rather surprised how little these students knew of their nearest environmental surroundings. One student, who I asked where his food comes from, said "The super-market". Another student, asked where his household rubbish goes, said "The bin at the end of the sidewalk." I was delighted, then, to see that many of the people who responded to my survey included two or three local environmental facts which they thought every pagan should know. I have assembled them all into one teaching for the sake of this collection.

After having put these pieces together, it suddenly occurred to me that these things everyone should know refer not only of the biological environment. They speak also of the *social* environment. They speak of the hidden hierarchies where some people get more respect and attention and prestige than others. They speak of the need to be sensitive to people's moods and feelings. They speak of the need to know who in the community is knowledgeable, generous, and reliable, and who is a troublemaker, or even a threat. Many of the teachings in this collection have double meanings like this; but I shall leave it to the reader to discover the rest of them for herself.

A good and honourable person need not fear death... (§ 184)

This teaching, like a few others, was assembled from the contributions of several informants. I asked some of them what things they thought worse than dying. Here are a few of their answers:

- "a life of long-term severe pain due to some injury or disease."
- "A lonely life, with no friends or family to talk to."
- "Poverty, oppression, living in fear, being constantly put down because you're a woman, or because you're Native, or from another country, or just from the poor side of town."
- "A life where you put too much value on material things, and you spend all your time chasing the American dream of getting rich without working for it."

The first response may seem unsurprising. But I was intrigued by the characterisation of unfulfilling human relationships and unjust social orders as worse than death. In further conversation with some of these informants, it was clear that in their thinking, someone who finds herself in such situations should not just 'give up'. Rather, it was emphasised that she should work to change her situations, to the best of their ability. Right from the beginning, with the story of Aradia, modern paganism has supported the idea that oppression should be resisted. But especially in reference to medical issues, it was also emphasised that it is pointless to prolong life for the sake of prolonging life. Most of my informants claimed that participating in the "circle of life", with honour and love and other virtues (c.f. § 83), is more important than perpetuating one's biological functions. It may follow that pagan moral thinking does not rule out choices like doctor-assisted suicide, or euthanasia. But to explore this implication properly, I shall have to write another book.

A Viking Death Invocation. (§185)

This piece was imparted to me by half a dozen people who responded to my survey. The text as it appears in this collection comes from the 1999 film *The 13th Warrior*, directed by John McTiernan. In the film, the wife of a clan chieftain who recently died recites it while being lifted three times over a makeshift wooden wall. She was symbolically looking over the barrier that separates the mortal world from Valhalla, the hall of the heroic dead. Later in the film, the main heroes recite it again a moment before engaging an enemy tribe in battle. The film was based on the novel *Eaters of the Dead* by Michael Crichton, which in turn was based on two historical sources. One was the early Anglo-Saxon epic story of *Beowulf*. The other was the account of Ibn Fadlan, a 10th century Arabian explorer who traveled along the river Volga, and wrote an account of the early Russian tribes which he met on the way.

I think it is elegant to end this collection of pagan folk wisdom with this piece, for two main reasons. One is because it is associated with death. Most informants who mentioned it said that they have heard people use it at funerals. Some described its use by people who thought they were about to die: those who were suffering terminal diseases, for instance, or those who had been involved in car accidents. One informant said that as a British soldier in Afghanistan, where he fights the Taliban almost every day, he recites it to himself every time he goes out on patrol. As a death-recitation it may be compared to similar expressions in other spiritual cultures, such as the Islamic "Allah Akbar", or the Jewish "Shemah Yisrael". Other invocations in this collection (such as §130, "You shall know them..."), also sometimes serve this purpose.

The second reason it is appropriate to close with this saying is because it is a modern day, twentieth century creation that has made its way into the folklore of the movement, and taken on a life of its own. Another of my informants, for instance, didn't know that it was written for a movie. Inserting 'the Summerland' for 'The Halls of Valhalla', he insisted that it was an ancient invocation. But while I think it is important to acknowledge the real origin of such things, I think it may be wrong to try and stop people from using them just because they are historically 'mistaken'. For the folklore of the pagan community is a living thing. It grows and changes. It learns things from various sources and makes them its own. Despite the recent origin of this particular piece, it has become a part of the living heritage of the community.

Eleventh Movement:

Circle-Songs

"If Music be the Food of Love, Play On, Give Me Excess of it..."
Having attended Pagan ceremonies of various kinds in five
different countries, I am always impressed by the way Pagans use
music and song, both in ceremonies and at gatherings and
parties. I keep hearing several of the same concepts and senti-
ments expressed in the lyrics, and sometimes I hear the same
tunes and melodies as well. But I'm also sometimes surprised at
how many Pagan groups use recorded music, or never sing at all,
and equally surprised at the reactions provoked when someone
tries to sing instead. But most of the time, people say things like,
"I wish I knew more Pagan chants and songs", or "We Pagans
should sing more". Well, I quite agree. Singing together is one of
the ways that a group of like-minded people becomes a unified
community, able to share and build and live together. I decided,
therefore, to put together as large a collection of pagan songs as I
could.

First I dug out my old 'ring-binder of shadows', my collection
of notes and scraps which I started up when I first encountered
the Craft. I had written down the lyrics of all the songs I had ever
heard performed in a ritual, even if only once, over the space of
about a dozen years. Then I wrote and distributed my survey.

Where I have been able to determine authorship, I have
mentioned the author's name in the collection. (I wrote §196 and
§ 255 myself: some friends of mine really liked them and put them
in their response to my survey.) Yet it is my view that once
something attains the status of folklore, it belongs to everyone.
And this does not take anything away from the author. An
artifact of folklore gains in value the more it is used and shared.
It is not like a material commodity that becomes scarcer as more
people use it, like petroleum. Rather, as it is passed on and

enjoyed by various people in all the different ways people meet each other, it creates more and more value in people's lives. Similarly, people subject it to endless creative variations, and this increases its value exponentially. And thus, surely, benefits the author too.

In terms of its musical arrangement, most of these songs are very simple: the melody might have only three or four notes, and the chord progression may consist of a few one-tone modal drops. Some of these pieces, such as "We approach the Sacred Grove" (§300) were asserted by my informants to be new lyrics to the tune of old English plainsongs or mediaeval madrigals: again, very simple, almost minimalist in melody and chord progression. Perhaps this is a deliberate arrangement, in order to accommodate people's different vocal ranges. For more confident or experienced singers, it permits a great many possibilities for harmonic variations and spur-of-the-moment improvisation.

The circle-songs and wisdom teachings constitute a large part of the pagan community's shared vocabulary. And that vocabulary also includes a lot of excellent silliness! As one of my informants said:

> There is a lot of 'filk' in the Pagan liturgy – not to be discounted for all that. Pagans are rare in their willingness to take the piss out of their gods and not consider that an inappropriate relationship. This marks their relationship with 'deity' as markedly different from most mainstream faiths. Great filk will never die. (Em Poore, personal communication, 30 December 2007)

Some of the 'filk' takes the form of inside jokes. If some event or circle begins late, or if someone shows up late, it is because he's on Pagan Standard Time. If the ritual is slow and somber, we say the priestess has Raised the Pancake of Power. In response to a militant Christian saying 'Jesus loves you', the good pagan responds 'But not the same way Aphrodite loves me!' Pagans take their gods seriously precisely by not taking them seriously all of the time. I am including a few of the best satirical 'revisions' here among the comments. But the very best pagan filk is, alas, unpublishable.

Barre Toelken wrote, "A traditional item (whether oral or material or gestural) is folklore only when it is actually used or performed in its indigenous set of live contexts." (Toeklen, *Dynamics of Folklore*, pg. 38). The songs presented here, therefore, need to be heard *as songs*, performed at a pagan gathering, to be understood properly. The beauty of these songs may not be obvious when they are presented as words on a page. But I'm sure that it will be easy to see the literary poetry, and the earnest heartfelt belief, in many of them.

Songs that Honour the Gods

§ 186. "Circle Round"
In the moonlight (sunlight)
Listen to the Lord and Lady
Call their children.
(Jim Allen / Circle Sanctuary)

§ 187. "Kore's Chant"
She changes everything she touches, and
Everything she touches changes.
(Starhawk)

§ 188. (Variations of Kore's Chant)
We are changers,
Everything we touch can change.

Her name cannot be spoken, Her face was not forgotten

Her power is to open, Her promise can never be broken.

Everything lost is found again
In a new form, in a new way
Everything hurt is healed again
In a new time, in a new day.

§ 189.
We all come from the Goddess
And to her we shall return
Like a drop of rain
Flowing to the ocean
(Z. Budapest)

§ 190.
We all come from the Horned One
And to him we shall return
Like a flash of light
Shining from the firey sun.
(Tamarra James)

§ 191.
Hoof and horn, hoof and horn
All that dies shall be reborn
Corn and grain, corn and grain
All that falls shall rise again
(Ian Corrigan)

§ 192. "The Goddess Chant"
Isis Astarte Diana Hecate,
Demeter Kali Inanna!
(Deena Metzger)

§ 193. "The God's Chant"

Pan Poseidon Dionysus Cernunnos,
Mithras Loki Apollo!
(Tamarra James)

§ 194.
Danu Cerridwen Epona Morrígan,
Blodeuwedd Brighid Rhiannon!
(Aislin Avalon)

§ 195.
Brigit, triple flame, be within me
Tonight, tomorrow, and forever.
Tonight, tomorrow, and forever.

§ 196.
Lugh, the mighty sun, be within me
Tonight, tomorrow, and forever
Tonight, tomorrow, and forever.

§ 197.
Mother daughter sister lover
Hear us, hear us
It is you we seek within us
Goddess, guide us.

§ 198.
Father brother son and lover
Hear us, hear us
It is you we seek within us
Horned one, help us.
(Tamarra James)

§ 199.
The Earth is our Mother

We must take care of Her
The Earth is our Mother
We must take care of Her

Hey yana, ho yana, hey yan-a
Hey yana, ho yana, hey yan-a

Her sacred ground we walk upon
With every step we take
Her sacred ground we walk upon
With every step we take

§ 200.
The Sky is our Father
We must take care of Him
The Sky is our Father
We must take care of Him
(Adapted from an Aboriginal Hopi song)

His sacred air, we're breathing in
In every breath we take
His sacred air we're breathing in
In every breath we take

Hey yana, ho yana, hey yan-a
Hey yana, ho yana, hey yan-a

§ 201.
Gods and Dead and Mighty Sidhe,
Powers of earth and sky and sea.
By fire and well, by sacred tree,
Offering we make to ye.
(Isaac Bonewits)

§ 202.
Earth Mother, great spirit within me
Earth Mother, bless us with peace
Earth Mother, we are your family
With thanksgiving, we care for thee

For I am one with all
As Her spirit flows through my soul
For peace is all I know
In perfect faith, I let it go

Earth Mother, great Goddess so gracious
Earth Mother, your love is our light
Earth Mother, the light of our oneness
With thanksgiving, your family unites

§ 203.
Old and Strong
She moves on and on and on
Can you feel the spirit?
She is like the mountain,
She is like the ocean,
She is like the river,
She is like the wind,
She is like the mountain,
Old and strong.

§ 204.
Hecate, to thee I pray
Guide me through my darkness
Hecate, to thee I pray
Hold me in the night

In waning moon
Darkness grows
In my blood
Life force flows

Time to rest
wounds are healed
Look to self
All's revealed

§ 205.
Midnight deep
Lunar hung
Moon is high
Now becomes

Power of dark
Goddess breathe
Show us now
Visions meant to be

§ 206. "Brigit's Well"
We will never
Ever lose our way to the well
Of Her memory

And the power
Of Her living flame
It will rise,
It will rise again.

She is hidden,
But her children have
Not forgotten,

They still worship her.

In the meadow,
When the moon is full,
And the fire
It will rise again.

Like the grasses
Through the dark, through the soil
To the sunlight
We will rise again.

§ 207.
Lady, lady, lady, listen to my heart's song
Lady, lady, lady, listen to my heart's song
I will never forget you, I will never forsake you,
I will never forget you, I will never forsake you,

§ 208.
Ancient mother, I hear you calling,
Ancient mother, I hear your song
Ancient mother, I hear your laughter
Ancient mother, I hear your tears.

§ 209.
Mother moon, shine down on me.
I am you and you are me.
We are part of everything.
We are part of everything.

§ 210.
Daughter can you hear me?
Son can you hear me?
In the wind

In the flame
In the rain
In the earth beneath your feet
Can you hear me?
If you look to the world for the love that you seek
Look inside and that is where you'll find me
Can you hear me?
Listen and you'll hear me.
(Rauncie Ryan)

§ 211.
Mother Earth, hear me calling.
I'm your daughter, you're my home.

Sister Moon, hear me calling.
In the night, you're not alone.

Father Sun, hear me calling.
Let your strong light shine in me.

§ 212.
All my ancestors stand by me
Teach my spirit to be free.

§ 213.
Old ones hear us
Old ones rejoice
We are the children sending a voice
No more destruction, no more remorse
Dancing the heartbeat back to the source.

§ 214.
Dionysus, father of the vine,
Hear the dancers of the hill,

Sing evoé for the holy wine.
(Tamarra James)

§ 215.
Autumn time, red leaves fall,
While the weeping sky looks overall
Demeter sadly walks the land
The dying grasses in her hand.

§ 216.
O great spirit, sun, moon, sky and sea
You are inside and all around me.
(White Buffalo Society)

§ 217.
Earth mother, we honor your body
Earth mother, we honor your bones
Earth mother, we sing to your body
Earth mother, we sing to your stones

§ 218.
Waves Crash, Hoof Beats On The Sand - Epona
Winds Gust, Manes Ablaze Go Free - Epona
White Mare, Spirit Of The Wild - Epona
(Evo Domingues Jr.)

§219. "The Lady's Bransle"
She will bring the buds in the spring, and laugh among the
   flowers
In summer's heat her kisses are sweet, she lies in leafy bowers
She cuts the corn and gathers the grain, when the leaves fall all
   around her
Her bones grow cold in wintertime, she wraps her cloak around
   her.

(Hope Ahern)

§ 220.
Grandmother, Spider Woman, Arachne
Grandmother, Spider Woman, Arachne
Join us together, help us to be free
Join us together, help us to be free

§ 221.
Mother I can feel you under my feet
Mother I can feel your heartbeat
Father I can see you as the eagle flies
Spirit won't you take me higher

§ 222.
Hecate, ancient one, dark mother take me in,
Hecate, ancient one, let me be reborn

§ 223.
The horn, the horn, the Hunter's horn
Is not a thing to taunt or scorn.

§ 224.
She's been waiting, waiting,
She's been waiting so long
She's been waiting for her children to remember and return.
She's been waiting, waiting,
She's been waiting so long
She's been waiting for her children to remember and return.
Blessed be and blessed are the lovers of the lady.
Blessed be and blessed are Maiden Mother Crone
Blessed be and blessed are the ones who dance together
Blessed be and blessed are the ones who dance alone.
(Paula Walowitz)

§ 225.
Birgitta Birgitta
goddess of the flame
Birgitta Birgitta
priestess of the flame
awaken the flame
within my being
awaken the sacred fire
within my being
(Lisa Theil)

§ 226.
Lady Brigid of the Bards
Blessed Fire of Inspiration
Spark the flames within our hearts
Lead our creative exploration
Lady Brigid hear our song
As we give offerings of praise
Let your blessings make us strong
that we may serve you all our days.
(Peggy Kaan)

§ 227.
Come, Daughter of Eternity,
Come, Brigit of the Flame,
Come, Sister of Infinity,
Bring healing to the lame.
Bright as the Sun above,
Song of the well
Crafter of hearts and minds,
We love you well.
(Arlene Davis)

§ 228. "Triple Goddess Song"
Honoured maiden huntress
Artemis, Artemis
Maiden, come to us.

Silver shining wheel
of radiance, radiance,
Mother (Full Moon), come to us.

Honour queen of wisdom
Hecate, Hecate
Old one, come to us.

§ 229 "Snake Woman"
(solo voice) Snake woman, shedding Her skin
(all) Snake woman shedding her skin
Shedding, shedding, shedding her skin
Snake woman shedding her skin
Shedding, shedding, shedding her skin

(solo voice) Bird woman taking flight
(all) Bird woman taking flight
Taking, taking, taking flight
Bird woman taking flight
Taking, taking, taking flight

(solo voice) Star woman shining bright
(all) Star woman shining bright
Shining, shining, shining bright
Star woman shining bright
Shining, shining, shining bright

(solo voice) Moon woman riding the night
(all) Moon woman riding the night

Riding, riding, riding the night
Moon woman riding the night
Riding, riding, riding the night

(solo voice) Blossom woman opening wide
(all) Blossom woman opening wide
Opening, opening, opening wide
Blossom woman opening wide
Opening, opening, opening wide

(solo voice) Snake woman, shedding Her skin
(all) Snake woman shedding her skin
Shedding, shedding, shedding her skin
Snake woman shedding her skin
Shedding, shedding, shedding her skin

§ 230. "Circles"
Around, and around, and around goes the good earth
And all things much change as the seasons go by.
We are the children of the Lord and the Lady,
Whose mysteries we know yet we never know why.

§ 231. "Spring Strathspey"
Sweetly it drew me, the sound that went through me
As if sure it knew me: a maiden-song, laughing long.
I'm sure that I hear it! O let me draw near it!
I want to be merrily courted in spring.
(Gwydion Pendderwen)

§ 232.
Round and around and around we go,
Sometimes fast and sometimes slow
Round and around and around the ring,
Of the summer-born king.

(Gwydion Pendderwen)

§ 233.
Fur and feather and scale and skin,
Different without but the same within
Many of body but one of soul
Through all creatures are the Gods made whole.
(Sable)

§ 234.
Horned one, lover, son
Leaper in the corn
Deep in the mother
Die and be reborn.

§ 235.
Green man come, green man go,
Green man, green man,
The sun shines down upon his leaves,
Green man, green man,
And now it's time for him to lead,
Green man, green man.

§ 236.
Cernunnos, Horned One!
Cernunnos, King of the Sun!
Herne the Hunter, and Hunted One,
Stag God of the Earth.
(Silver on the Tree)

§ 237.
Blessed is She who brings the life to the land
Blessed is She
Flow out from your sources, sacred river

Blessed is She.

§ 238.
Maid of Battle, maid of skill,
Maid of wisdom, maid of will,
We will follow and fulfill,
Hail to thee, Athena!
(Tamarra James)

§ 239.
Lugh Lamhfada, Sage of Skill,
Sun and Harvest, Spear of Will
Lugh Lamhfada, with your might,
Bring us all your blessings bright.
(Aislinn Avalon)

§ 240.
Holy Water, Sacred Flame,
Brighid we invoke our name,
Bless my hands, my head, my heart,
Source of healing, song and art.

§ 241. "Hymn to Her"
She will always carry on.
Something is lost, something is found
They will keep on speaking her name
Some things change, some stay the same.
(The Pretenders)

§ 242.
Full moon, shining bright, midnight on the waters
O Aradia, Diana's silver daughter,
(Tziporah Klien)

§ 243.
I am the ocean, and the ocean is me.
I am the Goddess, and I am the sea.
Everything opens when I open me.
Everything opens when I open me.

§ 244.
And Sisters of the East, we see you flying in the sky,
You are Sacred, and you are looking at us.
We pray to you, pray to you,
You are Sacred, come join with us.

And Sisters of the South, we see you shining with the fire...
And Sisters of the West, we see you flowing with the sea...
And Sisters of the North, we see you sitting on the earth...

§ 245.
Thank you, Mother Earth,
Thank you, Sister Water.
Thank you for my birth,
Thank you from your daughter.
Thank you, Brother Sun,
Thank you, Air in motion.
Thank you, everyone:
Earth, fire, wind, and ocean.

§ 246. "A Poplar Stood by the Road Side"
The sound of the kankles from below the roots,
The bees were buzzing in the middle
The falcon's children at the summit
A group of brothers rides on by
Please stop, young brothers
Behold the falcon's children
Listen to the buzzing bees

Listen to the ringing kankles
The kankles ring for our dear father
The bees, they buzz for our dear mother
The falcon's children grieve for our brother

§ 247.
Goddess shining from our eyes,
Arms raised up toward the skies,
Bodies moving to the beat
Rhythms pounded from our feet,
Hail to all who gather here!
Welcome all and have no fear!
We have come with one desire,
To play our drums and dance the fire!
Join us and you will see,
We are all here in Unity.
(Lupa Bardy)

§ 248.
There is nothing without one conscious spark.
First differentiate, then to reunion hark!
Respective dances fire, and still rests earth,
which mixed, to water and air give birth.
Self, not-self, one many, within without,
time and space, motion and form, a redoubt.
Our sex gives life, and we eat a death sentence.
Of nature's law these are the whole great essence.
In name of this mystery,
our ancestors, Gods, kith and kin,
the meaning of life, the universe, and everything,
let us all join hands to sing and dance merrily,
that we thus celebrate our differences,
in light of common similarity!
(Shawn Fryer)

§ 249. "The Crann Uball Ancestor Song"
Those who have fallen and who've lain down forever,
You whose stars have risen to the dark sky together,
Hear my call through our orchard, through all the trees before me,
Sacred ground here is marked, through all realms we are guarded,
So surrounded.

§ 250. "Hunter's Howl"
Rushing running through the wood
The she-wolf howl is understood
The pack they hear her hunting cry
The sacred game begins

Hi hi, de de,
hi hi, de li,
hi hi, de de de li de li
Hi hi, de de,
hi hi, de li,
hi hi, de de de li de li

Running wolf, blue blazing star
Tell the spirits who we are
Worthy we be, tell them why
We pledge the sacred promise

Forest see us, aren't we brave
Aren't we worthy of the prey
We honour them and hold them high
Waste not their sacrifice

Feathers fly, legs run the ground
Hunters life to prey is bound
Fins and flippers swim the flow
Know earth, sea and sky

Death feeds life, life breeds death
Respect all those who give their flesh
Nothing wasted, each we're bound
Our lives to theirs

Hunters' moon, She's riding high
Illuminates from darkened sky
Sacred wheel of life and death
Give and take we need you

The hunted hears the hunters' cries
The maiden moon runs through the skies
The sun He shines upon them both
Who's predator and who's prey?

Nothing wasted, honoured well
The promise sacred must be held
Only worthy hunters find
The chance to turn the wheel.
(NaTasha Bertrand)

§ 251. "Love Song"
Running lover wild and free
Running lover come to me
You I seek through the brightening air
Come to me save me from despair

City's ways take a heavy toll
On my body and my soul
Food I do not know nor trust
Air is full of toxic dust

You are wild and you are free
On your natural food you feed

You are healthy, you are strong
You run so fast on your legs so long

Forest dweller how I fear
Oh my love, that your death is near
Hunters press and hunters push
Their hounds do chase you through the bush

Oh my love can you feel my need
As I seek thee through the trees
Come to me for it's you I track
I will both honour you and sing you back

I'll shoot the arrow fast and true
Oh my love, straight into you
May you not suffer long in pain
Death be quick, good my aim

Antlers, skin and flesh and bone
I will transport to my home
Your flesh will feed me through the year
Your skin will keep me warm my dear

Running lover can't you see
How again I will need you to live and breathe
Come my love, answer my cry
Come my love, to me to die
Hi de ho, lo de li,
Come my love,
Oh to die.
(NaTasha Bertrand)

§ 252. "Thanksgiving Round"
The summer is over; the Goddess has changed

Her robes turned to tatters, her beauty has waned
She calls us to take up our tools and our toil
To manifest vision, to make our dreams real.
(Em Poore)

Songs That Honour the Earth and the Natural World

§ 253.
Cold dark and lonely,
Locked deep within my own fears,
No key to free me,
Waiting for the sun.
(Tziporah Klein)

§ 254.
We are going to Valhalla,
We are going to Valhalla,
We are going to Valhalla,
When the Valkyries take us home!

§ 255.
Spirits of the eastern wind, we call unto you
All over the morning sky, we call unto you.

§ 256.
All the air is sacred, every breath we take.
All the air is sacred, every breath we take.
Unite the people, we are one.
Unite the people, we are one.

§ 257.
We are the walking breath. We are the spirit of the earth,
We are alive and walking, where we are is beautiful.

§ 258.
Wearing my long white feathers as I fly.
Wearing my long white feathers as I fly.
I circle around, I circle around
The boundaries of the Earth
(Navajo Ghost Dance.)

§ 259.
Burn fire burn: desire, desire!
Flame higher flame: now let the change come!

§ 260.
Spirits of fire, come to us!
We will kindle the fire
Spirits of fire, come to us!
We will kindle the fire
We will kindle the fire!
Dance the magic circle round
We will kindle the fire
We will kindle the fire.

§ 261.
We circle around the fire
To Raise the Cone of Power
To bring what we desire
So Mote it Be.

§ 262.
Burn fire
Burn within me
Kindled from eternal fire
All the people
That I see
All the people

Part of me
One flame
Many parts
A simple fire of flaming hearts
Guide my footsteps, feed my soul
Wherever I may go

§ 263.
Fire transform me
Bring me to my passion
Fire transform me
Bring me to my passion
I chose Life!
I choose Courage!
I choose Life!
I choose Courage!
To dance among the flames.
To dance among the flames.

§ 264.
I am the ocean, and the ocean is me.
I am the Goddess, and I am the sea.
Everything opens when I open me.
Everything opens when I open me.

§ 265.
The great sea
Has sent me adrift
It moves me
As the weed in a great river
Earth and the great weather
Moves me
Have carried me away
And moves my inward parts with joy.

(Inuit shamanic song)

§ 266.
River, she is flowing, flowing and flowing
River, she is flowing down to the sea.
Mother, carry me
Your child I will always be.
Mother carry me down to the sea.

Wind, she is blowing, blowing all blowing
Wind she is blowing, through the trees.
Wind, wind carry me
Our spirits shall always be.
Wind, wind carry me, so I can be free.
Moon she is waning, waning and waiting
Moon, she is waiting for us to be free.
Sister moon watch over me
Our spirits shall always be.
Sister moon watch over me until we are free.

§ 267.
Powers of the Earth,
Power taking form.
Rising to rebirth,
Rising to be born.

§ 268.
Dark Earth
Silent stone
Tangled root
And green leaf, oh
High peaks, magic herbs
Cold springs rush and forest grow
Mountain Mother come to me

I receive you merrily
Guide my footsteps, feed my soul
Wherever I may go.

§ 269. "Witches' Song"
Weave the magic
By the moonlight
Dance and sing the witches' song!
(Selena Fox)

§ 270.
Come, sweet summer, humming buzzing, like a sated bee,
Sniff the pollen, suck the nectar, summer humming, come to me!
(Morgan, Amrita, and Rhea Eilinel)

§ 271. "Pentacle Song"
Hey ho, pentagram glow
Guard this hearth, this home, this land,
And we shall be merry.
Hey ho, pentagram glow
Bring us peace, and health, and light,
And we shall be merry.

Hey ho, pentagram glow
Speed our love, our strength, our power
And we shall be merry.

Hey ho, pentagram glow
Grant our dreams, our wish, our will,
And we shall be merry.

Hey ho, pentagram glow
In North in East, in South, in West
And we shall be merry.

(Selena Fox)

§ 272.
Air moves us
Fire transforms us
Water shapes us
Earth heals us
And the balance of the wheel goes round and round
And the balance of the wheel goes round
(Reclaiming Collective / Cathleen Shell)

§ 273.
We are reclaiming the air (fire / earth / water),
Giving the air divine names

§ 274.
We are one, in our grove,
upon the earth, within the sea, beneath the sky.
We are joined, to send our call,
to the honored dead, to the spirit folk, to the blessed gods.
We praise thee, in one voice, in our sacred grove.
We are one.
(Ian Corrigan.)

§ 275.
The Earth, the Air, the Fire, the Water
Return Return Return Return
The Earth, the Air, the Fire, the Water
Return Return Return Return
I-ay I-ay I-ay I-ay
I-oh I-oh I-oh I-oh
I-ay I-ay I-ay I-ay
I-oh I-oh I-oh I-oh

§ 276.
Air I am, Fire I am,
Water, Earth, and Spirit I am.
(Andras Corben Arthen)

§ 277.
Earth is my body
Water my blood
Air is my breath, and
Fire my spirit!

§ 278 "Welcome the Elements"
Welcome the air and the fire and the water
Welcome the earth and the spirit that's within
Welcome the directions and elements, all sacred things
And honour their connection to that which is within.

Welcome the east, inspiration and intellect
Welcome the air, and the clarity that's within
Welcome the south, creative will and passion
Welcome the fire, and the energy within

Welcome the west, intuition and emotion
Welcome the water, and the empathy within

Welcome the north, the senses and the body
Welcome the earth, and the harmony within
Welcome the centre, infinity, eternity
Welcome the spirit, divinity within.
(Pali A'Kala)

§ 279.
In Balance with the moon and the sun and the earth
With my body and soul I will bring forth new birth.

§ 280.
Spirit of the wind, carry me
Spirit of the wind, carry me home
Spirit of the wind, carry me home to myself.

Spirit of the sun, warm light healing me,
Spirit of the sun, carry me home,
Spirit of the sun, carry me home to myself.

Spirit of the sea, flow with me,
Spirit of the sea, flow with me home
Spirit of the sea, flow with me home to myself

Spirit of the land, carry me
Spirit of the land, carry me home,
Spirit of the land, carry me home to myself.

Spirit of the trees, at peace,
Spirit of the trees, at peace with me,
Spirit of the trees, at peace with me within myself
(Star Williams / Todd Allen)

§ 281.
The ocean is the beginning of the Earth
The ocean is the beginning of the Earth
All life comes from the sea
All life comes from the sea

The wind is the beginning of the world
All joy comes from the air

Fire is the beginning of the world
All pow'r comes from the flame

Water is the beginning of the world
All life comes from the sea

The Earth is the beginning of the world
All strength comes from within.
(Delaney Johnson [5 years old at the time!] and Starhawk)

§ 282.
Rain comes falling down
Trees reach for the sky
Leaves grow on the trees
Breeze shakes the leaves
Seeds in the air,
Rain falling down, falling down.
(Silver on the Tree.)

§ 283.
Morning glory song!
Morning glory song!
Sing, supernova!
Shaking out his golden hair,
Spreads his goodness everywhere.
Morning Glory Song!
(Silver on the tree)

§ 284. "The Mill Chant"
Air breath and air blow, make the wheel of magic go,
Work the will for which we pray,
Eo deo ha hey yay.
Eo deo ha hey yay.

Fire blaze and fire burn, make the wheel of magic turn,
Work the will for which we pray,
Eo deo ha hey yay.

Eo deo ha hey yay.

Water heat and water boil, make the wheel of magic toil,
Work the will for which we pray,
Eo deo ha hey yay.
Eo deo ha hey yay.

Earth without and earth within, make the wheel of magic spin,
Work the will for which we pray,
Eo deo ha hey yay.
Eo deo ha hey yay.

§ 285. "The Wheel Chant"
Power of wind and power of air,
Power of mountains, bleak and bare,
Turn the time of night and day,
And spin the wheel, au-ri-ay.

Power of flame and power of fire,
Power of all our heart's desire,
Light of dark and light of day,
And spin the wheel, au-ri-ay.

Power of ice and water free,
Power that hides in depths of sea,
Turn the tide of night and day
And spin the wheel, au-ri-ay.

Power of stone and power of earth
Power that shapes our place of birth
Weave the web of night and day
And spin the wheel, au-ri-ay.

Songs That Honour the Human Community

§ 286.
We are a circle, within a circle
With no beginning, and never ending.
(Rick Hamouris)

§ 287.
You hear us sing, you hear us sigh;
Now hear us call you, spirits of air and sky.

Inside our hearts, there lies a spark
Love and desire, a burning fire.
Within our blood, within our tears
There lies the altar of living water.

Take our fear, take our pain
Take the darkness into the earth again.
(Rick Hamouris)

§ 288.
Round and round we go,
We hold each other's hands,
And dance around in a circle.
The day is done,
The dance just begun.

§ 289.
Strand by strand, hand over hand,
Thread by thread, we weave the web.
Weave and spin, weave and spin,
This is how the work begins.
Mend and heal, mend and heal,
Take the dream and make it real.

§ 290.
Every step I take is a healing step,
Every step I take is a healing step.
Healing, healing, healing my body,
Healing, healing, healing the land.

§ 291.
Let it begin with each step we take,
And let it begin with each change we make,
And let it begin with each chain we break,
And let it begin every time we awake.
(Starhawk / Reclaiming Collective)

§ 292.
All my life's a circle
Sunrise and sundown
The moon rules through the night time
Till the daylight comes around
All my life's a circle
And I can tell you why:
Seasons spinning round again,
The years keep rolling by.
(Harry Chapin)

§ 293.
We are a circle, we are
One to another, we are
Moving together, we are one
(Marae Price, Shakina Mountainwater)

§ 294.
I am spirit and I flow in you.
You are spirit and you flow in me.
(Marae Price)

§ 295.
It's the blood of the Ancients that flows through our veins
And the forms pass, but the circle of life remains.
(Charlie Murphy)

§ 296.
Pour the Waters, raise the cup,
Drink your share of wisdom deep.
Strength and Love now fill us up,
As the Elder Ways we keep.

§ 297.
Come to the land, the holy land,
The land that has welcomed our people.
Come to the land, the beautiful land,
May we root in her ever deeper.
(Marae Price)

§ 298.
Come we now as a people,
To gather at the Sacred Well,
Come we now as a people,
Together in the warmth and the light of the Flame.
(Ian Corrigan.)

§ 299.
Come and be one, become one, be one, be.
Come and be one, become one, be one, be.

§ 300.
We approach the sacred grove
With hearts and minds and flesh and bone
Join us now in ways of old
We have come home.

(Sean Miller)

§ 301.
Fire's burning, fire's burning
Draw near, draw near
In the glowing, in the glowing
All sing and be merry!

§ 302.
Listen to the sound, to the sound of your heartbeat
Listen to the sound of your heartbeat's drum.

§ 303.
By the waters, the waters of Chalice Well
We lay down and wept, and wept for Avalon
We remember thee, remember thee, remember Avalon.

§ 304.
Stars we are and stars we will be,
Circling through eternity,
Stars we were and stars we remain
Walking on this earthly plane

§ 305.
There is a river of birds in migration
A nation of women on wings
(Libana)

§ 306.
In the city, throughout the country
The moon shines women's light,
In the city, throughout the country
We're taking back the night
(Pashta Marymoon)

§ 307.
Under the full moonlight we dance
Spirits dance, we dance
Joining hands, we dance
Joining souls rejoice!
(Libana / Karen Beth)

§ 308.
Break the mask
Burn the husk,
Free the Spirit
From the dust!

§ 309.
Truth is the fire that breaks our chains.
We'll rise with the fire of freedom.
Healing is the fire running through our veins.
We'll stop the fire of destruction.
(Starhawk)

§ 310.
Seed of what I wish to be,
Grow and bud and bloom in me.

§ 311.
Chalice and flame, cauldron of change,
We are the power to heal and reclaim.
(Linda Pintl)

§ 312.
We come from the mountain
Living on the mountain
Go back to the mountain
Turn the world around!

We come from the fire...
We come from the city...
We come from the ocean...
(Harry Belafonte)

§ 313.
Woman I am
Spirit I am
I have no beginning and I have no end
I have the infinite within my soul
All this I am.

§ 314.
Let the Beauty you love, be what you do.
There are hundreds of ways to kneel and kiss the ground.
(Jalalludin Rumi)

§ 315.
Hie, Hie, Hou, Hou! Dance ici, dance lá, jou ici, jou lá!
Hie, Hie, Hou, Hou! Dance ici, dance lá, jou ici, jou lá!

Translation:
Hey, hey, ho, ho! Dance here, dance there, play here, play there!
(Claimed by an informant to be a mediaeval witch's chant from
    northern France and the Isle of Guernsey)

§ 316.
Eko, Eko, Aradia
Eko, Eko, Hecate Freya
We'll teach your children, year after year,
To love with their hearts, and live without fear.
(Kenny Klien)

§ 317.
My skin, my bones, my heretic heart
Are my authority.
(Catherine Madsen)

§ 318.
Let the people live their lives
As if it were a song
For singing out of light
Provide the music for the stars
To be dancing circles in the night.
(Translated from a Russian folk song)

§ 319.
I believe that the day will come
When we will (all) work as one,
I believe that the time will come
When our Will will be done,
our Will will be done,
our Will will be done

§ 320.
We are children of the Earth, and
We come from different places
We are sculptured and formed
By the hands of time.

We are children of the Moon, and
We invoke her different phases
Ebb and flow like the tide,
Dancing to her song.
We are children of the sun, and
We mark his different seasons,
Rise and fall with the day,

Shining with his light.

§ 321.
We are the old people
We are the new people
We are the same people
Stronger than before.
(Morning Feather and Will Shepherd)

§ 322.
I am the Mabon, I am the child
I am Yir, the golden bough.
I am the dart that the yew lets fly.
Three pure rays, the pillars of light.
I am the wren, the king of birds
I am Bard, the teller of lies.
I am the song within the heart.
I am the light that will never die.
I am the stars, within the void,
I am the Aion, the Mabon, I am the child...
(Silver On The Tree)

§ 323.
By Fire and by Water, between the Earth and Sky,
We stand like the World-Tree rooted deep, crowned high.

§ 324.
Power of the Spirits, flowing through me
Power of the Spirits, shining in me
Power of the Spirits, growing with me

§ 325.
We are the power in everyone
We are the dance of the moon and sun

We are the hope that will not hide
We are the turning of the tide.
(Starhawk)

§ 326.
We are the flow, we are the ebb
We are the weavers, we are the web.
We are the warp, we are the weft,
We are the needle, we are the thread.
(Starhawk)

§ 327.
May the love we're sharing
Spread it's wings
And fly across the Earth
And bring new joy to every soul
Who is alive

My the blessings of your grace, my love
Shine on everyone
And may we all see the light within
Within, within

§ 328.
We are blessed with the waters of life
And the air that we breathe
Will bring us freedom
And the fire that we kindle tonight
On this sacred earth
Will bring us together
Spirits together
(Alex DelBusso.)

§ 329.

We are one with the Mother,
We are one with the earth,
We are one with each other,
By our lives, by our birth.

§ 330.

Beware, there is magic all around you
Beware, there is magic all around you
Beware, there is magic all around you
Awake, rejoice, and see!

§ 331.

My love is a garden enclosed
A sacred (sealed) fountain
A well of living water, and
All green is our bed.
(The Song of Solomon)

§ 332.

We give thanks for unknown blessings
Already on the way.

§ 333.

All I ask of You
Is forever to remember me
As loving you.
(Sufi Chant)

§ 334.

We swear by peace and love to stand
Heart to heart and hand in hand
Mark, O Spirit, and hear us now
Confirming this our Sacred Vow.

§ 335.
We all fly like eagles,
Flying so high,
Circling the universe
On wings of pure light.
Oh wey chi-chiya, Oh wey yi-yo.
Oh wey chi-chiya, Oh wey yi-yo.
Where we walk is holy,
Sacred is the ground.
Rivers mountains, forests,
Listen to the sound.
Oh wey chi-chiya, Oh wey yi-yo.
Oh wey chi-chiya, Oh wey yi-yo.

§ 336. "Avalon"
It's a long long walk to Avalon
Down a road that few have seen
It's a long long time since the bard has sung
And the earth was wild and green

First the winter snows lay nature to bed
In the icy breath of the year
Then the springtime sun shines upon my head
And I know I have nothing to fear

It's a long long walk to Avalon
Down a road that we can see
It is not so far, nor is it gone
Avalon's in you and me

§ 337
All Beings of the Earth
Sing the healing song, rising.
Will the healing fire, changing.

Swim the healing deep, feeling.
Walk the healing Earth, being.
(Lynn Stone, Andras C. Arthen, Deirdre P. Arthen, Sherry G.
   Arthen)

§ 338
Powerful song of radiant light
weave us the web that spins the night
Web of stars that holds the dark
Weave us the Earth that feeds the spark

Strand by strand, hand over hand
Thread by thread we weave our web
(Pandora, Starhawk, Rose May Dance)

§ 339
Spiraling into the center,
The center of our soul,
The center of our soul,
We are the weavers
We are the woven ones
We are the dreamers
We are the dream

§ 340
On the same wheel we spin
Into (out of) life and out (in) again
One is many, many one
Brewing in Her cauldron

§ 341
We are the witches who will never be burned
We are the witches who have learned what it is to be free

Higher and higher and higher
Fire's strength we will reclaim
Higher and higher and higher

Fire of love is burning bright
Higher and higher and higher
Flickering and dancing in the night
Higher and higher and higher

Weave your power with the wind
We will charge and we will spin
Higher and higher and higher

§ 342
Our hands will work for peace and justice
Our hands will work the land
Our feet will trace Her moving patterns
Let us dance and bless the land

Gather round the harvest table
Let us feast and bless the land

Take the gift of love and death
Take the gift of blood and bone

Weave the circle breath by breath
Build the vision stone by stone.
(Thorn Coyle, Starhawk)

§ 343
We are alive, as the earth is alove
We have the power to fight for our freedom
If we have courage we can be healers
Like the sun, We shall rise

(Rose May Dance, Starhawk)

§ 344
If the people live their lives
As if it were a song, for singing out of light
Provide the music for the stars
To be dancing circles in the night.

§ 345
Wandering in the deep of the night
A thousand birds take flight
And our dreams are born
On the wings of change.
We are weaving the world tonight.
(Suzanne Sterling)

§ 346
Goodnight fair witches
Lay down your head and rest
Lay down your weary head and be the mountain's guest
The stars will guide you, your dreams will do the rest
So I bid you goodnight, goodnight, goodnight.

§ 347.
Gone, gone, gone beyond
Gone beyond, beyond
Hail the goer!
(Traditional Buddhist funeral chant)

§ 348.
Walk with wisdom from this hallowed place.
Walk not in sorrow, our roots shall ere embrace.
May strength be your brother, and honor be your friend,
And luck be your lover until we meet again.

(Sable)

§ 349.
Join your heart once more with your comrades
Ere you turn your face to the wind
And walk the road from this holy place
In the company of friends.
(Marae Price)

§ 350.
Perfect love and Perfect trust
Joy be shared by all of us
Merry meet and merry part
Truth and goodness (wisdom) in our hearts

§ 351.
May the long time sun shine be on you
All love surround you
And the pure light within you
Guide your way home.

§ 352.
Lord and Lady guide the homeward
Steps of parting friends,
Merry meet, merry part,
And merry meet again.
(Jackie Gilhooley)

§ 353.
We have gathered in their name
Now we sing them home again.

§ 354.
From fire to water, to earth and to wind

It's a circle of light, a dance without end
So Merry meet, and merry part, and merry meet again.
Merry meet, and merry part, and merry meet again.

§ 355.
Perfect love and Perfect trust
Joy be shared by all of us
Merry meet and merry part
Truth and goodness in our hearts

§ 356.
May the circle be open but unbroken
May the love of the Goddess be ever in your heart.
Merry meet, and merry part, and merry meet again!
(Starhawk)

Notes about the Circle Songs.

Circle Round. (§186)

This was the very first pagan chant I ever heard performed. The day was a sunny August afternoon, in a conservation park north of London Ontario, and I was only nineteen years old. The organizers of the ceremony were busily putting things together in the ritual space, while about fifty people were talking and relaxing nearby, paying no attention. When the ritual presenters were ready, their signal to the others was simply to start singing this song, as a three-part round. One by one people took the hint, gathered at the ritual circle and joined in. About five minutes later everyone was assembled, and the ceremony begun.

"I am the Mabon..." (§322)

I learned this piece while attending a private pagan gathering, and only much later found that it had been composed and recorded by "Silver On The Tree", a pagan musical group based in England. It was frequently sung during the middle-portion of ritual, while wine or other sacramental foodstuffs were being distributed. The idea was apparently to keep people busy while they were waiting their turn!

The content of the lyrics is consistent with the teachings, symbols, and styles of contemporary British Druidry. Here are explanations of some of them. "Mabon" is the name used in the British druidic community for the holiday of autumn equinox. It is also the name of a Welsh god, Mabon ap Modron, 'The Son of the Mother", the divine child of the goddess who brings to humanity the good news of her transformations.

The "dart that the Yew lets fly" is death. The symbol works in several ways. English longbows were traditionally made from the flexible and durable wood of the yew tree. Indeed the English Longbow was the weapon of mass destruction that won the battle of Agincourt! These trees were planted in avenues near church-yards in order to have a ready supply of wood for the manufacture of new bows. Moreover, the yew tree is the last tree of the Ogham, the magical tree-alphabet used by Druids and other Celtic seekers. The tree is associated with death as it exudes a mild poison from its bark. But it is also one of the longest living European trees, and its branches can reach down, plant themselves, and become new trees. A sapling of Yew can also grow from the dead stump of its parent. Therefore the Yew tree has been adopted by contemporary Druids as one of the primary symbols of death and mortality, yet also birth and renewal.

Note that in all cases the language of identity is used to introduce each sacred theme: "I am". This is the language of The Mystery, the deity who dwells within.

Kore's Chant. (§187 and §188)

This very well known chant was composed by Starhawk, author of *The Spiral Dance* and probably the most prominent and well known American witch of her time. I first heard it performed at an outdoor festival where a Wiccan priest sang it while leading three hundred people in a spiral dance. It was the second most frequently mentioned song in my survey results: only one other, "We are a circle" (§286), was mentioned more often.

Philosophically, the message of Kore's Chant is simple, even elemental. The lyrics assert only that Kore, the daughter of Demeter and the goddess of springtime and flowers, changes everything: for better or worse, for good or ill. But the lyric doesn't mention Kore by name, so each singer can attribute it to any goddess she likes, or she can treat it as a personal affirmation. The poem also leaves it open whether the goddess is the agent of change, or whether she is the embodiment of a natural process for which no personal agency truly exists. But either way, it suggests that changes in the world are *intelligible:* they are part of the story of the goddess Kore.

There are numerous variations contributed by 'Reclaiming', the feminist spiritual activist community which Starhawk more or less founded. I have included several in this collection (as §188). But I wish to draw attention to a line in one of them: "Her name cannot be spoken". This line affirms that the being of the goddess is in some sense ineffable: to express her being in words is to diminish her somehow. This idea also appears in artistic depictions of the Goddess: she is often wearing a veil, a cloak, a hood, or some other garment that conceals her face and body. Middle Eastern goddesses, in particular, are frequently depicted in contemporary pagan art as wearing veils. This has nothing to do with chastity or modesty, but rather has to do with mystery. She is hidden because she cannot be described. Instead, she can be represented artistically. Better still, she can be met face-to-face, in a first-order experience of the sacred.

Songs for the Goddess and the God together (§189 to §200)

According to one of my informants, a leading priestess in her community for more than thirty years, these pieces began as songs in honour of the Goddess, and only the Goddess. But someone, somewhere along the way, thought it was important to add a verse in honour of the God, in order to add 'balance'. Sometimes two different male-God verses were composed by two different people, without knowledge of each other. Therefore, there are often more chants for Him, then there are for Her, even though the song was originally composed for Her! Nonetheless, in each case, the Goddess' part is sung first. In this short sequence, each Goddess chant is followed by the God-chants that accompany it.

"Hoof and Horn" (§191)

This is one of the god-chants that was composed to balance a goddess chant. Composed by Ian Corrigan, one of the leading figures in Arn Draiocht Fein (an American druidic organization), it expresses the divinity of the circle of life, and the promise of rebirth. The story of The God is the story of the game animals in the woods and the hunter who chases them. It is the story of the crops in the fields and the farmer who harvests them. The god is he who kills and is killed, who dies and is reborn. He does this not to save us from sin or from evil. He does this so that we can *eat*. The gods in contemporary paganism are personifications of the cycle of life. And that is not to confirm or deny that they exist as persons with whom one could have a spiritual relationship. But it is to assert that their presence may be found in the food chain and other ecological processes. They are found in plant and animal habitats, both natural and man-made. Wherever the great immensities of birth, death, and organic transformation and renewal are found, whether in human activities or in natural events, there the presence of the gods may be found too. The personification of such processes with the names and stories of gods is a pagan's way of proclaiming that they are worthy of being celebrated.

As an aside, I also received a satirical revision of this song:

Milk and honey, milk and honey,
Send us great big heaps of money!

The Goddess Chant: "Isis, Astarte..." (§192)

The author of this piece, Catherine Madsen, has written numerous longer songs that are well known at Bardic circles. This particular piece began life as the chorus of "Burning Times", a song about mediaeval women accused of witchcraft by Holy Inquisition. The song made it outside Pagan culture and into the mainstream when it was recorded by Christy Moore, the well known Irish folk musician. There are several variations of this chant, some (like §193) recite the names of male deities from a variety of cultures, and some (like § 194) recite the names of goddesses from just one cultural pantheon, in this case the Celtic nation.

Brigit's Well: "We will never..." (§206)

This was one of the most popular pieces in my survey. The double reference to a well and to fire identify it as a song of the Celtic goddess Brighid, who had these attributes. I had the first and second stanza in my own collection; the third was contributed by an anonymous person responding to my survey.

"We all come from the Goddess..." (§189)

This piece is often sung together with the next one in the collection, "Hoof and Horn" (§191), either one after another as a single song, or at the same time almost like a round. One informant told me that this one was composed by Ian Corrigan, a leading figure in the American druidic community. Another informant attributed this chant to the American feminist author, Z. Budapest. But I later learned that this piece, like many others, began as a Goddess chant, and later on an addendum in honour of the Horned God was added by someone who thought that the song needed to be 'balanced'. In the case of this piece, there are not one but two male-god-honouring addendums: the other one is "We all come from the Horned One" (§190, composed by Tamarra James). These two Horned God songs were composed separately, but somewhere along the way they came together, and now people often sing the three of them as one.

Circles (§ 230)

This song is actually the chorus of a longer song with several verses, and it is usually performed outside of rituals, during the 'after party' as a performance piece. However, many of my informants described the use of the chorus as a stand-alone ritual song. To the best of my knowledge it was written by Catherine Madsen: but the lyrics and melody were borrowed from a folk song by Alan Bell, called "Windmill", about the countryside of Holland. Here's the original chorus:

Around, and around, and around went the big sails,
Turning the shafts, and the great wooden wheels.
Creaking and groaning, the mill-stones kept turning,
Grinding to flour the good corn from the fields.

The original song is not a pagan song, but it too is a song about food production, community, and good life. It has the kind of simple gentleness that hearkens the mind back to a (possibly fictitious) past golden age of pastoral simplicity. It too is about the perfect happiness that can be found in the most simple of earthy activities.

Many pagan musicians are in the habit of taking perfectly good traditional folk songs, with lyrics that are already beautiful and deeply spiritual, and turning them into pagan devotional songs. There's nothing inherently wrong with this practice. But in my experience the very best bards are those who create their own melodies. And I think it is also important to learn, and to respect, the folklore tradition of one's country and people and history. When I go to pagan gatherings, I regularly perform the music of Canadian folk song writers like Stan Rogers and Gordon Lightfoot for that reason. Folk music traditions are one of the most important sources of shared history and experience and life; they are, indeed, one of the ways we learn who we are.

The Lady's Bransle (§219)

This song came to me from a number of sources. Its lyrics had been published by journalist Margot Adler in her 1979 study of the American pagan community, *Drawing Down the Moon* (on pg. 474). This song celebrates the turning of the seasons, and is generally performed on one of the eight festivals of the pagan ritual year. And just for fun, here's a filk version of this song, called "The Lady's Brothel":

She will bring the bugs in the spring, and laugh when she's

deflowered,

   When she's in heat, she'll give you a treat, But you'll be disembowed.

   She rots the grain and brings tomain, when pagan folk displease her,

   Then moons and suns all burn their buns, In vain attempts to please her!

Spring Strathspey (§231)

Gwydion Pendderwen was a well known Pagan bardic performer from California who died in the year 1982. His many original songs have become part of the standard repertoire of pagan bards all over the English speaking world. Indeed, a line from another of his songs appeared in this collection as a wisdom-teaching (§141). Spring Strathspey is the chorus of a larger song, usually performed not during ritual but in the party afterwards, but sometimes the chorus is performed in ritual on its own. The song tells the tale of a young girl who is more or less seduced by the Welsh god Myrddin. It is thus comparable to the sweet ethereal baudiness of folk songs like "The Gypsie Laddie" (§26) and Robbie Burns' poem, "Corn Rigs" (§27).

"Green Man..." (§225)

I first collected this one at the Hill of Tara Festival, in Ireland, in 2004. It was sung at the event by Gemma McGowan, a ceremonial performer, who told me she heard it while attending a Witch's Ball in Croydon, south of London, England. On the occasion I first heard it, it was used as a processional song, which the ritual performers sang while leading the community from a staging area to the ritual circle. At a second ceremony I attended in Germany about a year later, I heard it again, also used as a processional song. In both cases there was an actor clad in a Green Man costume and mask. The Irish Green Man simply walked near the head of the procession in a methodical, devout kind of way. The German Green Man danced and ran around flamboyantly. He occasionally chased attractive women or small children, only to be restrained by handlers dressed as Celtic warriors.

By the Waters (§303)

This piece is sung to the tune of a Jewish song which laments the Exile in Babylon, and which was recorded by Don McLean (of 'American Pie' fame). The original lyrics are as follows:

> By the waters, the waters of Babylon
> We lay down and wept, and wept, for thee Zion
> We remember thee, remember thee, remember thee Zion.

Like this Jewish original, the Pagan version laments a loss: in this case, the loss of the (perhaps fictitious) idyllic pre-Christian pagan societies where the Goddess was worshipped freely, and where 'female' values, such as caregiving and nurturing, had the highest place. Since the hill of Glastonbury Tor is one of the alleged resting places of King Arthur, as well as the Holy Grail, therefore many pagans believe it is the mythical Isle of Avalon itself, and the site of an ancient goddess temple. The monastic garden of Chalice Well, mentioned in this song, is a short distance away. This thesis was explored in Marion Zimmer Bradley's novel, *The Mists of Avalon*, which tells the Arthurian myths from Morgan le Fay's point of view.

"A poplar stood by the road side" (§246)

This is an English translation of a traditional song from Lithuania. My informant, a fist-generation Canadian of Lithuanian descent, explained that it tells the story of the world tree, and the organization of the universe. In her words:

> The ringing of the kankles from under the roots is the image of

the world of the old, the wise and the dead. The buzzing bees in the middle symbolise the world of the working and toiling people. The falcon's children at the top represent the heavens, the world of warriors and heroes. The pivotal meaning of the daina is the universal importance and harmony of these three parts.

(Maritja Kunkaitis, personal communication, 2006)

Two hunting songs (§250 and §2451)

These songs both express the spiritual relationship between a hunter and her prey animals. Since the author, NaTasha Bertrand, is a practicing conservation hunter (and former vegetarian!), these songs are based on direct personal experience. Here is how she describes the relationship between a hunter and her animals, and the spiritual significance of these songs, in her own words.

The Hunter's Howl is not a teaching song, more like a reminder of the philosophy and ideals. An example: "hunter's life to prey is bound" is a reminding slogan. If I am not binding myself, involving myself in the management and maintenance of that animal's needs, health, habitat, population, etc, then I have no business hunting any of that animal. When I do kill an animal, I must maintain the relationship, my involvement, for at least another year. If that animal's population is too low, I must not hunt it, even if the regulations state that it is OK to do so. Hunting is not about the killing, it is about being willing to acknowledge that humans are part of nature, and are responsible for so much of nature being destroyed, and choosing to consciously take part in conserving the nature that remains by being active within it according to law and conservation ethics. For me, this is the core of Conservation Hunting. (NaTasha Bertrand, personal communication, 27 December 2007)

Concerning her second hunting song included here, "Love Song" (§251), she explains:

> This is my love song to Whitetail Deer. I alter it slightly, depending on the hunting circumstances, each time. It has been answered. It is very powerful, and only works when it is true. I have sung this version of it in non-hunting public a few times, and each time at the end several people come forward and kneel, some crying. (NaTasha Bertrand, personal communication, 27 December 2007)

Opening Songs (§286 to §301)

According to most informants, these songs are performed at the beginning of public rituals, for reasons which should be obvious. Their purpose is to affirm community togetherness and solidarity. It is significant, perhaps, that many of them use the symbolism of the circle. The circle is the most elemental of all geometric shapes. There are no corners, and no angles. All its points are directly connected to each other, and are the same distance from the centre. The circle is also a natural shape: it appears in the sun and moon, in the horizon, in bird's nests, in flowers, in bubbles, and in the pupils of our eyes. A circle, in the Pagan world-view, is a model of the cosmos. It seems natural, therefore, that the circle is used by a wide variety of cultures for meetings and gatherings where values like equality and companionship are affirmed. For example, here are the words of Heheka Sapa, more widely known as Black Elk, one of the most well known leaders of the Dakota Nation. This passage comes from an autobiography which he dictated in 1930.

> Everything the Power of the World does is done in a circle. The Sky is round and I have heard that the earth is round like a ball and so are all the stars. The wind, in its greatest power, whirls. Birds make their nests in circles, for theirs is the same religion

as ours. The sun comes forth and goes down again in a circle. The moon does the same, and both are round. Even the seasons form a great circle in their changing, and always come back again to where they were. The life of a man is a circle from childhood to childhood and so it is in everything where power moves. Our tipis were round like the nests of birds and these were always set in a circle, the nation's hoop, a nest of many nests where the Great Spirit meant for us to hatch our children. (McLuhan, *Touch the Earth*, pg. 42)

The most elementary ideas demand expression in the simplest and most familiar shapes. The image of the circle was the connection between the world in which Aboriginal people find themselves, and the way they configured the identity of their community. It appears in the Medicine Wheel, the symbol of a circle divided into four coloured quadrants, which correspond to the body, mind, heart, and spirit, to cardinal directions, and various teachings. The circle also appears in European cultures: for instance, in the circular shape of Celtic passage mounds and ring barrows. It appears in King Arthur's mythology as the Round Table which, rather like the Aboriginal council fire, also affirms that everyone who sits at the table is the equal of everyone else, and that no one is 'above' or 'higher' than anyone else. It should not be a surprise that the image of a circle features so prominently in the songs that are sung at the beginning of ceremonies. For the circle is more than a symbol: it is the representation of their most sacred values, and indeed the very meaning of their way of life.

We are a circle, within a circle (§286)
This song was the most popular in the collection: more than a hundred people offered it to me in their response to my survey. It was also offered in English, French, German, and Russian! Although this song is usually performed 'as is', one informant

showed me that it is only the chorus of a longer song. I have therefore included the verses separately (as §287). Most of the time, it is performed as part of the opening ceremony of a conference or other extended event. I think this wide distribution is a testament to the general consistency of pagan ideas around the world, and to the significance of the message this song expresses.

The message of this song is simple: it affirms that the community, not just each individual, may find its greater spiritual self in the whole of the world. For the song affirms that the human circle is a self-contained universe unto itself. We are a circle of people holding hands, and at the same time our circle is contained in, and part of, the larger circles of the world, such as the cycle of death and birth, or the horizon, or the earth's orbit around the sun. In this way the human community has a place and a home in the larger field of the universe. Furthermore this song has a cosmic imagination which reaches for the infinite: for the circle have no beginning, and never ends. Indeed the thirteen words of this song are, in my mind, a primary wisdom teaching, on par with The Mystery, and the Charge of the Goddess.

Songs for Taking Back the Night (§305 to § 309)

Every year, most cities in Canada and the United States have a "Take Back the Night" parade. It is a protest march, opposing violence against women and in support of women's interests generally. Men are not permitted to join the march, although they may cheer it on from the sidelines. The idea is that the night is being 'taken back' from those who have used the cover of the night to attack women and children. The songs in this sequence were originally composed by participants in the first Take Back the Night marches.

The Elements Round (§275)

This piece may also be compared to the Christian teaching that we are all dust, "and unto dust ye shall return". It asserts that life is transient, and that we shall all dissolve back into the base elements from which we came. But I think the pagan teaching is more optimistic and life-affirming. For in the Pagan way of thinking, the base element to which we return is not the dirt of the grave. Rather, we return to the living material of the Earth, the atmosphere, the food chain and other ecological processes, and to the sea. This piece therefore coheres well with other songs and wisdom-teachings which assert that each person is a part of a global body, and that each person may find her full and true Self in the whole of the world.

Incidentally, there is a comic variation of this piece which is worth mentioning:

The rent, the phone, the gas, the water
Return, return, return, return
I pay, I pay, I pay, I pay,
I owe, I owe, I owe, I owe…

"We are an Old People…" (§ 321)

This song often ends with a repetition of the last line, with a building of a sense of urgency and determination until the last repetition is almost screamed. The general sense of its affirmation is that Pagans see themselves, at least in part, as in solidarity with historical people who suffered or died as pagans. Especially included here are those who died during the Burning Times. The theme of solidarity with the oppressed goes back to the beginning of the modern movement. It also appears in Leland's *Aradia*, for instance. In that story, the goddess Diana sends her daughter Aradia to teach the witches how to strike back at their oppressors.

"Beware, there is magic" (§ 330)

This piece expresses the Pagan idea that the whole of the world is infused with energy, and that all things in the natural world can be taken as proper objects for our sense of wonder. In this way it can be compared with wisdom-teachings like "Here be dragons!" (§136) and "Goddess is alive, magic is afoot!" (§137) One informant offered a comic version of this piece:

> Beware, there are pagans all around you,
> It's a conspiracy around you!
> Beware, there are pagans all around you,
> And we look just like you!

"From Fire to Water..." (§ 354)

This piece is generally performed only at the close of a ritual, when the circle is 'taken down' and the Quarters are 'released'. The second line of the song is slightly changed, in accord with which of the Quarters is being addressed. In the East it is a circle of light; in the south, life; in the west, love; and in the north, law.

Esoteric Intonations

Some circle songs are not really songs at all. They are more like meditative invocations: the seeker 'intones' a deep resonating note with each phoneme, for as long as her breath can sustain the sound. The purpose here is to stimulate a mild trance-state in the mind. The phonemes themselves are either the names of deities, or single phonemes representing those names. The language may not be in a living modern language: it might be a dead language, like Latin or Anglo-Saxon, or in an invented esoteric language like Enochian. There isn't much point in reproducing many esoteric chants in a collection like this one, where the purpose is to study the meaning of the lyrics. But just for fun, I'll mention three that appeared in my survey.

- "Io Evoeh", alleged to mean 'All hail', or 'Spirits gather'
- "Ap ap anno, Irute!", alleged to mean 'Goddess returns from the west'

- "I – A – O", phonemes representing the first letters in the names of the Egyptian gods Isis, Apophis, and Osiris.

But it is even possible that these chants mean nothing at all, and they are intoned only for the sake of the physiological and psycho-spiritual effect that intoning them can create. The purpose of these intonations, all my informants agreed, is also 'to summon the presence of the deity'. Esoteric phonemes like this also sometimes appear as part of other chants with sensible lyrics, such as The Mill Chant (§284) and The Wheel Chant (§285).

"Cold Dark and Lonely" (§253)

This rather bleak song is usually sung only in the winter months, for instance at Winter Solstice and its nearest neighbors on the calendar. It is never used at any other time of the year, and never sung at the end of a ceremony. Something more cheerful almost always follows it, as many pagans find it depressing and prefer more lively affirmations.

I collected two variations of the third line. The variation offered here, "No key to free me", seems to be the more common one. The second variation is "No one can see me". Although the lyric is indubitably dour compared to other pagan songs, I think it is remarkable for its honesty. Loneliness, abandonment, unwelcome solitude, and sheer *undifferentiated waiting* are experiences nearly everyone can recognise and sometimes must endure. Its presence in this collection is important: it shows that pagans do not dwell solely on the easy and gratifying side of things, as in an escapist fantasy. In fact pagan music incorporates the whole range of human emotional experience, including sadness and dejection. Yet this piece is also, in a strange way, a positive song. The last line, 'waiting for the sun', should be understood as a promise of renewal. Most pagans understand spiritual experiences in terms of cycles like sunrises and seasonal changes. The song places the singer in a dark and unhappy place, but at the same time gives her hope. No pagan song or affirmation or wisdom teaching known to me removes or denies the possibility of hope. This hidden optimism makes this song the most beautiful in the collection.

Going to Valhalla (§254)

I recently heard this song performed on the last night of Kaleidoscope Gathering 2007, and the theme that year was "Vikings – and the places they visited". A dock in the shape of a Viking longship had been built on the lake. At two o'clock in the morning, on the last night of the festival, a hundred people or more were still happily drumming and dancing around the bonfire. Then a group of Vikings (or festival staff in costume, whichever you prefer!) danced in a procession into the circle, carrying the longship's huge draconic head and tail. They paraded them around the circle a few times while everyone sang the chorus of "We are going to Valhalla". Then the head and tail were dropped in the fire! The song changed to a chant: "The ship! The ship! The ship is on fire!" I saw clearly for a moment the face of one of the Vikings, who is also one of my best friends, smiling brightly, absolutely blissful. The burning of these pieces of the longship became our offering, our sacrifice, our tribal celebration, our sacred affirmation of the goodness of the transience of life. For that night, we were all one tribe, and we were back in the world of mythology again, and we were going to Valhalla, and life was very good.

I have paired this one immediately next to "Cold Dark and Lonely" because both of them express a relationship to death. But while the former piece laments the transience of things, "Going to Valhalla" joyfully celebrates that transience. It positively *delights* in the fact that we are all going to die some day. It's a silly song, with some very silly verses, performed at an up-beat rhythm that is easy to dance to.

"Air I Am..." (§276)

This piece, composed by Spanish-American druid Andreas Corben Arthen, was also one of the most popular pieces to appear in my survey. Along with it appeared two outstanding filk versions. The first, attributed to Prudence P, goes:

> Sam I am, Sam I am,
> I don't like green eggs and ham!

And the second, created by Michael Nabert, goes:

> Air, the pipe, Fire, the match,
> Water, beer, and Earth, the meat!

My informant told me that this particular variation is intended only for "Men's Mysteries"!

Songs from popular culture

Quite a few songs from popular culture have made it into the pagan musical repertoire. "We come from the mountain" (§312) was originally composed by Harry Belafonte, 'the King of Calypso'. Several informants told me that they started using this song after seeing Belafonte perform it on television's The Muppet Show! Also appearing in this collection: "All my life's a circle" (§292) by the American folk singer Harry Chapin, and "Hymn to Her" (§241) by The Pretenders, from the album *Get Close*. It seems that anything which expresses the magical power of circles, or landscapes, or living things, and so on, can become part of a pagan's repertoire of spiritual songs and teachings. The genius of the pagan community is its ability to gather ideas from a very eclectic variety of sources, and fit them together into an artistically coherent whole.

"Holy Water, Sacred Flame..." (§240)

My informant for this piece said: "As a devotee of Brighid, I really like this one, I only wish it didn't sound like London Bridge Is Falling Down!" (Aislinn Avalon, personal communication)

Closing Songs (§346 to §356)

As is surely obvious, these pieces are generally performed at the end of rituals. The saying "Merry meet, merry part, and merry meet again!", which appears in two of them, is a common parting affirmation. It appears in Gardner's Book of Shadows as the last line of the standard text of a Wiccan ritual. It is used to mark the end of rituals and ceremonies, and is also frequently used when people go home at the end of a gathering, festival, or party.

Twelfth Movement:

A Commentary

The Idea of a World-View.
The English word 'world-view' is a translation of the German word *Weltanschauung*, originally coined by the philosopher Albert Schweitzer. Alternative translations include 'world-conception' or 'theory of the universe'. It is the central concept in Schweitzer's 1923 work, *The Decay and the Restoration of Civilisation*. Here is how he defined it:

> The greatest of the spirit's tasks is to produce a theory of the universe. What is meant by a theory of the universe? It is the content of the thoughts of society and the individuals which compose it about the nature and object of the world in which they live, and the position and destiny of mankind and of individual men within it. What significance has the society in which I live and I myself in the world? What do we want to do in the world? What do we hope to get from it? What is our duty to it? The answer given by the majority to these fundamental questions about existence decides what the spirit is in which they and their age live. (Schweitzer, *The Decay and Restoration of Civilisation*, pg. 80-1)

A world-view is thus more than a group of beliefs about the nature of the world. It is also a bridge between those scientific or metaphysical beliefs, and the ethical beliefs about what people can and should do in response to the world. It is the intellectual narrative in terms of which the actions, choices, and purposes of individuals and groups make sense. It therefore has indispensable practical utility: it is the justification for a way of life, for individuals and for whole societies. And we cannot live without one. As Schweitzer says, "For individuals as for the community, life without a theory of things is a pathological disturbance of the higher capacity for self-direction." (*ibid*, pg. 86)

Schweitzer says that the purpose of a world-view is to preserve and edify civilisation. This assertion gives him a tool with which to judge a world-view: for not all world-views are all equal. Some are more conducive to the survival and the edification of human life than others. As an example he claims that once the ancient Roman Empire's world view was dominated by Stoicism, "the fate of the Mediterranean peoples was sealed. Thinking based on resignation, magnificent as it was, could not ensure a progress in a world-wide empire." (*ibid*, pg. 83) This is a partly misleading statement, since the early Roman empire was also highly imperialist. Its leaders believed that Rome had a special mission to bring universal peace and civilisation to the world. But Schweitzer's larger point must not be missed in the details. A world-view can have a distinctive character and identity, just as a person does. That character makes it fit or unfit for the task of preserving civilisation. Stoicism, the dominant world-view of the Roman empire (at least after Emperor Marcus Aurelius, if not before), is a world-view of passive resignation. It was therefore unsuited to the task of preserving the empire. Therefore, the empire was rendered vulnerable to internal corruption and external attack, and due to that vulnerability, it eventually fell.

In order to fulfill its task of preserving and edifying civilisation, Schweitzer says a world-view must have three particular qualities. First, it must be the product of sustained rational thought. "Only what has been well turned over in the thought of the many, and thus recognised as truth, possesses a natural power of conviction which will work on other minds and will continue to be effective. Only where there is a constant appeal to the need of a reflective view of things are all man's spiritual capacities called into activity." (*Ibid* pg. 86-7.) This is stipulated in order that it may help people come to an understanding of the world, and of one another. A world-view derived from unreflective instincts and impulses, in his view, cannot properly reflect reality, nor will it have sufficient power to motivate people to take action. Second, a functioning world-view must also be optimistic; and third, it must be ethical. Optimism he defines as the preference for existence over non-existence, and the affirmation that life is inherently valuable. As he says, "From this [optimistic] attitude to the universe and to life... originates activity directed to the improvement of the living conditions of individuals, of society, of nations and of humanity." Ethics he defines as "the activity of man directed to secure the inner perfection of his own personality." (*ibid* pg. 94) These last two points go together: for Schweitzer, they are the most important criteria which separate an acceptable world-view from an unacceptable one.

The reason for beginning this commentary with a description of the idea of a world-view is this. I claim that the literary testament of the contemporary movement, with all its eclectic borrowings and strange variations, expresses a valid a world-view in Schweitzer's original, philosophical meaning of the term. Although in many ways that world-view is multifaceted, with not one but several distinct threads of narrative, still it fulfils the criteria of being rational, optimistic, and ethical. The rationality of the pagan world view is born of *artistic and aesthetic integrity*. Its optimism is in its consistent affirmation of the inherent goodness of life. And its ethical dimension reveals itself in many levels. The Wiccan Rede offers a practical morality of personal freedom for yourself, and non-malevolence toward others. The Mystery, and other related teachings, offer a deeper and more contemplative morality based on identifying the earth as your body, and the Goddess as your own innermost spirit.

In this commentary, as in this whole book, my purpose is simply to describe and explain that world view, clearly and comprehensively, and in the best possible light. But the task of passing judgment upon it belongs to you.

The Word

In most contemporary pagan traditions, the experience of the sacred is asserted to be ineffable. It is a first-order, first-person experience that simply cannot be imparted or described in words. It belongs to the individual person who experiences it, and to no one else. This idea is reminiscent of the teaching in the first line of the Tao Te Ching: "The Tao that can be spoken is not the Tao". It may also be found in some Sufi teachings, for instance: "You who talk about Baraka may be the enemies of Baraka" (Shah, *The Way of the Sufi*, pg. 288). This implies that each person must seek out the presence of the divine on her own. Moreover, each person must make up her own mind concerning the meaning of the experience. No book or scripture or institutional authority could stand between you and the divine. This makes contemporary paganism attractive to individualist-minded people. But I think that the divine is *not* ineffable. People can, and do, speak of the sacred all the time. Paganism may not be a religion of "the book". But it is a religion of *the Word*.

Let me start my explanation with a quote from Shakespeare: "What's in a name? A rose by any other name would smell as sweet." This is an important truth: but a name is not worth nothing. The name makes the rose stand out for a moment. It draws special attention to the object so named. Without the name, the rose would smell as sweet, and the experience of smelling it would still be pleasurable. But the name is the word that *recognizes* the experience of the rose for what it is, by making it count for something. Thus without the name, the experience would have no identity. This thing with the soft petals, the fragrant perfume, the sharp thorns, *is* a rose. The name, therefore, is an instrument of knowledge: by means of the name, we *know* what something is. Shakespeare's quote could be completed thus: "A rose by any other name would smell as sweet – but we would not know what that sweet smell is, nor what it means."

The first order of words, in the experience of the sacred, is the *naming* of the presence of the sacred itself. This naming differentiates the spiritual from the ordinary, the sacred from the profane. Even if it is admitted that the spirit cannot be defined, and that it may be a massive mistake to talk about it with words at all, it may still be acknowledged that the spirit can be named. The act of naming something, while not quite the same as defining it, is an indispensable means of understanding it, noting its significance, and even appreciating it. Much of the beauty of any religious culture is in the magical and wonderful names that it gives to our spiritual experiences. Pagans prefer to give spiritual names to environmental things: the sun and moon, the animals and plants, the landforms and seas, and so on, all have the names of gods and goddesses, for instance. They give divine names to such things that are beautiful, invigorating, and pleasurable to see. They name such things with which human beings are already engaged in various relationships. Some of these relationships are biological, such as food production, air and water purification, light and warmth and so on. Some are cultural associations. Through these relationships, the act of naming is neither accidental nor arbitrary.

Yet the act of naming is also an act of *will*. Someone who names something has made a choice: a choice of a name, the choice to make something stand out from the background of the world. She imposes that choice upon the thing so named. To name something with a spiritual name is thus not only to recognize and acknowledge its spiritual significance. It is also to *create* that significance. The bestowal of a spiritual name thus *contributes* something to the thing named, which may or may not have been there before. But it does not add something extraneous, or something which could be removed again later, as one might add an extension to a house. It is to add something that, once added, becomes an intrinsic part of the thing's identity.

The names we have for the things we declare to be sacred and spiritual, and the names we have for the relationships which bind people to them, constitute a kind of Testament. For by giving something a divine name, the seeker *attests* that the thing with the sacred name *is* a sacred thing. Any religious Testament, old or new, is an elaborate and extended act of naming the sacred. Having named the sacred, it can then be *narrated*: that is, we can tell stories about it.

Can the wonders of the world not speak for themselves? If all that makes something spiritual is the act of naming it, then the way may be open for an arbitrary relativism. Yet some things in the world appear to be spiritual 'already', that is, whether or not someone has named them so. The warmth of a summer breeze, the colours of the trees in autumn, the faces of our friends and lovers, can be spiritual revelations, with or without a name. The sunlight in the early morning, the moonrise over the sea, the first buds sprouted from the soil in springtime, the songs of the birds, all appear to speak to us, regardless of what names we use for them.

To reply to this question, may I return to a concept which I left undefined earlier: 'presence'. The presence of the rose is the softness of its petals, the sharpness of its thorns, and so on. This presence is what speaks to us. Presence is that which is 'given' to perception by the embodied qualities of things in the world. It is what we experience when we touch, smell, and gaze upon the rose. Things 'speak' to us because they are 'present' to us, here and now. And what do they say? "My thorns are sharp", and "My petals are soft", and "My fragrance is sweet", and "My colour is lovely". Note that in each case a relationship is presupposed between the rose and one of the five human senses. Qualities like sharpness, softness, sweetness, and so on, belong to the rose, but they make sense only if someone is touching the rose, smelling it, gazing upon it. These qualities constitute the voices and the vocabulary by which the things of the world 'speak' to us. The notion of 'speech' which I am using here is very broad indeed. After all, I am describing how plants, animals, stones, weather events, even the sun, can 'speak', even though they have no vocal chords. But to paraphrase Marshal McLuhan, 'the presence is the message.' Things speak to us when we look upon them, touch them, smell them, and hear them. A transmission of meaning is in progress: and the message is nothing less than the *assertion of being*.

A spiritual event is an assertion of the being of the whole world, in and through some particular object or event in the world. A spiritual experience is one in which a comprehensive Word of Being is spoken. That Word of Being is "I Am Here". It is not a rootless "I Am", of the burning bush, which can be a reality only as an abstraction. The Word of Being is a grounded "I Am Here. I stand before you, I face you. I am offering myself to you." The Word of Being is a practical reality for both mind and body. It is an experience of something in the world both abstract and also tangible. It is abstract in that more than the material presentation is suggested in the experience. It is tangible in that it is an embodied experience: it is something seen, touched, heard, smelled, and tasted.

At the same time, the Word of Being is "Yes." For the Word not only asserts the Being of the world, it also affirms its goodness. This I think is a necessary logical connection. Just as it is a contradiction to say 'Life is of no value' while at the same time continuing to eat, drink, breathe, avoid harm, and do all the things necessary to protect and preserve life, so it is also a contradiction to assert one's own being without at the same time affirming the goodness of one's own being. In short, the act of asserting something must necessarily be the act of asserting its goodness. If something was not worthy of assertion, it would not be so asserted. Even in ordinary gift-giving, such as at birthday parties, this principle is in play. To offer something as a gift to another is at the same time to presuppose that the thing offered as a gift is valuable (if, indeed, the thing is offered as a genuine gift!), and that the recipient is deserving. So it is with the Word of

Being. To speak is at the same time to assert the rightness, the justice, the excellence of the message.

There may be more complex levels, where the Word of Being also poses questions, and suggests possibilities. For the spiritual event also asserts itself as a participant in one's own being, insofar as a relationship with oneself may be possible. Indeed in the spiritual event the whole world appears to offer itself to you as a gift. Everything that 'presents' itself to you is a gift: it is a 'present' in the here and now. The first order of words, then, is the Word of Being, the 'I am here' which is spoken by anything and everything. When we hear that word, we call it a spiritual experience.

The name is thus the second, and not the first, order of words in the spiritual experience. The most basic of names is a logical place-holder, like "The One", or "The All", or "The spiritual experience", or even the word "God". This name does no more than conveniently differentiate some event as special and distinct from other, more mundane and banal events. This is a useful thing to do, so don't get me wrong here. But sometimes it is not enough to simply classify a spiritual event into a convenient logical category. We therefore also designate spiritual events with personal names: we *address* them with the names of gods and goddesses. The names of the gods are, on this level of   interpretation, designators for spiritual or mystical events in the world. But they are *personal* designators. As such they necessarily imply that the event is *not* a mechanistic process which can be described in an objective or disinterested way. Rather, it suggests that the event is a being with which one could have a person-to-person relationship.

We do more than bestow names on the spiritual revelations around us. We also offer personal responses. What I shall call the third order of sacred words are those which we render in prayers, invocations, ritual charges, songs, mantras, and the like. Think of the word 'spell' for a moment. It is a noun, referring to a recitation of magically potent words, intended to bring about some change in the world. It is also a verb: it designates the activity of creating words by arranging letters together. Not all of our spells and letters are language-bound. Some, for instance, are image-bound. Some are music-bound. For we also express the sacred with art forms. Music has a special privilege here, for reasons that will be described later. Painting, architecture, poetry, sculpture, dance, and physical touching are all ways of speaking too, because they involve a transmission of thought and intention and feeling. In other words, there is a Word expressed in *any offering of meaning from one being to another*. The Word of Being that expresses the sacred is like an energy, passed from mouth to ear, and from hand to hand. It is also like an activity of *sharing*. Indeed, a spiritual event gains in power and value as it is shared. It is not the sort of good which diminishes as it is divided up. Indeed it cannot be divided up. While it can be given, it cannot be given "away": one does not lose anything in the act of giving. It is not a strategic resource like petroleum, for which if some people have more of it, others necessarily have less. Like language itself, each person grows more rich with Being the more it is shared with others. In this way it becomes an unlimited and infinitely renewable resource. The wisdom teachings in this collection, as well as the stories of the Goddess presented earlier, constitute a sacred vocabulary of this third order. But this makes them no less important. They too are expressions of a sacred presence: they too are variations of the Word of Being. One who offers a wisdom teaching to another is acting, in part, as the mouthpiece for the comprehensive divinity of the world. Moreover, the third order of words can do something which is not done by the assertion of being alone: the wisdom teaching *interprets* the spiritual experience. The Word of Being, on its own, only asserts itself: it does not explain anything. But the wisdom teaching, the spell or invocation, the proverb, the motto of a deity, and so on, are expressed on the personal, social, or other practical level. Mythology can be included here too: mythology expresses the

Word of Being through storytelling. These things are able to *teach* and to *guide* in ways that the unqualified Word of Being cannot.

The Word of Being must be spoken aloud to have full effect. Indeed, many religious traditions insist that sacred teachings, stories, invocations, and so on, have to be recited out loud. The full impact of some testaments is not available to someone who reads it silently to himself. The Koran, for instance, cannot just be read: it has to be recited (and to many Muslims, it has to be *sung*). Similar observations can be made of Christians reciting the Old Testament Psalms with Gregorian Chant. And the Hindus also claim that the Vedas and Upanishads have to be recited or sung out loud to be experienced and understood properly. Therefore they have in their tradition a collection of thousands of *mantras*. Some are only one or two words long, some are complete sentences, and some are linked verses. The Indian philosopher Sri Aurobindo describes the importance of mantra as follows:

> The language of the Veda is itself a *sruti*, a rhythm not composed by the intellect but heard, a divine Word that came vibrating out of the Infinite to the inner audience of the man who had previously made himself fit for the impersonal knowledge. (Aurobindo, *The Secret of the Veda*, pg. 6)

In orthodox Hinduism, a person makes himself fit to receive the divine knowledge of the Veda by performing *puja* (the ritual offering of flowers, incense, buttermilk, honey, etc.), by meditating, sometimes by abstaining from meat-eating and sex, and ultimately by living in accord with Hinduism's moral teachings. But what I wish to draw attention to is Aurobindo's suggestion that mantras are words or phrases of power. When they are spoken or sung out loud, an energy is released (whether you know it or not) from the centre of the universe, expressive of the truth, carrying with it the presence of the Atman. It is capable of bringing about a new or changed reality; some say on a psychological level, some say on both psychological and on material levels. The singer has to understand that when singing a mantra, therefore, he's playing with fire. This may be why, by the way, at some point in the history of Hinduism, responsibility for reciting the most important and powerful mantras was handed over to specialists: the Brahmin, the priests. This may also be why so many Hindu traditions emphasize that certain things have to be learned from a guru, and can't be learned on your own. Of course, in popular Hinduism all kinds of people use mantras all the time, and there is nothing particularly elitist about it. But at some time in history, the most effective and powerful of mantras, the ones with the most *resonance* (to borrow a term from the physics of sound), were eventually memorized and written down, so that other practitioners and future generations could benefit from them. That's what the Vedas are: in large part, they are written records of mantras that were found by practical trial-and-error to work very well. And then people began to write theological, philosophical, and poetic commentary on those mantras.

In the spiritual thought of India, God is not a 'thing', nor exactly a person. Rather, God is an *activity*. God is a divine 'event', as well as a deity with a name and a personality. Western mystics often say the sensation of the presence of the Atman is an interior sensation: it is something felt within the mind and heart. In India, the divine is *embodied*; it is part of the material world. God is 'what happens' in the universe. Of course Hinduism also holds that the embodied world is an illusion, but never mind that for now: the point is that, as an embodied presence, the divine is something you can see and hear with your eyes and ears. The metaphysics is very 'minimalist' here: there is no need to posit the existence of afterlife realms or higher states of being, nor special modes of consciousness which are able to perceive it. It is enough to say that within, behind, or beneath things, there is an extra presence, something like a thought or a consciousness, which is very subtle, and escapes most people's attention. But with the right perceptual attitude, or under the right circumstances, or even when you least expect it, you can see it with your eyes. You can see the Atman manifesting itself in landscapes, weather events, trees, animals, the sun and moon, and so on. You can see it in the works of human hands too: such as in temple architecture, and statues and icons of deities, in paintings that depict scenes from mythology, and in the abstract symbolism of mandalas. You can see it in the face of the *guru*, the religious teacher, or more generally in the faces of other people. The point of meditation, and of *puja* and so on, is to help you to learn what you should be looking for. That's why Hindus offer *puja* to trees, to statues of gods, to the *guru*, and so on. In Tantrayana, the participants offer *puja* to each other: to their friends and loved ones, for they see the divine within their faces too.

The second, related point, more germane to the topic of words, wisdom teachings, and circle songs, is that the embodied, manifest presence of the Atman is also something that you can *hear*. Again, the metaphysics involved is very simple: you don't need to be in an advanced meditative trance-state to hear the divine, speaking in and with the sounds of the world. The word *mantra*, to most of us, denotes a special word or phrase, like a prayer and magic spell combined, which is recited during meditation or ceremony. In India it means a little more than that: it also means to *hear and to be heard* by the deity. It corresponds with *darsan*, which is to see and be seen by the deity. Both of those activities together, coupled with the offering of a gift, constitutes *puja*. So the *mantra* is not just the words that are spoken, but also the activity of speaking them, and the experience of hearing them.

There's a tradition of Hindu philosophy called the Mimamsa school, which is distinctive for suggesting that all sounds have an extra, mystical meaning. No relativism is suggested here: the extra meaning is not a matter of someone's choice or opinion, but is related to an eternal meaning and an ultimate reality. The word for this part of a sound is *shabda*. No human being creates or produces *shabda*, it is produced by the universe itself. It would be not quite right to say that every sound has a piece of *shabda* within it. It would be closer to the truth to say that every sound participates in the ultimate sound of the universe, the cosmic Word that pronounces the truth and order of things: that participation is *shabda*. Another philosophical school, called the Grammarians, accepts this theory but add that the cosmic order of the world manifests in the diversity of all the words that people ever say. Grammarians emphasise the diversity over the unity, although they do not deny the underlying unity. They also hold that every element of consciousness is attached to a word; there is no consciousness without words and without language, for words, language and consciousness is inextricably combined. But people can obscure the power of *shabda* inherent in words by, for instance, telling lies, being deceitful, by ignorance or absent-mindedness, even by malicious gossip. This, of course, has a detrimental effect on one's karma. Not only the experience, but also the content, of one's mantra, is therefore vitally important. Words are powerful things: words call forth realities and force the mind to acknowledge them.

While I was writing this book, I described this meditation on the Word of Being to a friend of mine. He listened patiently, and then he pointed to the window and said: "Have you seen what's out there?" His point was that this meditation cannot ignore social and environmental realities. What Word of Being was spoken by Hurricane Katrina? What about an earthquake, a forest fire, a tsunami? What sacred "Yes" is to be heard in human disasters like sexual violence and murder? How, if at all, can this meditation be sustained in the face of warfare, international terrorism, genocide, or any other form of organized political aggression?

In the Pagan world view, death is not evil, and not to be feared or avoided. Nor is it to be 'ignored' or 'bypassed' by emphasizing after-life realities where the soul may journey after death. A dignified death can say 'Yes' to life, for instance if the life of an animal or plant is taken so that we can eat. A funeral can often say 'Yes' to life, for instance if a particularly well loved person leaves behind a legacy of wisdom and knowledge that others may continue to enjoy. The whole of the cycle of life, death, and rebirth is acknowledged in paganism as a sacred activity, the working out of the divine presence in all things. Even a natural disaster, therefore, has a place in the organic functioning of the world, the totality of which is ultimately life-affirming and life-supportive. Were it otherwise, the planetary ecosystem would have digested itself and collapsed billions of years ago. Of course, since many pagans recognize the divine in the natural world, they are worried about climate change and global warming. Industrial pollution, car exhaust, and related human products, insofar as the contribute to creating more natural disasters than would normally happen, are therefore seen by many pagans as expressions of disregard or contempt for our environmental relationships. But otherwise, a natural disaster is as much a part of the world's Being, as much an immensity, as a natural wonder. It too can inspire amazement and magic, even if it also inspires fear for one's safety. It too is speaking its Word, by its presence: and its Word is, "Here I am — so what are you going to do about it?"

As to the question of whether there is a sacred 'Yes' in the actions of a violent criminal, I would like to say this. For any conscious, intelligent being that claims to possess free will, the sacred 'Yes' must be *chosen*. Each person's presence alone is still a sacred "I am Here" – but this Word of Being can only be positive and life-affirming if that person makes it so by his actions. A perpetrator of violence is someone whose Word of Being is life-negating, or egotistical, or even in pathological disorder. It is the Word of a person who thinks he can strengthen himself by weakening others. His actions aim to *impose* his presence on others; to possess them, or destroy them. This is not a natural or automatic process, like the organic functions of an ecosystem. It is a choice. Likewise, the actions that aim to *share* one's presence with others, and thereby respect and uplift them, is also a choice. I must therefore modify my thesis. A survivour of violence and trauma may find that there is no life-affirming 'Yes' in the presence of her attacker. Not all instances of the Word of Being, it seems, are beautiful and good. But there could be a 'Yes' in a trauma-survivour's choice of response to the occasion. Some people learn values like friendship and courage and perseverance only after they have endured a disease, a serious injury, a disability, or some other kind of trauma. (Having said that, there is no one in the pagan community who would wish such things upon others!) Not only learning, but also healing, may play a role here. Healing, in a pagan perspective, is the process of restoring a person's ability to speak a sacred 'Yes' in response to whatever losses, struggles, or traumas she has experienced.

The Song

The Word of Being, the "I am Here!" by which things and people are present to each other, is not necessarily a spoken word. It is also, very often, a word that one must *sing*. The Testament of contemporary Paganism cannot be written down (this book notwithstanding!). This is not because the testament is ineffable: rather, it is because the written word is not its proper medium. That proper medium is *music*. It may be better, therefore, to refine my account here yet again, and speak of a *Song* of Being.

Music features in so many of the important social and cultural events in our lives. Even in a modern, industrialized civilisation, music features in political ceremonies and affairs of state, such as the opening of Parliament, or the inauguration of newly elected governments. It appears in college and university graduations, when the professors, deans, and other important people parade to a stage accompanied by a fanfare. At my high school, which was in a town founded by Scotsmen, the parade of senior teachers and administrators are led to the stage by a bagpipe player, wearing full Highland regalia. Music also appears in sporting events: the singing of a national anthem just before a game begins. Major international tournaments, like the Olympics, will have pop stars, rock bands, or even opera singers perform at the opening ceremonies. Religious ritual has used music right from the very beginning. Some of the oldest religious buildings in the world, including Neolithic monuments like Newgrange, have extraordinary acoustic properties, suggesting that they were deliberately designed to produce or amplify certain kinds of sounds.

The production of sounds is a natural and normal activity for almost every living being in the animal kingdom. Indeed, every animal has within its body two built-in musical instruments. The first is the voice. Marvin Harris, an American anthropologist, suggested that the voice emerged as our primary means of communicating, winning out over posturing and touching and other things animals do to get their point across, because it enables us to communicate whilst we are busily doing something else with our hands. Food preparation, or play, or combat, or any other work performed with the hands, as well as rest, can continue uninterrupted while we are speaking. Having discovered that by making sounds we can do more with our hands, it is not a long leap to the next discovery, which is that we can do things with our voices too. Perhaps we started by imitating the sounds of animals, or of natural phenomenon like rain, wind, ocean waves, and thunder. As soon as vocalized phonemes became associated with experiences and events, the seed of language and of music was planted in the mind.

The other musical instrument all animals are born with is the heart. Within everyone's breast is a little drum, tirelessly beating out its rhythm. A normal human heart rate is sixty beats per minute, when at rest. We live our whole lives according to this rhythm: it speeds up when we are working or exerting ourselves, and slows down when at rest. Hence we automatically, *naturally* understand that fast rhythms mean action and excitement, and slower rhythms are more introspective.

Arguably, we have more music in us than that. The circadian cycle, which is the cycle of sleeping and waking, can be interpreted as a musical rhythm. The left-right, left-right action of walking produces a rhythm as obvious as a heartbeat. Breathing gives us a rhythm as steady as a heartbeat too.

Music, clearly, has a special relation to our minds and bodies. It resonates with our bones and internal organs. If someone was making a beat by thumping her foot and clapping her hands, one after the other, you would know instantly which was the down beat and which was the back beat. This is because it is already in the structure of your brain to hear music and understand it. Music has specific emotional effects: In the first few bars of any song, even before the singer has begun, we know right away whether we are hearing a rough, energetic song, or a soft romantic love song. Even the descriptive words I am using here, like 'rough' and 'soft', bear witness to the sensuality of music: we tend to describe it with the metaphors of touch, texture, and shape.

The brain's kinestethic motor cortex is closely linked to the auditory cortex: it augments the experience of sound by corresponding sounds to muscles in the body. Low sounds correspond to the muscles of the lower body, like the legs or abdomen; mid-level and high sounds to the arms and upper body. This effect also produces endorphins, and so certain kinds of sounds, especially the sounds which follow the resolution of dissonance or the completion of a melodic phrase, are accompanied by neuro-chemical events in the brain that manipulate our emotions.

There is also a side to music which is purely abstract and intellectual. It has to do with the mathematical relations between notes and rests, with harmony and resonance and dissonance, with the structure of melodies and the relation to the passage of time in a performance, and so on. The abstract side of music gains its significance and meaning by the coherence of its internal logic, not by its correspondence to a fact or an experience of the world. The degree to which music is mathematically complete is a major measure of its beauty and excellence. An early Greek religious and intellectual movement known as the Pythagoreans were the first people in Western civilisation to discover and exploit this. They found, for instance, that by using strings of different lengths, they could find the geometrical relations between musical notes. As we would understand it today, their experiments enabled them to measure *frequencies*, and find the relations between frequencies. They found, for instance, that two strings, one exactly twice the length of the other, will play the same note: the long string plays it at a lower pitch, and the shorter string at a higher pitch. Today we call this relation the octave. The Pythagoreans thought these relations were the key to understanding the universe itself. Being abstract and intellectual, being borne of pure logic, they were therefore not subject to the transformations of time and vicissitudes of fate and fortune, and therefore eternal, perfect, and divine. To a Pythagorean, God is a mathematician.

Music is thus a true universal language. The emotional response that good music can produce is also universal, for the simple reason that the neurology and physiology which music affects is basically the same for the entire human race. Its principles of internal logic, like rhythm, melody, and harmony, are things anyone can understand, since they depend on rational principles that can be grasped by anyone who is not missing his brain.

As almost all religious seekers know, music is one of the easiest ways to induce a trance state in the mind, as a preparation for a spiritual experience. A good grove can get a foothold in your consciousness whether you want it there or not. It lifts you from your present mental and emotional place and takes you elsewhere. Physiologically, it triggers the brain to produce various neurotransmitters from endorphins to hormones. And these physiological responses prepare the mind for further religious experiences. They might be interpreted as an invigoration of the energy in our 'other' physiology, the psychic physiology of the chakras and the meridians. Or it might be interpreted as a spiritual transportation-device that leads to contact with the divine. The philosopher Rudolph Otto, in *The Idea of the Holy* (1923), discusses the concept of "numinous sounds". These are sounds that have the certain hard-to-define property of creating or making possible an experience of the divine, because they sound as if they are coming *from* the divine. A numinous sound is a sound that attracts and demands your full attention: it raises up the hairs on the back of your neck, gives you shivers up and down your spine, and all over your skin. It sounds as if there's a *voice* definitely there, but it is coming from all around, from the very centre of the earth or the top of the sky, and from within the deepest part of your own being. Part of the reason that numinous sounds are effective may be physiological, as already described. But there is also a phenomenological claim here. A numinous sound is a sound which you experience as more than just a sound. It is a sound which *suggests realities beyond itself.* Just as a door left ajar suggests the room on the other side which you cannot yet see, and just as a hilltop suggests an unexplored valley on the other side, so does a numinous sound suggest that it is more than what meets the ear. However much you listen, there is more still to hear. To someone with the right attitude, the numinous sound provokes thought and ignites the imagination, and stimulates the sense of wonder.

Numinous sounds often depend for their power on social contexts. A car horn during rush hour is not a numinous sound; a Tibetan mountain horn is. Glasses clinking together as people drink a toast is not a numinous sound; a bell at the top of a church bell tower is. An economics professor lecturing on fiscal policy is not speaking with a numinous voice; a classically trained actor reciting a Shakespearean sonnet is. Most of the time, we recognise

334 A Pagan Testament

numinous sounds because we recognise the social contexts in which numinous sounds belong. But this, I think, takes nothing away from the experience. Indeed it may add to it: if we were constantly surrounded on all sides by numinous sounds (as in fact some spiritual teachers assert is the case), there wouldn't be anything special about the experience. Without the contrast to ordinary, utilitarian sounds, the very idea of numinous sound might not have any meaning.

The power of the numinous sound, by the way, is the main reason that various conservative or fundamentalist religions sometimes control the kind of music that their adherents are allowed to listen to. There might also be controls placed on whether or not they may dance to it, and what dances they can do. The reason is essentially political: the leaders of these religions have to be able to present themselves as the sole and exclusive suppliers of the numinous experience. This has nothing to do with spirituality, and everything to do with power, allegiance, and social control. For if people learned that through music they could obtain their own spiritual experiences, they would not have much need for authoritarian kinds of spiritual leadership.

Having said that, however, the most spiritually powerful music is usually music produced not individually but collaboratively: in bands, groups, choirs, and orchestras. Some physical aspects of sound like constructive interference and harmonic resonance simply cannot be produced by one voice alone (unless the singer is in a specially designed space). And obviously the more voices or instruments are added to the orchestra, the more possibilities there are for making different sounds, and exploring different musical relations like harmony, dissonance, resonance, and so on. With that comes extra physiological, intellectual, and emotional effects on the listeners and performers. These groups need leaders, orchestra conductors for instance, to keep everyone tuned to the same key, and in time to the same beat. Starhawk's categorical distinctions between different kinds of power may be useful here. The political control of a religious fundamentalist who won't let his parishioners listen to rock and roll, exercises what she calls "power-over". This kind of power is domineering, hierarchical, and in her view ultimately oppressive therefore. The members of a choir, or an orchestra, or a rock band, or a drumming group, and so on, collaborate with each other to make the most of their musical talents: they exercise "power-with". This kind of power is co-operative, non-hierarchical, and therefore, in her view, liberating.

It takes control to produce excellent music. But it is a sense of control in which you let go, lose yourself. It is the music that takes control of the performer, not the performer who controls the music. 'Power-over', of a sort, is still happening. But the performer is being controlled by the spirit. No one is being exploited or oppressed. Therefore, Starhawk calls it "power-from-within".

It is a great credit to Paganism, then, that of the five things mentioned in the Charge of the Goddess, 'make music' and 'sing' are two of them. Performing music is for me the finest of rituals, and its value only increases the more that it is shared.

Some of you may be familiar with the distinction between two kinds of art: the *Apolline* and the *Dionysian*. A quick way to distinguish these two categories may be like this. Apolline art is named for the Greek god Apollo, god of the sun. It is the art of high civilisation and reason. Its power is largely intellectual: it is subtle, refined, yet no less enchanting and sublime, like a half-misty day at sunrise. Dionysian art is named for Dionysus, one of the Greek gods of nature. His art emerges from wildness, passion, madness, and energetic release. His music is like a thunderstorm. Its power comes from natural forces, instincts, animal drives and passions, and a zest for life that does not rigorously exclude what is dangerous and frightening. This categorical distinction between these two kinds of art was invented in 1871 by the German philosopher Friedrich Nietzsche, and published in his first book,

The Birth of Tragedy: Out of the Spirit of Music. As he saw it, all art is a form of creative interpretation and representation of life. But this act of creation passes through one of two 'filters' or 'lenses'. Apolline art is life re-presented or re-created through *dreams*; Dionysian art, through *intoxication*. The artist reacts or responds to the reality of the world as re-presented to her in dreams, or in ecstasy. Both are forms of trance, or of altered consciousness or experience, but they re-present the world in different ways. Nietzsche emphasizes Dionysian art throughout his text, since he thought Dionysian experience doesn't get enough attention and respect. But all throughout *The Birth of Tragedy*, he insists that the best art is a product of both of them together. They complement each other, even while they also oppose each other. An artist who is able to achieve a marriage between the two can claim to have achieved true artistic excellence and greatness.

In any given work of art, therefore, there are not one but two forces: they both co-operate with each other and contradict each other, at one and the same time. Yet if this tension is pulled just right, *art* will happen: art which Nietzsche calls "the metaphysical activity of man". (*The Birth of Tragedy*, pg. 7-8) This, by the way, is an ancient wisdom: Aristotle's *Metaphysics* begins with a discussion of art and the senses. That's what I think is missing from the eastern mystical understanding of sacred music, as described earlier. It's not just that the mantra or the force of *shabda* makes the original spiritual forces of the world present to you. Rather, it's also that the activity of artistic creation, through the Apolline and Dionysian experiences of dream and of ecstasy, gives the spiritual world its very existence. In other words, art does not just represent the world, or give a manifest presence to its immanent sacred powers. Art also *creates* the world.

Here's the way Nietzsche's argument goes. The ancient Greeks knew that the world was a rough and unpredictable place. Human life, as they saw it, is contended by violent storms, dangerous landscapes, wild animals, human criminals, tragic twists of fortune, and the inevitability of death. Art is what helps us to *cope:* art helps us to accept this reality, and go on living in this difficult world, without caving in to resignation, or terror. Art helps us cope with the world by *justifying* human existence, elevating all these things to the level of the divine, re-presenting all human and natural life as if it is the life of the gods. Here are Nietzsche's own words:

> The Greeks knew and felt the fears and horrors of existence: in order to be able to live at all they had to interpose the radiant dream-birth of the Olympians between themselves and these horrors... In order to live, the Greeks were profoundly compelled to create those gods. We might imagine their origin as follows: the Apolline impulse to beauty led, in gradual stages, from the original Titanic order of the gods of fear to the Olympian order of the gods of joy, just as roses sprout on thorn-bushes. How else could life have been borne by a race so sensitive, so impetuous in their desires, so uniquely capable of *suffering*, if it had not been revealed to them, haloed in a higher glory, in their gods? The same impulse that calls art into existence, the complement and apotheosis of existence, also created the Olympian world with which the Hellenic 'will' held up a transfiguring mirror to itself. Thus the gods provide a justification for the life of man by living it themselves. (Nietzsche, *The Birth of Tragedy*, pg. 22.)

Nietzsche is presupposing the work of the philosopher Ludwig Feuerbach, a contemporary of his. Feuerbach wrote a masterwork text on religion, *The Essence of Christianity*, to show how religion is a re-presentation of ourselves and of human life in an idealized way. In other words, it is an act of projecting human qualities on to God. But where Feuerbach thought that this meant all religion is therefore a contemptible fraud, Nietzsche thought this is something to celebrate. A god, as he saw it (at least in his earlier

writings) is a reflection or representation of humanity *as*
something divine. That reflection or representation of human life
was a justification of human life. Here is how the passage from
The Birth of Tragedy continues:

> Amongst the Greeks the 'will' wished to contemplate itself, in
> the transfiguration of genius and the world of art; in order to
> glorify themselves, its creations had to feel worthy of glorifi-
> cation. They had to see themselves in a higher sphere, without
> this contemplation seeming either a command or a reproach. It
> was in this sphere of beauty that they saw reflections of
> themselves, the Olympians. (*The Birth of Tragedy*, pg. 24.)

It's also important to understand that when Nietzsche wrote *The
Birth of Tragedy*, he wasn't just calling for a revival of the heady
days of Greek myth and art and drama. He thought that just such
a revival was already happening. In fact he thought it was
especially personified in three artists: Johann Wolfgang von
Goethe, Ludwig van Beethoven, and Richard Wagner. His book is
actually dedicated to Wagner, whom he knew personally. Their
friendship, by the way, was not to last. After Wagner composed
the opera *Tristan and Isolde*, Nietzsche thought that Wagner had
caved in to Christian sentimentality, and wanted nothing more to
do with him.

Nietzsche's understanding of the Apolline Dream and the
Dionysian Ecstasy offers something which we do not find in the
Eastern idea of the Mantra. With music, as with art, we do more
than conjure up or call forth or participate in a pre-existing divine
reality. We actually become involved in *creating* that reality. And
yet we do not create our world out of nothing. We re-fashion our
world from the way we respond to how it appears to us, first of
all in dreams, visions, trances, intellectual contemplation, and
meditative feelings, and secondly in ecstasy, intoxication, passion,
sexuality, release, and even blind insanity. Because through art

we are co-creators of reality, we can therefore survive the unpredictability of fortune and the tragedy of death. We can even heal ourselves, and lift ourselves up: from beings who aim for mere survival, to beings who aim for civilization and excellence.

In the great collection of Pagan circle songs, it seems there is already a wisdom-tradition, mostly orally transmitted, in which the movement's most important beliefs, principles, proverbs, and ideas are expressed with great clarity and beauty. I want to know if there is a way for contemporary Pagans to find the Apolline and the Dionysian power of the mantra in their own circle songs. To do that, we might return again to a first question: Why does music move us? Most people, when asked why a certain piece of music moves them, answer by saying, "because I like it." And then when asked why they like it, they just repeat themselves: "I like it because I like it." I think this answer is honest, but not particularly informative. Logically, it's a circular argument. It tells us nothing, really, about what makes music likable. It merely expresses a strong personal preference.

Someone might add, if pushed, that musical appreciation is so rooted in culture and personal taste that what one person finds beautiful may be repugnant to another, and there is no way to establish any kind of music as universally or objectively beautiful. Western world people, for instance, often don't understand the subtleties and the painstaking precision that goes into traditional Chinese or Japanese music: to our ears, they seem to keep hitting the same five notes over and over again. On that basis it is often concluded that music and art and beauty is inherently personal, and so if you like something, then that's all there is to say about it. And then, as a final coup-de-grace, someone might conclude, "Beauty is in the eye of the beholder."

But if it is assumed from the beginning that musical taste is deeply personal, or relative to culture, then there may be no point in using music to reach out to other people and to share the experience. We would be forced to assume that other people are likely to have a different understanding of music, hand in hand with their different preferences, different emotional responses, and different experiences. Therefore we would have no obvious way to offer to each other our thoughts and feelings and expressions through music. But it is obvious that music *does*, in fact, bring people together. For one thing, music is often performed collaboratively. People make music in groups: from small barbershop quartets to hundred-piece symphony orchestras. There is also a collaborative relationship between a composer and a performer, even if the composer has been dead for two hundred years. And, of course, anyone who has ever been to a dance club or a rave understands the singularity of purpose – to dance – held in common by everyone there. People might say that they 'tune out the world' and 'lose themselves in the music', or that by dancing to the music they wrap themselves up in a private world. But it is still the case that everyone is responding in a similar way to the same sound. To claim that in the situation of a dance everyone is having their own different experience is to make a mountain out of a molehill. The fact is that the experience is common to everyone there, in its broadest and most general sense.

Where the first conclusion, "I like it because I like it" is misleading, the second one, "Beauty is in the eye of the beholder", is, in my view, even more misleading. The reality is that beauty always strikes you as if from outside. It grabs you, takes you away, shakes you up, holds you in a state of quiescence or of shock. Beauty catches you by accident or by surprise – if it were only the beholder's feeling or choice that rendered things beautiful, that wouldn't happen. It holds you in a state of aesthetic arrest, to use James Joyce' term; but you don't feel imprisoned. In fact you feel free. The only small bit of truth in the old colloquialism is that you have to be the sort of person who is open and receptive to the aesthetic experience. Context matters too: you are less likely to be struck by the art of a concert violinist if you find him in a subway station, instead of in Massey Hall. But it is beauty itself which takes over your world for a time—not only, nor simply, the emotional or mental act of beholding beauty. And sometimes beauty catches you even when you are unprepared. The full truth is that beauty imposes its presence on *you*, and holds you in *its* eye. Have you ever been unable to look away from a blossoming flower in a garden, a distinct building in an old part of town, a glowing ember in a fireplace? Have you ever been unable to turn the radio off because of the song being played? Have you never been forced to stop in your tracks because of a beautiful sunset in the sky, or a beautiful person walking by? If not, then you probably haven't yet had a genuine aesthetic experience. The truth is that beauty catches you unawares, surprises you, *arrests* you. It makes you stop what you are doing, and makes you want to do something else, or even to *be* something else. Beauty *arouses* the life within us, and flows it through every vein and muscle in the body, like a gentle flame, or else like a torrential shower. Only after that resurgence of life has happened does the eye of the beholder properly open.

Simple Advice.

The Wiccan Rede (§56, §111), among the small collection of pieces which comprises this pagan testament, is one of the few wisdom-teachings obviously presented as a statement of moral principle. The name of the piece, 'Rede', is normally taken to mean 'advice' (whether the etymology here is correct is unverifiable) and so it is not presented as a binding moral law. And yet most modern Wiccans certainly treat it as such. Commitment to the Wiccan Rede is one of the only criteria for membership in the largest Wiccan religious organisation in the United States, the Covenant of the Goddess. The whole of the Rede is essentially a poem, composed by Doreen Valiente probably around 1950, consisting of twenty-six stanzas of two lines each. The last two lines are the most well known, and are sometimes mistaken for the whole thing. "Eight words the Wiccan Rede fulfill: An it harm none, do what you will." (§56, §111) These two lines are usually treated by Wiccans as if it is a self-sufficient statement of ethics, at least on par with central statements of Christian ethics like the Golden Rule, "Do unto others as you would have them do unto you". These principles appear straightforward, clear, and practical. But if these principles are so simple, where did the library of commentary come from? Let it suffice for the current purpose to say that early Christians were interested in knowing more about the meaning of their ethical principles, and wanted to use them for larger, intellectual or contemplative purposes. For instance, they were interested to know whether Christ's commandments could be integrated with the various philosophical ideas inherited from pre-Christian civilisations like Greece, Rome, and various near-eastern societies. The Wiccan Rede likewise contains its own stock of philosophical questions.

The Wiccan Rede's central principle is 'harm none'. This is an essentially Utilitarian idea. It is no great surprise that Valiente hit upon it. For one thing, when Wicca was created it was an almost immediate media sensation. Tabloid newspapers were regularly reporting on pagan rituals, and following the lives of the participants of those rituals. Valiente may have wanted to send the message that Wicca is no threat to anyone or anything. With 'harm none' as its moral principle, there is no room for sacrifice, or cannibalism, or any of the other gruesome things associated with Witchcraft.

Another reason for the Utilitarianism of the Rede may be because, like Wicca, Utilitarianism was born in England, with authors like Jeremy Bentham, John Stewart Mill, G.E. Moore, and Henry Sidgewick. The last two authors were lecturing and publishing in Valiente's lifetime, although it is probably impossible to tell whether she was reading their books. But by her time, Utilitarian ideas were already well entrenched in the world-view of British culture. Utilitarian ideas were part of the world-view that made the Industrial Revolution possible. And the enormous amount of wealth and mechanical power provided by industrial-isation gave Utilitarian thinking a practical confirmation. For Utilitarianism and industrialisation are alike in that the primary location of value is an action's consequences and *results*, whether material or immaterial. Utilitarianism is a moral theory which states that the right action is that which results in the best conse-quences. The best consequences are those which cause the greatest benefit and the least harm, to those affected by the action. In the words of John Stewart Mill, whose expression of the Utilitarian central principle is one of the classics:

> The creed which accepts as the foundation of morals, Utility, or the Greatest Happiness Principle, holds that actions are right in proportion as they tend to promote happiness, wrong as they tend to produce the reverse of happiness. By happiness is intended pleasure, and the absence of pain; by unhappiness, pain, and the privation of pleasure. (Mill, *Utilitarianism*, pg.118)

On this Utilitarian theory, actions are to be judged right or wrong only by their consequences. Nothing else matters. Right actions are, simply, the ones with the best consequences. In at least one respect, this was a revolutionary idea for its time. Prior to Bentham, the vast majority of thinkers in the Western tradition held that actions were judged according to laws or standards of duty, received from some conception of pure reason, or human nature, or divine command. Utilitarianism sweeps all of that aside. For Utilitarians, there are situations in which some action can be right, and in other situations the same action can be wrong; this is determined by the amount of pain and pleasure the action causes, or can be expected to cause. Utilitarianism is thus very flexible. Since it is not primarily a morality based on rules and duties, it can provide relief to those who think that rule-based or duty-based systems of morality are oppressive, dogmatic, or constraining (leaving aside the possibility that 'harm none' can be a kind of a rule in itself).

'Harm none' is similar to a variation of the basic Utilitarian principle, usually called 'negative Utilitarianism', which states that we should concern ourselves not with the maximisation of happiness but primarily with the minimisation of harm. While it is categorically impossible to 'harm none', to minimise suffering and pain is perfectly plausible as a general moral principle. This is the kind of Utilitarianism asserted in the 20th century by G.E. Moore, and in the ancient world by Epicurius. Another form of it is known to us as the Hippocratic Oath. Crafted around 430 BCE, the Oath was taken by all medical doctors at the beginning of their careers. It calls upon them to swear to the gods Apollo and Aesculapius "to help the sick to the best of my ability and judgment" and to "abstain from harming or wronging any man by it" (*Hippocratic Writings* pg. 67). But this was a professional obligation for doctors, not as a comprehensive ethical statement for all people. Still, 'harm none' has intuitive appeal: for people are often more able to tell what harms or sufferings they want to avoid, than what benefits or pleasures they want to pursue. It might be hard to decide whether Matt Halischuck's happiness when he scored the winning goal for Canada in the 2008 World Junior Hockey tournament is as good, or better, or not as good, as the happiness my sister experienced when each of her children were born, or the happiness I experience writing poetry. But many people would also say it is painful to be injured in a hockey game, to give birth to a child, and to read my poetry. And it is much easier to measure which of these three examples is the most painful. We are often more sure of what we do not want, than of what we do want. When faced with some range of choices, it is usually easy to tell which one will result in the least harm. It is thus very well suited to handle most of our practical ethical problems.

However, 'Harm none' is weak in this very important way. A

life dedicated to nothing more than 'harming none' could successfully bring the least possible amount of harm into the world without involving any of the things that make life worth living. Such a life could successfully harm none and yet miss out on art and music, love and friendship, education and learning, or even spiritual discovery. The Wiccan Rede is utterly incapable of offering any advice at all concerning how we are to live, nor how we should plan our lives. Nor can it tell us anything about what things or experiences make life go well. It tells us what 'bads' to avoid but not what 'goods' to pursue. It therefore does not offer any positive goals to strive for, nor any purposes to live for. And yet these are the very things that a person wishing to lead a spiritual life needs to know most. One could go through the whole of life harming none, or causing as little harm as possible, and yet never achieve any state of mind or style of life worthy of being called 'spiritual'. Indeed, a life dedicated to the personal goal of minimising harm would be a very mundane, ordinary, and boring life, remarkable only for the amount of work it requires. That, it seems to me, is fundamentally contrary to the historical understanding of 'paganism', with its Dionysian celebration of 'the good life': feasting and drinking, singing and dancing, and sexual indulgence, and the pursuit of human excellence in almost any kind of endeavour. There isn't a hint of 'harm none' in any of these things. Yet they are a part of the classical and romantic picture of the pagan life. Instances of this picture appear frequently in the folklore collection in this book. Furthermore, there are several traditions and practices which Paganism which affirms the way death is necessary for life, and the way life is intertwined with death. Traditions associated with hunting are chief among them. We can also look to harvest traditions like the "Corn King", the human effigy made from sheaves of freshly cut wheat, which is ceremonially set on fire. 'Harm None' has no place in these traditions.

We need a principle which requires us to do more than just

minimise harm. We need a principle that not only denounces the wrong and the bad, but also affirms the excellent and the good. We need a principle that can explain what it means to pursue a spiritual life, and why it is right and good to pursue it. To find that principle, it is possible that we need look no further than the second half of the Wiccan Rede, and place emphasis on its other central principle: the Will. This principle is particularly important to those who came to paganism through feminism: as the feminist theologian (thealogian?) Carol Christ wrote, "In a Goddess-centred context, the will is valued. A woman is encouraged to know her will, to believe that her will is valid, and to believe that her will can be achieved in the world, three powers traditionally denied to her in patriarchy. In a Goddess-centered framework, a woman's will is not subordinated to the Lord God as king and ruler, nor to men as his representatives." (Carol Christ, "Why women need the Goddess", cited in Reid, "Between the Worlds", pg. 52). But the Will became important to paganism not through the influence of feminism, but rather through the influence of two German philosophers and an English occultist, as we shall now see.

Crowley

It has been shown by Ronald Hutton, among other historians, that the early formation of Wicca was heavily influenced by the work of a certain infamous occultist of the time named Alistair Crowley. He was the author of several fiction and non-fiction books on magic, creator of at least one occult society which still exists today, self-styled "Great Beast 666", and general havoc-maker of all things "upright" and "proper" in Merry Old England. W.B. Yeats referred to him as "half lunatic, half knave". Wicca's inheritance from Crowley is, on the whole, patchy and inconsistent. Ron Hutton wrote that:

> "There is certainly a lot of Crowley's work in the earliest known versions of the witch rituals, which may well be the

source of the whole rumour that he wrote them; but it appears in chunks, copied or slightly adapted from his earlier publications, and interspersed with other material which is not in Crowley's style at all. Such a pattern is far more consistent with composition by another person who borrowed from works of the magus." (Hutton, *Triumph of the Moon*, pg. 217).

But it seems clear that the Wiccan Rede's assertive side, 'Do what you will', comes from him. It is virtually unchanged from Crowley's own ethical statement, known as the Law of Thelema, or sometimes as Crowley's Law, which is: "Do what thou Will shall be the whole of the Law. Love is the law, love under will." (c.f. §107) This statement appears in a work entitled "The Book of the Law", supposedly dictated to Crowley by a disembodied voice called 'Aiwaz' on the 8th of April, 1904. Central to Crowley's occultism is the doctrine of the True Will, which according to him comprises in itself the whole of the Law. One's True Will is the interposition of greater, higher, or cosmic Will in and through one's own thought, actions, and choices. It is also the claim that everyone has a right to autonomy, to develop herself and her way of life according to her own choices and to the best of her potential. This is an interesting, inspiring idea. But in Crowley's writings it is not argued for, but simply asserted as a self-evident reality. Serious critical questions like "what if someone wants to develop a way of life that is cruel, sadistic, or evil?" never arise. Instead of explanations or discussions of the meaning and implications of his principle, Crowley offers us only the model of his own life. (Not that any other self-proclaimed prophet ever offered much more.)

Let us take Crowley's Law at face value. On the level of a simple first reading, the True Will is not something that can be followed like a "law". To be more precise, someone whose life was genuinely and fully animated by his True Will could not be a follower of Crowley. To be a follower of Crowley, one would have to agree with Crowley's ideas and emulate his life. But then one would not be engaging one's own Will, but Crowley's. And if one did not engage one's own Will, one would not be heeding Crowley's instruction. In order to fulfill Crowley's law, you must break it. And this is a logical paradox. But let us assume, charitably, that it may be a paradox of the intellectually satisfying kind. Perhaps this is Crowley's way of trying to prevent his followers from becoming dogmatic and fundamentalist. Less easy to explain away as a thought-provoking paradox is the matter of whether it is possible to do harm in the name of the True Will. What should be done if it is my True Will to abduct small children in order to abuse and murder them, as has been done by several high-profile criminals? Crowley's Law says that I should just go ahead and do it, just because it is my True Will to do so. It might be someone else's True Will to stop me. But are we to respect and honour people who act from their True Will, and thus we can exercise our own Will only insofar as it does not interfere with anyone else's Will? Or should we concern ourselves only with our own True Will, which is, after all, the most the Law tells us? If it really is my True Will to set fire to a meeting hall while Crowley's present-day followers are gathering in it, then it would be an offence against the True Will of the cosmos for anyone to stop me. The next person's True Will is also an interposition of the same cosmic Will, so it would be the next person's True Will to allow the destruction of the meeting hall. Or, someone might argue that committing arson is not in fact in conformity with my True Will, and that I am mistaken if think it is. But no one could argue that, since it is 'my' will, not anyone else's. Since it is 'my' True Will, I am the only one who can say whether it is or is not in conformity with the True Will of the cosmos. Or, if everyone winds up living more or less the same kind of life, having sought and discovered their True Will, then what is the point of calling it 'my' Will? At the end of the day, this line of thought is an impossible labyrinth of bombastic absurdity that ends up nowhere. I think we are better off without it.

The same may be said of his requirement that the study of the book of the law is forbidden, and that each person should read it only once and then destroy his copy. This requirement is found in the front-piece of the Book of the Law, which reads:

Do what thou Will shall be the whole of the Law.

The study of this book is forbidden. It is wise to destroy this copy after the first reading.

Whosoever disregards this does so at his own risk and peril. These are most dire.

Those who discuss the contents of this Book are to be shunned by all, as centers of pestilence.

All questions of the Law are to be decided only by appeal to my writings, each for himself.

There is no law beyond Do what thou wilt.

Love is the law, love under will.

(Crowley, *Magical and Philosophical Commentaries*, pg. 71)

Crowley may have written this to stop people from treating his writings dogmatically. But alternative interpretations of this requirement are possible. For instance, to forbid people from studying something is the same as to demand blind unquestioning obedience. It is to forbid people from enquiring and questioning, and that is one of the classic signs of mindless dogmatism. To claim that "all questions of the Law are to be decided only by appeal to my writings", as he does, is to disallow independent thinking and to proclaim infallible authority for his writings. But surely the addendum "each to his own" grants each reader some autonomy? Yes, but it is only a limited autonomy — the reader can interpret Crowley's writings on his own, but may turn to no other writings for help.

Certainly, Crowley was no fool, and knew the risks and perils of dogmatism. But I think it cannot be denied that the whole story is much more than that. Someone looking for a deep and ancient spiritual wisdom is often also looking for a voice of authority to provide it. The believer feels comfort and security knowing that the authority has put his or her seal of approval on whatever is believed. It was therefore important, for instance, for Gerald Gardner to claim that Wicca was an ancient tradition, transmitted with absolute secrecy through old families, and that he was a simple anthropologist reporting it objectively. Crowley offers that authority in his own person: he is the "Master Therion", the reincarnation of occultist Elphias Levi (so he claimed), and the gifted seer who channeled the Book of the Law from a divine being named "Aiwaz".

But the name of this divine being is the give-away. Ask Crowley who was the author of the Book of the Law, and his answer is "Aiwaz" (pronounced "I was!"). And that is not the only give-away. On the official seal of one of the ceremonial orders he founded, the A.:A.:, there are letters printed inside the points of an upside down seven pointed star. If read as a word starting on the left side, they form B.A.B.A.L.O.N. The Tower of Babel, near the city of Babylon, is the place where, as the Biblical story goes, all human languages were scattered and confused. To this day we say that someone who is talking nonsense is "babbling". Here is Crowley saying that his work is pure babble! Ladies and gentlemen, the Emperor had no clothes — and moreover, he knows he has no clothes, and he secretly laughs at those who praise his fashion sense.

The harm principle in the Wiccan Rede is one possible escape from the labyrinth of Crowley's Law. So long as I do not cause harm, I can do as I will. It cannot, therefore, be my True Will to commit violent crimes. This is the general pattern of liberal or libertarian thinking from John Stewart Mill onward: one person's right to do as she wills may not infringe upon anyone else's rights. It may be that Valiente was in her own subtle way attempting a poetic and spiritual interpretation of this classic statement of liberalism, and at the same time attempting to admonish and correct the Master Therion. She may have thought that acting upon the True Will must necessarily include respecting everyone through whom the True Will manifests itself, insofar as it is indeed the same True Will manifesting through us all. It cannot be the 'will' of the True Will to want to harm others who also embody the same True Will in themselves. This appears to me as a logical truism: for the True Will would presumably not intend to harm itself. Unfortunately there is nothing in the Rede itself to suggest that this was indeed Valiente's thinking at the time. As stated, the Rede simply asserts; it does not explain. Nor is there anything in Crowley's writings to this effect.

However, we are not at a loss. There are other conceptions of the Will that we can study as alternatives. For a number of 19th century German philosophers, at least one of whom Crowley is known to have admired, also had the Will at the centre of their philosophical attention. Let us look at two outstanding figures, Friedrich Nietzsche and his predecessor Arthur Schopenhauer, for another understanding of what it means to do what you will. We shall also see how the two authors were led to *very* different conclusions.

Schopenhauer

Arthur Schopenhauer's account of the Will is explained in the first volume of his two-volume masterwork, *The World As Will and Representation*, and it runs as follows. The will is that which gives to a person "the key to his own phenomenon", and "reveals to him the significance and shows him the inner mechanism of his being, his actions, his movements." (Schopenhauer *The World as Will and Representation*, pg. 100). The Will is knowable directly and objectively, and is inseparable from the knowledge of the body. For the will is just that immanent force or power which manifests itself as actions of the body. From there, Schopenhauer goes on to argue that the will is also the key to understanding every phenomenon in nature as well. For to his mind, will and representation are the only kinds of reality that we know; there is no other kind of reality to attribute to things in the world. A person engaged in a sustained introspective examination of how his own will appears to him (mainly as the volitional movements of his body) also finds that the Will is likewise present in the being of everything in the world.

> He will recognise that same will not only in those phenomena that are quite similar to his own, in men and animals, as their innermost nature, but continued reflection will lead him to recognise the force that shoots and vegetates in the plant, indeed the force by which the crystal is formed, the force that turns the magnet to the North Pole, the force whose shock he encounters from the contact of metals of different kinds, the force that appears in the elective affinities of matter as repulsion and attraction, separation and union, and finally even gravitation, which acts so powerfully in all matter, pulling the stone to the earth and the earth to the sun; all these he will recognise as different only in the phenomenon, but the same according to their inner nature. He will recognise them all as that which is immediately known to him so intimately and better than anything else, and where it appears most distinctly is called *will*. (Schopenhauer, *ibid*, pp. 109-110).

Here we have the idea that the will is the basic metaphysical ground of everything, standing outside of time and space, manifesting in everything in various degrees of intensity and perfection from the laws of physics and chemistry up to the conscious and free human being. One universal Will, at the centre of all reality: in this we have the prototype of Crowley's "True Will", but expressed with far more precision and clarity, and unencumbered by obscure occult symbolism, hedonistic egotism, and half-hidden leg-pulls.

However, the Will as Schopenhauer conceives it is the very polar opposite of how we today normally think of it. For us, as it was for Valiente, the will is the principle of autonomy, of freedom: yet it is more like a moral right than a cosmic unity. "Do what you will" can also mean just to do whatever you want to do, without the need for an authority to confirm your action. Schopenhauer claims that the appearance (German: *vorstellung*, "representation") of one's own body in motion is also the way the will appears, and also experienced simultaneously with the feeling of being a free being. But the will as a universal thing-in-itself is not a principle of freedom for us as individuals. The experience of our own will is, on this view, only the experience of the phenomenon of the larger, metaphysical Will of which everything is a phenomenon. The simple observation is this. We always think of ourselves as free in the moment we do something. But on looking back after having done it, it is always possible to explain the action as having been caused by some determinist force, be it psychological, physiological, or natural. We are determined by forces greater than our private will:

> "the individual, the person, is not the will as thing-in-itself, but is phenomenon of the will, is as such determined... Hence we get the strange fact that everyone considers himself to be *a priori* quite free, even in his individual actions, and imagines he can at any moment enter upon a different way of life, which is equivalent to saying that he can become a different person. But *a posteriori* through experience, he finds to his astonishment that he is not free, but liable to necessity..." (Schopenhauer, *ibid.* pg. 113-4).

For Schopenhauer, the cause-of-all-causes, even the cause of time and space itself, is the Will, of which we individual mortals are but one minor representation among many, like so many puppets on strings.

Schopenhauer's vision of the Will is alien to our own for another reason. He also claimed the Will is ultimately a source of suffering. The Will is suffering because it is always frustrated: it can never grasp that which it aims for, or as soon as it does, the thing once grasped soon perishes as all things in the embodied world eventually do. Otherwise the will immediately reaches for something else. As he says:

> This great intensity of willing is in and by itself and directly a constant source of suffering, firstly because all willing as such springs from want, and hence from suffering... Secondly because, through the causal connexion of things, most desires must remain unfulfilled, and the will is much more often crossed than satisfied. Consequently, much intense willing always entails much intense suffering. For all suffering is simply nothing but unfulfilled and thwarted willing. (Schopenhauer, *ibid*, pg. 363)

Note that the definition of suffering is the thwarting of the will: suffering arises when the will does not get what it wants. This Schopenhauer takes to be a perpetual condition — the will can *never* get everything it wants. The will gains temporary relaxation in artistic contemplation, especially *music* which he regarded as "a copy of the Will itself". But otherwise, one gains no respite from this ongoing and never-ending suffering. "The more intense the will, the more glaring the phenomenon of its conflict, and hence the greater the suffering." (pg. 395) Some kind of Christian, Hindu, or Buddhist asceticism is Schopenhauer's general recommendation for a cure, although he says that the "inner cheerfulness and true heavenly peace" that accompanies the denial of the will to life:

> ...must always be achieved afresh by constant struggle. For as the body is the will itself only in the form of objectivity, or as

phenomenon in the world of representation, that whole will-to-live exists potentially so long as the body lives, and is always striving to reach actuality and to burn afresh with all its intensity... for on earth no one can have lasting peace. (Schopenhauer, *ibid*, pg. 391)

This unhappy conclusion is not a non-sequitor. It follows properly and logically from Schopenhauer's first premises. (This conclusion can also be derived from Crowley's claims about the True Will, although Crowley never saw it.) The recognition of one's own will as the microcosm of a greater will to life is at the same time the recognition that the transience, mortality, and suffering of the world is a manifestation of the same will to life, and one suffers alongside it. "He knows the whole, comprehends its inner nature, and finds it involved in a constant passing away, a vain striving, an inward conflict, and a continual suffering." (pg. 379) In Schopenhauer's vision, the world is constantly in motion – an idea contemporary pagans might find familiar, as it appears so often in their wisdom teachings (c.f. §67, §147, §180). But his vision of a world in constant turbulent motion is a vision of pessimism and despair. Perhaps for that reason, Schopenhauer is not widely read anymore. John Leslie, a 20th century Utilitarian philosopher, suggested that his kind of pessimism, if it became widespread, could lead to apathy concerning the future of the human race. If enough people believed that the world would have been better off as a lifeless mass, like the moon, as Schopenhauer believed, it might be a short step to think that we ought to make it that way. And the denial of the possibility of lasting peace so long as we live embodied lives in the physical world troubles us, unless of course we believe in the possibility of lasting happiness in a paradise world after death.

Schopenhauer, for his part, did not.

Nietzsche

Let us turn then to the second conception of the will that was widespread at the time, the one we know Crowley appropriated: Friedrich Nietzsche. The Gnostic Catholic Church, the organisation founded by Crowley to carry forth his ideas, treats Nietzsche as a major saint in its divine pantheon.

Schopenhauer's thinking was admired by Nietzsche, at least for a while. By the time of writing one of his masterworks, *Beyond Good and Evil*, Nietzsche had made up his mind that Schopenhauer got the idea of the will entirely wrong. Agreeing that the Will is the key to understanding everything, but that most philosophers (and especially Schopenhauer) are deeply mistaken about what it is, he wrote that:

> Schopenhauer only did what philosophers are in the habit of doing—he adopted a *popular prejudice* and exaggerated it. Willing seems to me to be above all something *complicated*, something that is a unit only as a word... (Nietzsche, *Beyond Good and Evil*, pg. 25)

Actually, Schopenhauer adopted an idea imported from Hinduism, the *Atman*, and found European words for it; although it is also true that Schopenhauer didn't choose the term 'will' at random. Almost a century earlier, Immanuel Kant had already placed the autonomy and freedom of the will at the heart of human life and ethics, even going so far as to claim that the will is the only thing in the world which is good without qualification. Fichte, just after Kant, also placed the will at the centre of a constantly changing, turbulent and transient universe. Nietzsche exposes the idea of the Will as containing more depth and more complexity than any of his predecessors ever saw. For implicit within the notion of 'will' is, among other things, the notion of something that *commands* and something else that *obeys*. We also find, contrary to Schopenhauer, that the successful discharge of the will is *pleasurable*. In Nietzsche's words:

> "Freedom of the will" — that is the expression for the complex state of delight of the person exercising volition, who commands and at the same time identifies himself with the executor of the order — who, as such, enjoys also the triumph over obstacles, but thinks within himself that it was really his will itself that overcame them. In this way the person exercising volition adds the feelings of delight of his successful executive instruments, the useful "under-wills" or under-souls — indeed, our body is but a social structure composed of many souls — to his feelings of delight as a commander. (Nietzsche, *ibid*, pg. 26)

Nietzsche's enormous contribution to human thought is the systematic exposure of all our hidden beliefs. Most of them he finds to be false, contradictory, self-serving, and worthy only of ridicule. The entire edifice of the western 'enlightenment', the part-discovery, part-declaration, that the world is fully comprehensible to human reason, and that morality can be justified by means of reason, is utterly demolished. More valuable than that is his honest and direct examination of the wide empty space which his act of demolition left behind. But let us look at what he claims can fill that empty space. Nietzsche's explains the hidden structure of the will as a structure of command and obedience. Not that this is an illegitimate explanation. The will is indeed the capacity to express oneself through force and power, among other things. And this capacity exists within each of us, just because we are alive — or indeed, as Schopenhauer thought, it *is* what we are, we live within *it*. But Nietzsche also interprets his capacity for freedom as a relation of *supremacy*: "In all willing it is absolutely a question of commanding and obeying." (Nietzsche, *ibid*, pg. 27) Here Nietzsche is already laying the foundations for a larger vision to occupy the empty space left by his demolition of the foundations of western philosophy and religion. That vision is the *Ubermensch*, the "Superman" or the "Over-man", the man whose superior will to power enables him to overcome the tempestuous emptiness of the world, to declare meaning by force of character. Nietzsche believed that life had no intrinsic meaning, and so our only real choice is to rely upon the authority of other people to supply a sense of meaning, or else try to create our own. The Ubermensch is the man who has the will to create a meaning of life for himself, and impose it on his world, and in so doing create himself. (I do mean 'man' here, and not something more gender-neutral like 'humankind'. Nietzsche was contemptuous of women and believed them incapable of the will to power.) The Ubermensch does not remain resigned to the lack of meaning in the world, nor does he accept meaning imposed upon him by others. For that is the character of the 'slave morality'. Slaves are those who lack Will, and therefore must accept the meaning offered to them, or imposed on them, by the masters. This Nietzsche took to be something like a general law of nature.

> Even the [social] body within which individuals treat each other as equals, as suggested before—and this happens in every healthy aristocracy—if it is a living and not a dying body, has to do to other bodies what individuals within it refrain from doing to each other: it will have to be an incarnate will to power, it will strive to grow, spread, seize, become predominant—not from any morality or immorality but because it is *living* and because life simply *is* the will to power... "Exploitation" does not belong to a corrupt or imperfect and primitive society; it belongs to the *essence* of what lives, as a basic organic function; it is a consequence of the will to power, which is after all the will of life. (*ibid* pg. 203)

The Ubermensch, then, is a figure who *necessarily* dominates and exploits and sacrifices other people, as part of his expression of

Will. In order to be able to create himself, and impose his new meaning upon his life he has to be able to impose it on others as well.

We have three conceptions of the Will here, all of which were common currency among intellectuals around the time of the formation of Wicca. In chronological order, they are:

- *Schopenhauer's Will to Life:* the principle of primordial unity within everything, which manifests as a constant striving towards unattainable goals, and hence is a source of suffering;
- *Nietzsche's Will to Power:* the quality of character possessed by the 'noble soul' or the 'aristocratic class' enabling one to create one's own meaning and purpose, and entitling the possessor to impose his will upon others;
- *Crowley's "True Will":* a conglomeration of both the Will to Life and the Will to Power, described using the vocabulary of Cabbalistic occultism, lacking the comprehensive vision of both Nietzsche and Schopenhauer, and subject to several internal contradictions.

I may seem to have summarily dismissed a principle which is vitally important to contemporary paganism. But my point is just that paganism has inherited all three of these conceptions of the will, with all of their merits and their flaws. It may take a generation or two for the pagan understanding of the Will to overcome the problems described here. Certain feminist pagan writers may have already seen the way forward. Carol Christ, for instance, wrote that "in the Goddess framework, Will can be achieved only when it is exercised in harmony with the energies and wills of other beings." (cited in Reid, "Between the Worlds", pg. 53). Let me turn to another important pagan concept, which for Wicca exists in a strange relationship with the will, and which clearly calls for harmony between beings: the ability to love.

Acts of Love and Pleasure

To speak of love in any way other than through poetry and symbolism may appear totally misguided. For love is complicated. It resists being defined. Some part of its beauty dies when it is pinned down by an analytic definition, like a butterfly in a display-case. For love does not normally strike us as the sort of thing that can be examined under the microscope, with its internal organs dissected, to have its essence catalogued once and for all. With regard to ethics, there is a special kind of problem here. I think everyone would agree that love is, among other things, a passion, an attraction, an affection, a drive—at least that much about it can be pinned down without killing it. Love is surrounded by related flowering trees like pleasure and pain, happiness and sadness, beauty and grotesqueness, peace and action, decisiveness and hesitation, permission and taboo. The list goes on. The special problem with love is this: emotion cannot be commanded. It can only emerge from freedom and from freely made feelings and choices. How, then, can love be a duty? How can we tell someone that they ought to be happy? The answer is that we cannot. It is a deep contradiction to make love into a law. Moral statements like Crowley's Law (§112), and even the Christian commandment to "Love your neighbour as yourself" are, on one level, deep contradictions. Their poetic value is profound and indubitable, but their logic is most problematic. Some might argue that it is wrong to analyse such statements logically. But if we refuse to examine what it means to love, all we get from these statements is a vague rhapsodical sentimentality which may be emotionally satisfying but which ultimately teaches us very little. Philosophers shouldn't therefore surrender all talk of love to the poets. Love is built right into the very enterprise of philosophy itself: philosophy is *philia sophia*—the love of wisdom.

Some people might say that even though love cannot be commanded, still it exists in a tight relationship with the will. Schopenhauer conceived of the will as a cosmic primordial unity, thus placing everyone in a necessary relationship to other beings, and hence in a necessary relationship with love. His conception of the Will demands that we treat individuality as an illusion, and think of ourselves as all different expressions and manifestations of the same Will. Through this understanding, he believed, we are enabled to experience the suffering of other beings as though it is our own. Thus we are motivated to love other beings, and to come to the aid and rescue of beings who suffer. In his words:

> For the veil of Maya has become transparent for the person who performs works of love, and the deception of the *principium individuationis* [principle of individualism] has left him. Himself, his will, he recognises in every creature, and hence in the sufferer also... To be cured of this delusion and deception of Maya and to do works of love are one and the same thing; but the latter is the inevitable and infallible symptom of that knowledge. (Schopenhauer, *The World as Will and Representation*, pg. 373).

This is one of the ideas he learned from Hinduism and the wisdom of the east; it is his word for 'the Veil of Maya' (illusion). Love for others arises from the recognition of primordial unity with others. Love and the universal Will to Life therefore go together — and so there is no question of love under will, as there is for Crowley. Love has nothing to do with law. The passion, the commitment, the sincerity, of an act of love makes the act noble and excellent, not its fulfillment of a rule or a duty. Love is thus beyond any analysis of moral right and wrong. One of Nietzsche's own aphorisms observes, correctly I believe, this very teaching: "what is done for love goes beyond good and evil".

Love features prominently in the most important single text in modern paganism: the Charge of the Goddess. Some of the key proverbs from the Charge are about love, such as "ye shall dance, sing, feast, make music and love, all in my praise" (§81), and "my law is love unto all beings". The latter commandment is an echo of Crowley's Law of Thelema, and a recurrence of the impossibility of codifying love as a law. We might interpret this as saying that 'love unto all beings' is what substitutes for divine commandments in Wicca. The best known mention of love in the Charge of the Goddess is this one: "Let my worship be within the heart that rejoices; for behold, all acts of love and pleasure are my rituals" (§82). It is a credit to Paganism that love should feature so prominently in its most important and most beautiful statements of spiritual identity. Here, actions of love and pleasure are elevated to the status of a ritual, that is to say, a communion with the Goddess. As a ritual, as a communion with a deity, love is set apart from matters of moral law. But as if to provide further clarification, a list of eight qualities of character and behaviour are added which must 'therefore' be a part of the committed Wiccan's life: "Let there be beauty and strength, power and compassion, honour and humility, mirth and reverence within you" (§83). It appears that possession of these traits enables one to love, and are a part of the meaning of love. Thus they enable one to consummate a relationship with the Goddess. These eight virtues are paired off, as if to present them as natural complementary opposites akin to male and female, sun and moon, day and night, and the like.

The deep opposition between love and commandment is thereby avoided. Love goes beyond law, beyond ethics, beyond any kind of analysis, criticism, and judgment. It is based not upon a law but on a recognition of primordial spiritual unity. But if love has no relationship to law, or no relationship to ethics, it might be possible to harm people in the name of love, and thus escape blame or punishment. We may think we know intuitively or instinctively what love is. But there is a great deal of evil that can be perpetrated in the name of love this way. Stalkers and rapists claim to 'love' their victims—so how do we know they are mistaken about their intuition of love, and we are not mistaken about ours? This problem can arise if we claim to 'just know' what love is, and then say nothing more about it. So let us continue to examine love, and the relation of love to ethics. And of course we need to examine the remaining echo of the deep opposition between love and commandment. The statements "My law is love unto all beings", make love "in my praise", "Love is the law, love under will" — are they not plain absurdities on par with "Love your neighbour as yourself"? Is not Crowley's whole statement rendered self-negating by the placement of love *under* the unfettered discharge of will? To what extent, if at all, is this problem overcome by the elevation of love to that which obtains communion with the Goddess? *What, after all, is love?*

We can be fairly confident that the conception of love which is in play in Wicca's early testament is that which was espoused by the *Ordo Templi Orientis* (O.T.O.) of which Crowley and (briefly) Gardner were members. The O.T.O. started in Germany in 1904, as an offspring of mystical Freemasonry, and included among its inspirational sources the writings of the occultist Elphias Levi, the Tantra and Yoga that had been imported to Europe from India by the mid 19th century (which also inspired Schopenhauer), and the myths and legends surrounding the mediaeval Knights Templar. According to Ronald Hutton, the European branch of the O.T.O. contacted Crowley in 1912 and asked him to be the O.T.O. leader for England. He agreed, and immediately started re-working some of the rituals, and by 1947 he was regarded as in charge of the whole organisation. (c.f. Hutton, *The Triumph of the Moon*, pg. 222.) What did Crowley and his O.T.O. make of love?

When researching the answer to this question, I was first struck by what a small role 'love' actually plays in Crowley's thought, and how rarely he talks about it. One of Crowley's biographers said the following:

Crowley's 'Do what thou wilt…' phrase was to be augmented by another saying, 'Love is the law; love under will'. It was an extension of the know-thyself doctrine for which Crowley stood, yet many of his critics have incorrectly interpreted both dicta as being a license to moral permissiveness. That said, it must be admitted there were times when Crowley himself chose to interpret them this way, too. (Booth, *A Magick Life*, pg. 187)

How can 'Love under will' be an extension of the idea of self-knowledge? One line that stands out in my mind from the Book of the Law, in which the Law of Thelema originally appeared, is this one: "For I am divided for Love's sake, for the chance of union." (Crowley, *The Book of the Law*, line 29.) Crowley was almost certainly aware of the Hindu idea that the world was created when a primordial being split itself into separate parts, for instance into a male and female pair which then mated with each other to give birth to all living things. It did this in order to quell a feeling of loneliness and to experience the joy of recognition and reunion. It is an ancient, profound idea, of which I shall say more elsewhere. The appearance of this idea in Crowley's work is, unfortunately, the only really lucid and comprehensible thing I have found in the whole body of Crowley's work. Most of Crowley's magical writings are poetic yet at the same time confusing and cryptic, exploring various correspondences among symbols in a way that almost overwhelms the reader with information. This is often deliberate: it is an excellent way to separate sycophants from genuine seekers. But other passages are hopelessly obscure. For instance, Liber CLVI of the "Holy Books of Thelema" says:

Thou hast love; tear thy mother from thine heart, and spit in the face of thy father. Let thy foot trample the belly of thy wife, and let the babe at her breast be the prey of dogs and vultures. (Crowley, *The Holy Books of Thelema*, pg. 102)

If this passage is taken at face value, it clearly has nothing to do with 'dividing oneself for the chance of union'. One does not treat beloved family members that way. Perhaps there is a hidden symbolism at play, a symbolic subtext? There certainly is just such a hidden symbolism in a passage of Buddhism's great classic, the *Dhammapada*, which reads like Crowley's statement above, and may have been its inspiration:

> A (true) *Brahmin* goes scatheless though he has killed father and mother and two kings of the warrior caste. A (true) *Brahmin* goes scatheless though he has killed father and mother and two holy kings and an eminent man as the fifth. (*The Dhammapada*, XXI.5-6 (294-5)).

But in the Buddhist text it is fairly clear that 'mother' and 'father' are symbols for the psychological attachments of egotism and craving. Attachments like these, for Buddhists, are the main origin of suffering and of moral error. But other passages in Crowley's work conceal not deep spiritual truths but straight-forward eroticism. Parts of Liber VII are written to resemble the sort of noise one might make while having an orgasm. Chapter 69 of the "Book of Lies" is an instruction for performing fellatio. Again, this is Crowley having a good laugh at the expense of people who take his work too seriously. There is great wisdom in laughter. But there is only so much wisdom that can be taught by the court jester. Eventually one gets tired of being constantly humiliated. A mature seeker soon wishes to move on.

The word 'love' appears often enough in his autobiography, the *Confessions*, but mostly in reference to various paramours and how his love for them was always subordinate to his study and practice of 'magick'. For example, he describes the reason for the collapse of his relationship with an American woman named Alice as follows:

The secret of my strength was this, that love would always stand a shining symbol of my truth, that I loved spiritually the soul of mankind. Therefore each woman, be she chaste or wanton, faithful or false, inspiring me to scale the summits of song or whispering me to wallow in the swamps of sin, would be to me no more than a symbol in whose particular virtue my love could find the bread and wine of its universal Eucharist... always a moment has come when the woman had to choose between comradeship and catastrophe. For in truth, there was no Aleister Crowley to love; there was only a Word for the utterance of which a human form had been fashioned. (Crowley, *The Confessions*, pg. 239)

In the 'spiritual love of the soul of mankind' which Crowley claimed to possess, individual people disappear, and become symbols of abstract principles. But surely this is to miss the point of love! People deserve to be loved for who they are. And to take oneself as not a person but 'a Word' fashioned in human form, is the height of hubris and arrogance. This claim can only be uttered by someone who is basically incapable of seeing others as equals, or even as persons. No wonder so many of Crowley's 'Scarlet Women' left him. We can affirm that in the experience of sex and love a gateway opens to a presence that seems to come from beyond the here and now. Yet we can affirm this without at the same time failing to love each other as individuals, which is, after all, how everyone deserves to be loved. When I wrote earlier of the Word of Being, therefore, I wrote of that which each person offers to others by their presence alone. Nothing impersonal is implied there. It follows that each person can be a Word to another, and a source of spiritual meaning, whilst remaining herself.

So much for Crowley. But there are other places where we can look for an understanding of the idea of love that is in play in contemporary paganism.

Hinduism and Tantra

Hindus do not think of themselves as 'pagans'. But western paganism has a lot in common with Hinduism, not the least of which is a three thousand year old tradition of venerating female deities. And many of India's goddesses are respected and honoured by pagans in the western world. Indeed paganism seems to have a great deal in common with an unorthodox system of Hindu and Buddhist thought, called Tantrayana. In the Western world today, especially since the first English translations of the *Kama Sutra* were published, Tantra is associated with sexuality. In India, it is associated more with the worship of the Goddess and the practice of magic. To be clear, Tantra accepts the basic premises of 'everyday' Hinduism, such as the unity of the Atman and the illusory nature of the visible world. Tantra also agrees that the main source of human suffering (samsara) is psychological attachment to transient and illusory things, and that we may be released from this suffering by releasing those attachments. Its chief distinction, however, lies in the different means to achieve its spiritual goals. A well known story among Tantrikas (practitioners of Tantra) tells of how a hero named Vasistha practiced yoga, meditation, and many forms of physical asceticism for six thousand years. When after all that time he did not receive a vision of the Goddess, he grew angry and told his father he was going to curse Her. His father stopped him, and explained that his idea of the Goddess was completely wrong. 'The Goddess is the substance of the Buddha's enlightenment', explained the father. 'She is beautiful, kindly, compassionate, and above all she is loving.' Vasistha tried again, this time following his father's advice.

In the end She appeared to him, in the bodily form of Sarasvati, the holiest Goddess of ancient Brahman Vedic wisdom – an appropriate iconic shape for a Brahmin like him. She told him he was still a long way off the proper track, and that he ought to learn the 'Kula' method of religion; that is, the Tantrik tradition. She said he could not hope to get anywhere by mere yoga and asceticism, not even to glimpse Her proper feet. 'My worship', She said, 'is without austerity and pain!' (Rawson, *The Art of Tantra*, pg. 15).

Tantrayana is a spiritual path in which ecstasy and pleasure are considered valid means to achieve *moksha*, 'liberation', or *nirvana*, 'extinction'. I think it is best understood as a kind of protest movement: its primary 'target', so to speak, was the schools of Hinduism and Buddhism which called for fasting, celibacy, strenuous forms of yoga, and other highly demanding physical and mental disciplines. It asserts that the point of all of the rules, precepts, rituals, ascetic practices, and so on, is to help the seeker find spiritual release from her suffering. If the rules and precepts co not contribute to this purpose, or even become attachments in their own right, then they need not be followed.

Tantra also targeted the caste system, in which each person is born into one of four categorical groups roughly corresponding with occupations, and with social prestige and status. Strictly speaking, the caste system forbids people to marry outside of his or her caste, or pursue an occupation assigned to another castes. Tantra rejects this system. In the words of research Indra Sinha:

What all Tantras [Tantric scriptures] have in common is that they are scriptures for the common folk, unanimous in rejecting the elitism of caste Hinduism. This is in part a reflection of the fact that the great Mother Goddess and her consort Siva have dark aboriginal origins, and were for a long time not admitted to the Vedic religion... Tantra offered a sort of tabloid religion, full of fun, enjoyment, magic and properly awe-inspiring ceremonial. (Sinha, *Tantra: The Cult of Ecstasy*, pg. 16.)

Tantra, therefore, can be described as the practice of Hindu spirituality without the physical and psychological asceticism, and without the caste rigidity (there is also a Tibetan Buddhist form of Tantra). In the place of those things, Tantra uses five specific sacraments, called the Panchamakara: they are *mada*, wine, *matsya*, fish, *mamsa*, red meat, *mudra*, herbs and grains, and *maithuna*, sexual intercourse. Each of these five sacraments are specifically forbidden by various orthodox Vedic Hindu teachings. They are asserted to be spiritual traps which leave the practitioner further entangled in the wheel of Samsara (attachment and suffering). Therefore some practitioners use substitutes like honey, cow's milk, or roasted fruits. Others treat them as symbols for theological concepts and ideas: wine becomes a symbol of 'knowledge that intoxicates', fish becomes the symbol for the currents of psychic energy which flow in the body, and so on. But most Tantric circles use the real things. Here is Indra Sinha again:

> The Tantras, powerful in their devotion to the goddess, with their promises of liberation from the torment of endless rebirth, of occult powers to be won, and in their frank enjoyment of worldly pleasures, exercised a strong appeal for the masses excluded by birth and caste from the higher levels of Vedic worship. As a result, they were often strongly condemned by the brahmanical hierarchy. (Sinha, *Tantra: The Cult of Ecstasy*, pg. 18.)

I believe that contemporary paganism, and in particular Wicca, might someday become the Tantra of the western world. For one thing, it too is a kind of protest movement. It rejects mainstream Christianity's doctrine of Original Sin, its narrow-minded notion of family values, its 'divine command' morality, among other things. Paganism is often critical of modernity and 'progress' insofar as such things cause the loss of heritage and cultural identity. It is also a protest against forms of religious practice that demand the suppression of certain natural human instincts and experiences, especially including the libido. It protests against the unequal and sometimes violent treatment of women, from inter-personal harms like offensive name-calling, job discrimination, and wife-abuse, to the male-domination of the highest levels of political and economic power. Finally, modern Paganism protests against the destruction of the environment. For the Earth is seen by many pagans as humanity's shared home, the body of the Goddess herself, and the source of our most important spiritual revelations. Doreen Valiente agreed that modern paganism has a reactionary element: in 1989 she wrote:

> In a sense, the rebirth of witchcraft is a rebellion. It is being carried out by those both young and old who are no longer content to get their religion from the churches or their opinions from the newspapers; who are, moreover, profoundly disillu-sioned with the scientists who promised us Utopia and gave us the nuclear bomb. (Valiente, *The Rebirth of Witchcraft*, pg. 207).

Another connection between the two paths may be historical. Indra Sinha, the aforementioned researcher, believed that Tantric ideas may be largely responsible for the Greek festival of the Dithyramb. The connection is in part through the symbol of the God with the Horns, who in Greece was Dionysus, and in India was Shiva. Both began as consorts of a Great Goddess: Dionysus mates with Cybele, Mother Goddess of Phrygia; and Shiva with Parvati, 'daughter of the mountain'. Both gods wear the horns of bulls on their heads in their earliest representations. Shiva, depicted without horns in later representations, is accompanied by his companion animal Nandi, a white bull. (c.f. Sinha, *Tantra*, pp. 32-3). Furthermore, the stories of Dionysus relate how as a child he was taken to a place called Nysa, to be raised by nymphs. The name 'Dionysus', he observed, simply means 'the god of

Nysa'. Tradition held that Nysa was 'somewhere out east'; and most authorities regarded it as an imaginary mythical place. But Sinha believed that the mysterious place of Dionysus' youth was a real mountain in the Hindu Kush, called Mount Koh-e-Mor. For one thing, the geography of the area matches the legendary description of Nysa. And for another, when Alexander the Great conquered the area, he encountered a people called the Nysaeans, who honoured a hunting god named 'Nisa-deva' — a name which also means 'the god of Nysa'. (c.f. Sinha, *Tantra*, pg. 46). Sinha also raises a similar point about the worship of the goddess:

> Some scholars have been struck by the similarity of the word 'Tara', a name shared by an important group of Tantric goddesses, with the names Astarte, Ishtar, Atargatis and Ashtaroth, the renowned Mother goddess of Canaan. It is not just the goddess names which resemble one another, but the manner of their worship. It is clear that, from the very earliest times, sacred sexuality has played a part in the worship of the great Mother. (Sinha, *Tantra*, pg. 32)

Tantra in the east, and the Dithyramb in the west, Sinha concludes, probably came from the same source. That source was an Aboriginal fertility-religion practiced by tribes in the area that is now known as Pakistan and Afghanistan. These people apparently worshipped an Earth Goddess and her half-animal consort. Over the centuries this religion transformed into sophisticated mystery traditions that offered spiritual illumination and release to their practitioners. Yet the two central divine figures survived in various ways: they are, indeed, almost the same as the Great Goddess and the Horned God whom contemporary pagans honour to this day.

Let me return to the matter of what Tantra can contribute to the western Pagan understanding of love. Hindu Tantra and western Wicca appear to share, as a first philosophical premise, the claim that *spiritual illumination and release can be achieved in activities that are inherently enjoyable and loving*. Teachings from the Charge of the Goddess, already mentioned, attest to this. Some of its mottos would likely be instantly recognisable to any eastern Tantrika. The requirement to perform (some) rituals in the nude (§80) would probably also be familiar. In fact, between Wiccans and Tantrikas, the same word is used to designate ritual nudity: "skyclad". That is to say, the seekers in the ritual circle are clad only in the sky. And some of the same reasons are offered to explain ritual nudity: each seeker lays herself bare before the gods, hiding nothing. Finally, like Tantra, the *Charge of the Goddess* recommends five 'panchamakara' of its own: dancing, singing, feasting, making music, and love (§81). The last one, Love, common to both Tantra and Wicca, has a special place here. Sexual lovemaking is obviously enjoyable just as is it. Both Tantra and Wicca enrich the experience by treating it as a re-enactment of the actions of the gods, when the world was first made. In contemporary paganism, the re-enactment of this activity of the gods is called the Great Rite (§53).

The essence of Tantra, according to Rawson, is its assertion that "the human sexual libido is in some sense identical with the creative and beneficial energy-essence of the universe." (Rawson, *The Art of Tantra*, pg. 28) The universe is the body of a primordial deity, the Atman, and a product of the lovemaking of the gods. This idea appears in the Wiccan 'Great Rite', or 'Sacred Marriage', for instance. It appears in Dion Fortune's teaching that "all gods are one god" (§138). Similarly it is reflected in circle-songs that celebrate the presence of the gods 'within' the singer, such as "Bridgit triple flame" (§195) and "Fur and feather" (§233). The Atman is the seed of yourself that you find within others, and the seed of others that you find within yourself. All the many gods, goddesses, heroes, spirits, and even monsters in the Hindu pantheon are faces of the same Atman, just as you and I are. And the Hindu imagination is prolific: its art and literature has literally thousands of deities! But this assertion does not treat people as mere instances of theoretical principles or abstract concepts. It still treats people *as people* in themselves, who deserve to be loved for who they are. For one thing, Tantra is very practical: "things done come first, interpretations later" (Rawson, *The Art of Tantra*, pg. 31). But secondly, and more importantly, the Tantrik seeker is one who finds that 'bhoga is yoga', or *delight is religion*. We accomplish spiritual illumination and release by participating in the lovemaking of he gods. We participate in the lovemaking of the gods by loving each other: sharing food, drink, music, art, poetry, emotional support, practical help, advice and thought, sexual pleasure, and any other gift of beauty and enjoyment.

Sufism.

Another important influence on the western pagan under-standing of love, often overlooked, is Sufism. It appears to be a form of Islam, and has flourished in the Muslim world for centuries, but there are doubts about whether it really is a part of Islam at all. It accepts the six pillars of Islamic faith: God exists, God is One, there are Angels, there are Prophets, there is a Day of Restoration, there is Fate. However, Sufi understands these pillars as "recorded in the mind and experienced in the heart". (Shah, *The Way of the Sufi*, pg. 309.) Obeying divine commands, and accepting the authority of the Koran at face value, therefore, is not what matters. Furthermore some of Sufism's methods to arrive at that understanding are, in strict Muslim terms, heretical. For instance, one of the most famous pieces of Sufi literature, *The Rubáiyát of Omar Khayyám*, is full of praise for wine (whereas the Koran forbids the use of substances which impair one's ability to make sound judgements.). Like Tantra, Sufism is a path of ecstasy: it too finds music, dancing, poetry, and especially love, is the way to find God.

The connection to Wicca is as follows. Gerald Gardener was a close friend of the committed Sufi practitioner and author, Idries

Shah. In fact Shah ghost-wrote Gardner's biography, which was formally attributed to Jack Bracelin (c.f. Hutton, *The Triumph of the Moon*, pg. 205). Shah also published his own book of ceremonial spellcraft, entitled *The Secret Lore of Magic* (1957). In other publications he claimed that Sufism was among the most important influences on modern pagan witchcraft, as well as on important Western authors like Shakespeare, Gurdjieff, Ouspensky, Hans Christian Andersen, and many others. (Shah, *The Way of the Sufi*, pg. 21, 44) He argued that Sufism flourished in Spain while it was ruled by Arabs. From there Sufi ideas spread into southern France and inspired the movement of romantic poets known as Troubadors, but the change of language diluted its essential content. (Shah, *The Sufis*, pg. 360) The material and literary evidence for this possibility did not emerge until after his death. As historian Bettany Hughes has described, the court of the Alhambra, in the Arab capital of Spain, included a choir of singing girls. When the Moors were expelled from Spain, these girls were captured as prisoners of war, and distributed by Ferdinand and Isabella to other crowned heads of Europe as gifts. Hughes suggested that these Muslim singing girls may have inspired court musicians and other talents to compose songs on sophisticated themes like courtly love and romance.

Sufism is not a structured or deliberately systematic tradition. Its basic doctrines and practices are transmitted from teacher to apprentice mainly in the form of stories, poems, proverbs, jokes, songs and dances, and fragments. But a number of clear themes present themselves consistently. The major theme is, of course, love. Shah says,

The association between love and poetry, between the poet and the musician, and between these and the magician in the widest sense, runs through Sufism, as through the Western tradition which it undoubtedly contacted and reinforced. It is as if the twin streams of the ancient teaching mingle on this dimension, far removed from the coldly rationalising intellect. The objective of the poet-lover-magician is not, however, in Sufism, merely to be absorbed in the effulgence of the truth which he learns. He is transformed by it, and as a consequence has a social function – to inject back into the stream of life the direction which humanity needs in order to fulfill itself. (Shah, *The Sufis*, pg. 364)

The connection to love and poetry here is also a connection to social responsibility. A Sufi love-poet has his rapturous experience with divinity, but then he must return to earth to teach by example. However, to say that a Sufi has a 'relationship' with God is to miss the point:

The individual who equates love with divinity is a barbarian from the point of view of the person who has found the connection with the reason of life... those who have glimpsed the Sufi experiences realise that the multiple meanings contained in such a work of art are there, so far as the human being is concerned, in order to lead him to a true perception of what the inner reality is. It is the perception of this inner reality which enables him to take himself forward to the greater evolution which is the destiny of man. (Shah, *The Sufis*, pg. 365)

For a Sufi, as Shah appears to portray them, love and the poetry of love is the instrument not only for getting in contact with the 'inner reality', with God, but also the instrument for teaching others how to do so as well. Love is more uniquely suited for this purpose than anything else. It would be incomplete to say that love is thus 'just an instrument', that its value is just as a teaching tool for imparting spiritual ideas. It is, rather, "a common denominator for mankind", and therefore "with the analogy of love, and the literary use he makes of it, [the Sufi] can help to bridge the gap in understanding for others who are at an earlier stage of the Path." (Shah, *The Sufis*, pg. 366).

Discussing Sufism in this way might be, in some measure, missing the point. Sufism is not taught by means of intellectual discourse; some say it cannot be taught by words at all. Rather, it is taught through poetry, music, and direct experience (usually with the aid of a teacher). There is a story concerning an 11th century Islamic scholar named Maulana, who even as a young man was regarded as a leading intellectual. One day he was riding his donkey into the market district, surrounded by his students. A wild-looking dervish, a desert-dwelling mystic, came up to him and asked him, "Which was the greatest: the Sufi mystic Bayazid, or the prophet Mohammed?" Maulana gave the expected answer: Mohammed, of course. But the man countered, "Then why did Bayazid say, 'Glory be to me. How high is my dignity!' And why did Mohammed say 'I have not known thee as I should?'" Maulana did not answer. Instead, he fainted. (c.f. Harvey, *The Way of Passion*, pp. 24-6).

In the Sufi point of view, Bayazid's exclamation is the greatest. It locates the dwelling-place of God within each person, and it expresses this truth with an exuberant life-affirmation. The statement struck Maulana like a thunderbolt: it changed his life forever. He spent the next forty days with the dervish, during which his entire world-view was shattered, destroyed, and re-built again. The wild man's name was Shams of Tabriz, and Maulana became one of the best known and loved Sufi poets in the history of Islam: under the name of Jallaludin Rumi.

Like most Sufi poets and mystics, Rumi says that the experience of God cannot be described. Still, he uses various interesting metaphors to guide or to help others have their own experience. The seeker is like the moth who willingly flies toward the candle, to be burned up completely. Rumi sometimes uses sex and sexuality as a teaching device: for instance by telling ribald stories about lustful kings or promiscuous sheiks. To those who might be bothered by such parables, he says: "Don't laugh at this. This loving is also part of the infinite love, without which the world does not evolve." (Barks, *The Essential Rumi,* pg. 55). Some of his poems express hostility to academic understanding: "An intellectual doesn't know what the drunk is feeling!" (*ibid* pg. 102). This is ironic, since Rumi was himself a respected academic before he became a Sufi poet. But I think his point is not that all intellectual knowledge is entirely useless. Intellectual training can make you 'ready' to learn what intellectual training itself cannot teach: "When you begin to work without full knowledge, you risk your life." (*ibid,* pg. 181.). Concerning the value of traditions and rituals, Rumi says, "the rules of faithfulness are just the door and the doorkeeper. They keep the presence from being interrupted." (*ibid* pg. 240-1). Again and again, Rumi insists that the experience of God cannot be described. But he does describe the *relationship* between God and the seeker: and he does so in terms that I think contemporary pagans would recognise as "The Mystery". There are many examples of The Mystery in Rumi's writings. This poem, entitled "Say I am You", (*ibid.* pg. 275-6) is one of the best.

I am the dust particles in sunlight.
I am the round sun.

To the bits of dust I say, *Stay.*
To the sun, *Keep moving.*

I am morning mist,
And the breathing of evening.

I am wind in the top of a grove,
And surf on the cliff.

Mast, rudder, helmsman, and keel,

I am also the coral reef they foundered on.

I am a tree with a trained parrot in its branches.
Silence, thought, and voice.

The musical air coming through a flute,
A spark of a stone, a flickering

In metal. Both candle,
And the moth crazy around it.

Rose, and the nightingale
Lost in the fragrance.

I am all orders of being, the circling galaxy,
The evolutionary intelligence, the lift,

And the falling away. What is,
And what isn't. You who know

Jelaluddin, You the one
In all, say who

I am. Say I
Am You.

A true Sufi's sense of self is so dissolved into the presence of God
that there is longer any distinction between them.

The contemporary Pagan movement could become a kind of
Sufism of the west. It too uses ecstasy – dance, poetry, music, love
– as a path to the discovery of the divine. It too is interested in a
special kind of spiritual experience, in which the relationship
between a seeker and his god is that of two lovers. In the most
intense experience, the lover finds his beloved within himself, and

himself within the lover. Indeed, two Sufi love songs appeared in my folklore survey (§314 and §333). I shall leave the last word on Sufism to Rumi himself. His teaching on the meaning of love can be summarised in this simple aphorism (*ibid*, pg. 185): "The way you make love is the way God will be with you."

The Dwelling Place of Divinity

We have explored Tantra and Sufism in order to find a means to answer the question, What is love? As the Sufis say: love is the disappearance of yourself in the presence of God, the finding of God within yourself. As the Tantras say: love is the activity of the gods which created the universe, which continues to sustain it, and which is found within yourself and within each person you meet. Both of these Eastern traditions were important influences on Wicca during its formative decades, and both continue to exert a strong force upon its present development. But let us bring this discussion back to the Western world. Although it is right to learn from the East, we would do a great disservice to both traditions if we merely dress up Eastern ideas in Western clothes.

In *The Myth of the Eternal Return*, Mircea Eliade wrote about how in 'primitive' societies (that was the unfortunate word he used) a sacred act is an act which has a precedent in the culture's mythology, and especially in its *creation* mythology. In his words:

> The archaic world knows nothing of "profane" activities; every act which has a definite meaning—hunting, fishing, agriculture, games, conflicts, sexuality—in some way participates in the sacred... The only profane activities are those which have no mythical meaning, that is, which lack exemplary models. (Eliade, *The Myth of the Eternal Return*, pg. 28)

Eliade's point here is twofold. One is that an action is a sacred action when it is a repetition of an action of a god, originally performed at the beginning of time. The other is that nearly every sort of action has this mythological precedent, even the most ordinary acts. People in the ancient societies described by Eliade lived in an almost constant state of ritual. We see this in the way Black Elk described the importance of the circle. It was the elementary shape of his world, and so it was important that the layout of his community followed the same shape. The circular tipi itself, and the arrangement of a group of tipis in a circle, was a repetition of the cosmic circle of the whole world. A prophet of the Dakota Sioux named Tatanka-Ptecila said "The tribe always camped in a circle and in the middle of the circle was a place called Hocoka, the centre." (McLuhan, *Touch the Earth*, pg. 43). We also find this in the 'circles' in which contemporary pagans perform various rituals, from invoking the gods to sharing a meal.

The process of 'modernisation', Eliade goes on to say, involves a whittling down of the sacred, so that fewer and fewer acts have a precedent in mythology. But here comes the really clever bit:

> For the traditional societies, all the important acts of life were revealed *ab origine* by gods or heroes. Men only repeat these exemplary and paradigmatic gestures *ad infinitum*...When a captain goes to sea, he personifies the mythical hero Aori. He wears the costume which Aori is supposed to have worn, with a blackened face (and in a way prematurely) the same kind of *love* in his hair which Aori plucked from Iviri's head. He dances on the platform and extends his arms like Aori's wings... A man told me that when he went fish shooting (with bow and arrow) he pretended to be Kivavia himself. He did not implore Kivavia's favour and help; he identified himself with the mythical hero. (Eliade, *The Myth of the Eternal Return*, pg. 32-3)

The important line in this passage is the last one. The fisherman did not simply invoke the aid of the primordial fisherman from the mythology. He was not praying for the god to grace him with good luck or to guide his hand. Rather he imagined himself to *be* that primordial fisherman. The seeker does not meet the deity face to face. Rather he becomes the deity, incarnate on earth, or else incarnate in his mind, if only for a short time. This is a very interesting way of approaching divinity. There is a spectrum of practice here, with children's role-play at one end, and at the other the assumption of the identity of the deity as one might don a mask or a costume. In both cases, character and identity is the concept holding the event together. The person conceives of him or herself as being a certain kind of person, a character in a divine drama. Within that conception her actions are rendered both intelligible, and also sacred.

Some might thing that this idea has been long forgotten in modern times, or abandoned when we become adults in modern times, but this is not always the case. And anyone who has children knows what I mean. When children play games among each other, they are very often *role play* games. The playground becomes for them the environment in which their character properly lives: it might be a climbing-bar in a sandbox, but to the child it is a forest, a spaceship, a palace, or nearly anything which the fantasy requires. In the course of the role play, the child imposes an act of will upon things in the world. When I was a child I had a stick which was to me Excalibur itself, the Sword in the Stone, and I treated it accordingly. Similarly, a platform half way up a tree that was across the road from my house was Camelot Castle. But sometimes my bicycle was a levitating "speeder", and a nearby forest was the "Moon of Endor". This act of will is also exercised upon the child's own image of who he is. Children do not simply, or only, imagine themselves to be meeting with their favourite characters from movies, television, sports, popular culture, or pure imagination. They often imagine that they have *become* that character, and then they do the things that character is best known for doing. They act out that character's story, and experience the story from the first-person perspective. In this way, the world becomes populated with extra presences that are very much real in the child's mind. The mythology has changed. It is no longer Kivavia the fisherman-god, but a character from an adventure cartoon or movie. It might be Luke Skywalker. But the basic principle is the same.

Adults carry this practice on in their own way. Last winter my teenage brother and I watched a hockey game on television. I saw that one of the goaltenders had two eagle heads painted on either side of his helmet. My brother informed me that early in his career, that particular player was so good at catching airborne pucks that his fellow players said he had the eyes of an eagle. So he had the eagles painted on his helmet. It occurred to me that this may be not much different than the way in which the warriors of some aboriginal societies would wear animal claws on their clothing. Doing so would enable the warrior to partake of the strength and ferocity of that animal while hunting or while on the warpath. I don't believe that the hockey player in question thinks of the eagle eyes on his helmet as a magical item. More likely, he sees it as a statement of his identity, his badge of honour, his proclamation to others of who he is and what powers he possesses. Even so, it is still an example of what anthropologists sometimes call a fetish—an object used in shamanic magic that bestows power upon its possessor because of its association with a special animal, or plant, or deity, or natural force. Its function is not to fill a person with power as if filling a bucket with water. Rather it helps its possessor to *identify* with some greater power, and so partake of its spirit and its being.

This principle of *divine identification* is particularly apparent in the pagan ceremony known as "drawing down the moon". The purpose of the ritual is to 'draw down' the spirit of the Goddess herself upon the body of the human priestess. In effect the priestess becomes like a spirit-medium: the goddess 'possesses' her body for a short time. What the person says or does during the ceremony, then, is treated as the words and actions of the goddess. This practice also appears in Hindu Tantra (c.f. Rawson, *The Art of Tantra*, pg. 100) and was discussed by Margaret Murray in her thesis on mediaeval witchcraft, as well as by Frazer in his study of magic, The Golden Bough. It appears in Greek tradition: in the invocation to Apollo which was performed by the Oracle of Delphi, for instance. The initiates of Demeter may have practiced it at the Eleusinean Mysteries. Arguably, the same principle appears in Shakespeare's play, *Macbeth* (1603). There is a scene in which the prophetic witches (three of them!) conjure the spirit of Hecate, the Greek goddess of the night and the underworld. In Wicca the rite of Drawing Down the Moon is often followed by the recitation of the Charge of the Goddess, or by the Wine Blessing, which symbolises sexual intercourse. In Tantra it was often followed by the sacrament of *maithuna* itself. (c.f. Rawson, *The Art of Tantra*, pg. 100)

Drawing Down the Moon is the most intimate, direct, and personal kind of contact with a deity that a person can have. Nothing stands between the seeker and her goddess: not the social authority of a priest, not the intellectual authority of a scripture and tradition of interpretation, not even the formalities of the ritual itself if the circumstances are right. The priestess herself, in whom the goddess is invoked, has the most intimate experience of all. First she is put into a mild trance state. This might involve some combination of repetitive chanting; incense or candle light to change to the atmospheric condition of the room; costumes, veils, and masks to help the postulant 'let go' of her inhibitions (or even her identity); and other psychological devices. The words of the invocation alone carry neuro-linguistic force for some people, and merely speaking them with the right tone of voice can put some people into trance. Once the presence of the goddess is established, the people attending the ritual can pose questions to her directly, receive answers immediately, and make up their own minds about the meaning of what the goddess tells them.

It may be useful to compare this idea to the Judeo-Christian teaching that human begins are 'made in the image of God'. This is an interesting and profound idea: it is, in many ways, the foundation of the duty of respect and love which Christians owe to their neighbours. Yet it sits uneasily alongside other teachings, such as the Doctrine of Original Sin, or the teaching that 'you are dust, and unto dust you shall return'. A human being, in this Judeo-Christian world view, is still a creature of clay, ash, soil, and dust, nothing more. And while it may be wonderful that a mass of dust could be fashioned into the image of God, still it remains a mass of dust, and can never be more than that. Further, it remains weighed down by the burden of Original Sin. Unless, of course, your Christianity is of the more esoteric character, such as that which was espoused by mystics like Meister Eckhart. I think the Pagan teaching is much more life-affirming and uplifting. Attached to this teaching there is no denial of our mortality. Yet there is also no suggestion that the acknowledgement of mortality need imply any imperfection, or any distance from God. A pagan may make a gesture of respect or thanks to the gods: but she never kneels nor bows her head to them. The relationship between humanity and the gods is not like that of a sheep to shepherd, nor a servant to master. It is more like the relationship between a parent and a child, as many of the chant-songs affirm. It is also the relationship of a student and teacher, a friend to friend, even a lover to lover. It is the relationship of artists, co-creating the world together.

The literary testament of paganism thus suggests an exalted view of humankind, and of womankind in particular. It proclaims that we are children of the gods, and that the human body, heart, and mind is the dwelling place of the goddess. In the pagan way of thinking, as expressed by its literary sources, it is good to be human. And that is so because, it is an instance of the general truth that life is good, whether it be animal, plant, or microbial life. It is good to be here on this Earth, good to be surrounded by the bountiful beauty that the Earth offers to us all. The paradigm of ethics which lies behind the crude Utilitarianism of the Wiccan Rede is this notion of one's body, heart, and mind as the dwelling place of divinity. We are called upon, then, to live up to this heritage: to live our lives in accord with the qualities and attributes of the deity we find within. This is a profoundly life-affirming view, full of confidence in humanity.

It may interest readers to know that this is a variation of a system of ethics known to modern philosophers as Virtue Theory. Here we have a way of articulating moral principles which pre-dates the Christian "rule-bounded" ethics that so many pagans have reject (often for good reasons). An ancient Greek, looking at the gate to the Oracle's temple, would have understood the instruction written there, the requirement to "Know Yourself" is a first-order principle to which one is called to respond. But not all answers would have been considered acceptable. It is not enough to say, "I am who I am", or some other obscure mystical-sounding claptrap, because that is precisely not to answer the call. That, rather, is to avoid answering that call whilst impressing gullible onlookers with the façade of wisdom. If someone can evade accounting for her life this way, we have good cause to doubt whether that person really knows who he is. What would have counted as an acceptable answer, in the minds of the ancient mystical philosophers who ordered the words to be cut above the threshold to divine wisdom, was a description of one's life. That description came first of all in terms of one's place in society, for as Aristotle said, "man is a political animal" (Aristotle, The Politics, 1.ii, 1253a1.). Secondly in was stated in terms of the character traits and personal qualities one has developed in the course of that life. The best of these qualities, the ones which are shared with the gods and which are useful and necessary for a flourishing life, are the ones we generally call the Virtues.

Virtue theory the system of ethics which we find in pre-

Christian heroic and philosophical literature, is the oldest moral theory in the Western philosophical tradition. In my view is still the best moral system with which to understand who we are, what it means to be responsible, what it means to be spiritual, and indeed what it means to be human. It places the location of moral concern not on the results of the agent's actions, nor on the following of rules, but on the agent's character. A preliminary statement of its basic principle might be that the right thing to do is the action which manifests a virtue, and a virtue is a mark of excellent character, a personal quality which a person needs in order to fully flourish as a human being and lead a happy, fulfilling, and worthwhile life.

The Charge of the Goddess lists eight specific human qualities: beauty and strength, power and compassion, honour and humility, mirth and reverence. It seems that the Goddess asks the Pagan to cultivate those qualities in her character. Norse groups have varying lists of nine Virtues, derived from texts like the *Havamal*, the *Voluspa*, or the *Eddas*. Irish wisdom-texts like the Testament of Morann and the Instructions of Cormac abound with lists of character-traits which community leaders can be expected to possess. The *Testament of Morann*, for instance, requires the 'firflaith', or true ruler, to be "merciful, just, impartial, conscientious, firm, generous, hospitable, honourable, stable, beneficent, capable, honest, well-spoken, steady, true-judging." (*Audacht Morainn*, section 55.) These lists may seem very haphazardly assembled, and it may not be clear what they all have in common. Aristotle provided a simple way to bring them all together: the Virtues are the qualities of character which a person needs in order to have a happy life, to live as completely as a human being can, to flourish and excel. I am glossing quickly over a matter that deserves a great deal more exploration. But by now my basic point should be clear: the tradition of ethics which a Pagan inherits is Virtue theory, in which what matters is not adherence to a moral rule, not even a rule like "harm none".

Rather, what matters is *being a certain kind of person:* a person who possesses specific qualities of character which makes one capable of fully flourishing as an individual human being and as a member of a human community.

Aristotle said that a human being has "something within him that is divine" (*Nicomachean Ethics*, 10.vii.8). To him, that meant a capacity for theoretical reason. This ability enables you to contemplate "all things in the earth and in the sky", as Socrates said; it enables you to grasp that which is eternal and unchanging, as do the gods. These dreams of divinity which unwind themselves in our lives are what make us both spiritual and also responsible. Thus Yeats says "in dreams begin responsibility" (Yeats, *Responsibilities*, 1914). Surely he was right. To be spiritual means, primarily, to be the sort of person who seeks answers to the great questions in life from the religious and numinous realm of human culture and experience, and especially our dreams of divinity. And it is also to be the sort of person who can give religious or numinous responses when questioned about her actions and her choices. To embark on a spiritual path is from the first moment to take upon oneself a peculiar group of virtues, that is, a group of habits, customs, and practices (I do not say 'beliefs' here), which are connected to each other in the right kind of way, and which we take to be the virtues of the divine. For instance they may be the skills and talents associated with a particular occupation or practice: warrior skills, musical skills, intellectual skills, and so on, which we take to be metaphors or symbols of divinity: hence one may say he is 'on the warrior path', or 'on the healer path'. We make a path which would otherwise be an ordinary path into a spiritual path by asserting that the virtues of the path are also the virtues of a divinity. They might be given to us by a divine source, which the Charge of the Goddess asserts itself to be with statements like "Listen to the Words of the Great Mother..." Similarly we might believe that they are the qualities and character-traits of certain gods whom we desire to emulate: the beauty of Aphrodite, the industriousness of Hephaestus, the wisdom of Athena, the courage of Ares, the justice of Zeus, and so on.

To lack these virtues is not exactly to be irresponsible. It is to be mistaken about what the virtues are, how they benefit their possessor, and to be mistaken about what constitutes the spiritual life. We are responsible beings — we are all beings who are able to respond when called upon to know ourselves. The person who lacks the virtues is the person who responds poorly, whose life lacks direction and so who gives an account of his life that lacks cohesion and sense.

To be responsible as a spiritual person, then, is to possess these divine virtues and to live one's life in accord with them. The Wiccan Rede, which I may seem to have swept under the rug, should be one's first stop for making most practical decisions. But for the purpose of imagining a spiritual life and then seeking to live that life, we need the Virtues. It is this process which will enable us to lead fulfilling, worthwhile lives. Indeed this process will enable us to touch the divine, and elevate ourselves from a mere member of the species to a fully fledged human being.

A few summary remarks.

There is something I find myself needing to do, almost physically needing to do, at least a few nights out of every year, and that is go to a pagan revel fire. There's nothing else like it in Western society in general. I need to walk barefoot down a path in a forest, in the dark, with only torches every dozen meters or so to light the way, and a friend at my side. I need to hear the sound of the drums in the distance, growing clearer and louder as I get closer. I need to see the fire from around the bend for the first time, through the trees, through the silhouettes of the dancers and drummers. I need to see the thirty or so dancers, the twenty or so drummers, the hundred or so other people hanging about as they take a break from the dancing to talk, flirt, laugh, share food and drink, share stories, share life. I need to see the stars above, and feel the wind on my arms and legs, feel a branch or two from the trees brush by my face. I need to see the smiles on the faces of the people who recognise me as I arrive. I need to have my djembe slung over my shoulder, and find a place among the other drummers there, maybe pat a few of them on the shoulder as they let me in. I need to take a breath or two as I look on the dancers, enjoy the sight of them, enjoy their smiles and laughter, the flirting they do with each other. I need to feel the heat of the fire on my face, coming and going as the passing dancers come between me and the fire and then pass on again. I need to dig my bare toes into the warm sand. And then I need to feel the music of the drums in my rib cage and my arms, and then I need to join the music, let my arms and hands do my talking, let my drum-skin be my voice, let my eyes close as I arouse the wonderful Goddess-given energy of life that dwells within me. Then I need to feel that energy make my arms and hands move as if of their own accord, in time with the rhythm of the tribe. The pagan revel fire is the Dionysian dithyramb of our time.

A worthwhile and satisfying life must necessarily include a sense of magic like that. By 'magic' here I am not implying anything supernatural. To my mind, 'magic' is the hard-to-define quality of the things which stir up mystical feelings like amazement, curiosity, imagination, and above all *wonder*. Magic is that which renders something beautiful in a spiritual sense. It is that which makes one feel as if the world is more than it is presently understood to be, and yet at the same time the world is working itself out in a good and beautiful way. Magic underlies the relationship between ourselves, and the greater immensities of birth and death. Thus the experience of being in the presence of something magical is an empowering, uplifting experience. Magic, understood this way, contributes *meaning* to life.

People can obtain the magic they need from many kinds of sources, but not all of them are life-affirming, or even rational. It is very possible, for instance, to create magic and wonder and purpose with a totalitarian political program. Such a program can take the form of the 'toughening' of criminal law and of punishments for even the smallest of crimes; the praise for the 'natural' talent and merit of the rich and the corresponding scorn for the 'natural' laziness and ineptitude of the poor; the scapegoating of outsiders and of those who criticise the program; the cultivation of an environment of fear, especially the fear of foreign attack; the assertion that the leaders have received a mandate from God and are therefore infallible; the assertion that obedience is a sign of patriotism; the integration or even union of state power with corporate power; the promotion of absolutist or fundamentalist forms of religion; and of course the belief in the manifest destiny of the nation. All of these things, especially when taken together in a comprehensive political program, are effective ways to create a sense of purpose and meaning in life. All of them are capable of offering appealing answers to the important questions of who we are, and what we are supposed to do with our lives. Yet they are also capable of justifying xenophobia, racism, sexism, witch-hunting, militarism and violence, even open warfare. They can result in the camps of Treblinka and Auschwitz, the gulags of Siberia, the military prisons of Abu Graib and Guantanamo Bay.

The very best alternative, the proper place where we should look for the magic we need to live, is the Earth. First of all, the Earth will never demand the sacrifice of our minds to a totalitarian political program. It will never scapegoat anyone, nor will it invent false pretences for war. And it will never demand faith or belief in abstract realities that cannot be proven or dis-proven to actually exist. For the Earth's only laws are the natural laws of ecosystems. Secondly, the Earth is already recognized in cultures all over the world as a profound source of magic and meaning. The landscapes of our planet form perhaps the most important substance of shared identity between people, alongside shared language and history. So much of a nation's culture and history is what it is because of the kind of climate and environment the people inhabit. And many landscapes around the world are loved by their people as holy lands, given to them by God, and still inhabited by the ghosts and bones of ancestors. In many places, a Goddess is, or once was, the personification of the land. She is the image that best represents humanity's various relationships to the Earth, and to each other. She is the figure that integrates those relationships into personal and public identities. She, therefore, is the one to whom we ought to look for our sense of belonging and purpose.

The contemporary pagan community, holding the Earth in such high regard as it does, is in a position to show the world what a spiritually aware, environmentally conscious, socially just, and artistically flourishing society looks like. The pagan community can create a social and cultural space where ancient noble ideas like 'inspiration and honour' are still preserved and practiced. A person who lives in this mythological and mystical way, who fashions herself in the image of the goddess within her, is someone I would like to call a great soul. We have met such a person already. She is benevolent and persevering, like Grandmother Anishnabe; passionate and curious, like Queen Inanna; protective and loyal, like Demeter; fierce and loving, like the Morrígan; contemplative and wise, like the three Norns; nurturing and caring, like the Goddess With No Name. These and other qualities are the values involved in the celebration and enjoyment of embodied life. The pagan community could give to itself the task of preserving these values, and other values of the so-called 'old' ways. For some day, the world may want them back again.

After-song

Beyond the open garden gate, we face
A rambling path through field and wood and hill,
That finds a distant unaccounted place
Where all is wild, yet all is very still.

In that good land we'll make our camping-site.
We'll pick wild cherries, hunt the questing-beast,
And laugh the whole long merry day. At night
We'll build a fire, and set a heroes' feast!

And sing the praise of ramblers gone ahead,
And sing the praise of ramblers yet to come,
And sing of all the living and the dead
Who ever loved, or did to love succumb.

Next morn, we'll wake beside our own front door,
And then we'll go a-rambling on once more.

Bibliography

Adler, Margot. *Drawing Down the Moon* (Boston: Beacon Press, 1979/1986)

Athanassakis, *The Homeric Hymns*, (Baltimore: Johns Hopkins Press, 1976)

Blain, J. *Nine Worlds of Seid-Magic: Ecstasy and Neo-Shamanism in North European Paganism* (London: Routledge, 2002)

Burr, ed., "The Witch-Persecution at Bamberg" in *Translations and Reprints from the Original Sources of European History*, Vol. III, Series for 1896, University of Pennsylvania.

Campbell, Joseph, *The Power of Myth* (New York: Anchor/ Doubleday, 1988)

Chadwick & Mann (trans.) *The Hippocratic Writings* (London: Penguin, 1983)

Crowley, *Magical and Philosophical Commentaries on The Book of the Law* ed. John Symonds and Kenneth Grant (Montreal, Canada: 93 Publishing, 1974)

Crowley, *The Confessions of Aleister Crowley* J. Symonds & K. Grant, eds. (London: Jonathan Cape, 1969).

Crowley, *The Holy Books of Thelema*, (York Beach, Maine, USA: Samuel Weiser, 1983)

Farrar, Janet and Stewart. *The Witches' Way* (Phoenix, 1984)

Foster, *From Distant Days: Myths, Tales, and Poetry of Ancient Mesopotamia* (Bethseda, Maryland: CDL Press, 1995)

Frazer, James. *The Golden Bough* (New York: Touchstone, 1996 [first published 1922])

Friedrich Nietzsche, *Beyond Good and Evil* trans. W. Kaufmann (New York USA: Vintage books, 1966)

Gray, E. (trans.) *Caith Maigh Tuireadh* (Dublin: Irish Texts Society, 1983)

Gregory, *Gods and Fighting Men* (Gerards Cross, Buckinghamshire, UK: Colin Smythe, 1970)

Hamilton, Edith. *The Greek Way* (New York: Norton, 1930)

Hutton, *The Triumph of the Moon* (Oxford University Press, 1999)

Johnston, *Ojibway Heritage*, (Toronto: McLelland and Stewart, 1979)

Kelly, Fergus (trans) *Audacht Morann* (Dublin: Institute for Advanced Studies, 1976)

Kinsella, T. (trans) *The Táin* (Oxford University Press, 1969)

Leland, *Aradia, Gospel of the Witches* (New York: Samuel Weiser, 1974)

Leland, Charles. *Aradia: Gospel of the Witches* (New York: Weiser, 1974)

Markale, Jean. *Women of the Celts* (Rochester, Vermont: Inner Traditions, 1986)

Matthews, ed. *News and Rumor in Renaissance Europe* (G.P. Putnam, 1959).

McLuhan, *Touch the Earth: A Self-Portrait of Indian Existence* (New York: Promontory Press, 1971)

Mill, J.S. *On Liberty and Utilitarianism* omnibus edition (London: Everyman / Oxford University Press, 1969)

Monter, William (ed.) *European Witchcraft* (Toronto: Wiley & Sons, 1969)

Murray, Margaret. *The Witch Cult in Western Europe* (Oxford University Press, 1921)

Murray, Margaret. *The God of the Witches* (Oxford University Press, 1931)

Ó h-Ógáin, Dáithí *The Sacred Isle: Belief and Religion in Pre-Christian Ireland* (Wilton, Cork, Ireland: Collins Press, 1999)

Reid, Sian. *Between the Worlds: Readings in Contemporary Neopaganism* (Toronto: Canadian Scholar's Press, 2006)

Toelken, Barre. *The Dynamics of Folklore* (Boston, Mass.: Houghton Mifflin, 1979)

Shah, *The Sufis* (New York: Anchor / Doubleday, 1964)

Shah, *The Way of the Sufi* (London: Penguin, 1974 [first published 1968])

Sri Aurobindo Ghose, *The Secret of the Veda* (Pondicherry: Sri Aurobindo Ashram Press, 1956)

Sturlson, The Prose Edda trans. J. Byock (London: Penguin, 2005)

Underhill, Evelyn. *Mysticism* (Oneworld Publications, 1999 [first published 1911])

Wolkstein and Kramer, *Inanna: Queen of Heaven and Earth*, (New York: Harper & Row, 1983)

BOOKS

O is a symbol of the world, of oneness and unity. In different cultures it also means the "eye", symbolizing knowledge and insight. We aim to publish books that are accessible, constructive and that challenge accepted opinion, both that of academia and the "moral majority".

Our books are available in all good English language bookstores worldwide. If you don't see the book on the shelves ask the bookstore to order it for you, quoting the ISBN number and title. Alternatively you can order online (all major online retail sites carry our titles) or contact the distributor in the relevant country, listed on the copyright page.

See our website www.o-books.net for a full list of over 400 titles, growing by 100 a year.

And tune in to myspiritradio.com for our book review radio show, hosted by June-Elleni Laine, where you can listen to the authors discussing their books.

mySpiritRadio